Hineini
in Our Lives

OTHER JEWISH LIGHTS BOOKS
BY NORMAN J. COHEN

Self, Struggle & Change:
Family Conflict Stories in Genesis
and Their Healing Insights for Our Lives

Voices from Genesis:
Guiding Us through the Stages of Life

The Way Into Torah

Hineini
in Our Lives

Learning How to Respond
to Others through 14 Biblical Texts
& Personal Stories

NORMAN J. COHEN

WITH CONTRIBUTIONS BY

RABBI LESTER BRONSTEIN • ALAN DERSHOWITZ
RABBI LAURA GELLER • RABBI NEIL GILLMAN • RABBI RICHARD JACOBS
LAWRENCE KUSHNER • PETER ASCHER PITZELE
RABBI SANDY EISENBERG SASSO • RABBI ZALMAN SCHACHTER-SHALOMI
RABBI HAROLD M. SCHULWEIS • PHYLLIS TRIBLE

JEWISH LIGHTS Publishing
Woodstock, Vermont

Hineini in Our Lives:
Learning How to Respond to Others through 14 Biblical Texts & Personal Stories

2003 First Printing
© 2003 by Norman J. Cohen

Library of Congress Cataloging-in-Publication Data
Cohen, Norman J.
Hineini in our lives : learning how to respond to others through 14 biblical texts & personal stories / Norman J. Cohen.
        p. cm.
Includes bibliographical references (p.   ).
ISBN 1-58023-131-4 (HC)
1. Interpersonal relations—Biblical teaching. 2. Interpersonal relations—Religious aspects—Judaism. 3. Vocation—Biblical teaching. 4. Vocation—Judaism. 5. Spiritual life—Judaism. 6. Jewish way of life—Anecdotes. I. Title.
BS1199.I55C64 2003
296.7—dc22

                                              2003015277

10 9 8 7 6 5 4 3 2 1
Manufactured in Canada

Published by Jewish Lights Publishing
A Division of LongHill Partners, Inc.
Sunset Farm Offices, Route 4, P.O. Box 237
Woodstock, VT 05091
Tel: (802) 457-4000   Fax: (802) 457-4004
www.jewishlights.com

To my teacher
at
Hebrew Union College–Jewish Institute of Religion:
Abraham Aaroni,
who was a model of
erudition, exemplary pedagogy, and *menchlichkeit*

Contents

Preface

Any number of times I have heard people quote Woody Allen as saying, "80 percent of life is simply showing up." Actually, Allen said: "80 percent of *success* is showing up," but the misquote does say a great deal about people's attitude. Most people feel that all we have to do is be physically present, whether in our professional roles or in our personal relationships, and that is sufficient. We can get by if we merely "show our face" to others.

The Bible seems to already anticipate this sense that "being there" is sufficient to ensure success when we read God's words beckoning Moses to ascend Mt. Sinai: "Come up to Me on the mountain and be there, and I will give you the stone tablets with the teaching and the commandments" (Exodus 24:12). The Divine's words seem to imply that by Moses being on the mountain, he would receive the commandments. However, a famous Hasidic master, the Kotzker Rebbe, asks why God had to further instruct Moses to "be there." Wasn't he already up on the mountain? The Kotzker suggests that God was telling Moses not to just be there physically, but rather to be fully present in the moment—mentally, spiritually, and emotionally. Moses' relationship with God will come to fruition in his receiving of the Ten Commandments if and when he is fully there, a covenantal partner with the Divine.[1]

We, too, must be fully present, responsive, and receptive to the other in our lives, whether it be God or the individuals whom we love—our parents, spouses, children, siblings, or friends—if we want to experience real happiness and fulfillment. And at a time when many of us are finding it overwhelming to face the violence, terror, and seeming hopelessness that is so much a part of the fabric of our everyday lives, we need even more to experience the sense of security, wholeness, and meaning that comes from significant personal relationships. By truly hearing and responding to the call of the other, whether human or Divine, by giving of ourselves, we grow in stature. If we are so caught up in ourselves that we are unable to engage others in significant ways, then we are relegated to living life on our own. We become the sole sources of joy and meaning in our lives.

The Bible can provide us with opportunities to reflect on our own relationships and how we relate to those close to us. By confronting biblical characters and their struggles to respond both to other human beings as well as to the Divine, we can find out about ourselves as husbands, wives, mothers, fathers, brothers and sisters, children, lovers and friends, and as people searching for meaning in a fractured world. The Bible can be an extraordinary means of self-reflection for us as modern readers, helping us to better understand who we are and who we can become.

Just as the biblical characters are called by God and by the others in their lives, so, too, are we. Beginning with Adam in the Garden of Eden, biblical characters are asked to respond within relationships.[2] Abraham, Jacob, Joseph, Moses, Samuel, and the prophets—in every generation individuals are called, either by God or by other human beings,[3] and each responds with the word *hineini*, here I am. Every moment of calling and response is a model for each of us, who must learn how to discern the call of the other and react to it appropriately. We are the Abrahams, the Moses, and the Samuels of our time, and we are challenged to hear the call and the cry as they did.

There are many important terms and word-symbols in the Bible that represent essential themes or values. Some of these we all can call to mind, such as *mitzvah* (commandment), *chesed* (favor), and *b'rit* (covenant). However, no single word is more well known, important, or powerful than the simple word *hineini*. While other key words convey umbrella concepts that undergird the entire biblical worldview, only *hineini* is spoken. It flows from the essence of the individuals who say it and teaches us much about who they are. It represents the ability to respond to the other within relationships. At times the

Rabbis emphasize that we respond to God, to the highest call in the universe, when we are present for those whom we love and know and with whom we are acquainted. Our response to the Divine should lead us to recognizing our obligations to other people. This one word—*hineini*—has been used by the Rabbis in our traditional texts as well by contemporary teachers and leaders to capture the essence of relationship from a Jewish perspective and to motivate modern Jews to act on behalf of others.

When the word *hineini* is uttered by biblical characters or by God, it generally connotes three main sentiments. First is the ability to be present for and receptive to the other, as we find when Isaac responds to his son Jacob in Genesis 27:18 and when God is ever-present for Israel in Isaiah 65:1. Second, the word indicates the readiness to act on behalf of the other, as evident in Abraham's reply to God's call in the story of the *Akeidah* in Genesis 22:1, and in Esau's willingness to hunt game for Isaac in Genesis 27:1. Finally, *hineini* at times indicates the willingness to sacrifice for someone or something higher, as we read in Genesis 37:13 when Joseph is willing to visit his brothers, knowing how much they despise him, or when God is present for humanity when we are willing to give of the depth of ourselves to others in Isaiah 58. The nature of our relationships is measured by our willingness to act for others or even to make sacrifices for others.[4]

Each of us can learn about who we are as we function within our relationships, by confronting and immersing ourselves in the biblical vignettes in which the term *hineini* is used. There are many places in the Bible in which variations of this term appear, most often in the form of *hin'ni,* which is used together with a verbal form. For example, in Genesis 6:17, God says, "I am about to bring *(hin'ni mayvi)* the flood waters upon the Earth." However, there are only fourteen such passages in which the term stands alone, unconnected to a specific action, and they are found in a range of biblical contexts and stories. The majority are found in the book of Genesis, involving Abraham, Esau, Jacob, and Joseph; one in the beginning of Exodus, with Moses at the Burning Bush; two in the books of Samuel, the first involving Samuel and Eli the priest and the second, David and Saul; and, finally, three passages in the book of Isaiah, when God calls out to Israel.

This book involves the attempt to characterize what each of these *hineini* texts can teach modern readers. By utilizing a range of classic rabbinic interpretations of each of these fourteen passages, along with probing modern questions to uncover the meaning latent in each of them, we will apply the messages of these intriguing biblical passages to our own relationships, as well as to our relationship with God, no matter how each of us defines the Divine power in the universe.

To gain added perspective on the meaningfulness and power of the fourteen texts, we asked well-known religious and academic scholars and leaders to share a personal anecdote associated either with one of the *hineini* passages or with the concept of *hineini* in general. These engaging personal stories demonstrate how the Bible can touch every human being.

It is our hope that these personal stories and biblical interpretations, written from the perspective of modern life, will have a powerful impact on the lives of all those who will read this book. May you, the reader, make it a part of who you are as we share this journey of discovery of personal meaning.

Acknowledgments

One time, when his brothers had gone to pasture their father's flocks in Shechem, Israel said to Joseph, "Your brothers are pasturing at Shechem. Come, I will send you to them." He answered, *"Hineini"* (Here I am).... So he sent him from the valley of Hebron. When [Joseph] reached Shechem, a man came upon him wandering in the fields. The man asked him, "What are you looking for?" He answered, "I'm looking for my brothers. Could you tell me where they are pasturing?" The man said, "They have gone from here, for I heard them say, 'Let us go Dothan.'" So Joseph followed his brothers and found them at Dothan.

(Genesis 37:12–17)

When Joseph sets out from Jacob's tent, having answered his father's request with the classic word of response within relationships, *hineini,* little does he know what is going to unfold. He thinks that he will merely go out to check up on his brothers, who are pasturing the flocks near Shechem, and he will probably be back in less than a fortnight. After all, how long should the trip from Beer Sheba to Shechem and back take? Joseph cannot foresee that his journey to Shechem is to be the first part of the four-hundred-year odyssey of slavery and freedom of the Jewish people. How is he to know that he will be sold to an Ishmaelite caravan by his brothers, be taken down to Egypt, wind up in prison, interpret dreams, and, as a result, become the viceroy of Egypt, and witness his family settling in Goshen? And, ironically, had he not encountered and responded to the man as he was wandering in the fields, the entire story might have turned out differently.

The individuals we encounter along the way—our loved ones, those with whom we work, even the stranger on the road—often determine in part what our life journey will be like. Yet, sometimes it is only in retrospect that we can appreciate the crucial impact that certain encounters have had on us and how they have shaped our lives.

My own personal journey, from being a chemistry major at Columbia College to my love for Torah study, Israel, and the Jewish people, and my desire to share my knowledge, passion, and commitment as a Jew with others, is the result of individuals along the way who have touched me deeply. I indeed have been blessed with insightful and wonderful teachers throughout my life—as a teenager in Young Judaea, a mainstream Zionist youth movement, at Columbia College, the Jewish Theological Seminary, the Hebrew University, and especially at Hebrew Union College–Jewish Institute of Religion in both New York and Cincinnati. As a rabbinical student and a Ph.D. candidate, I was privileged to study with many individuals who nurtured in me a profound love for Jewish texts. None, however, was more wonderful to me than Abraham Aaroni, my rabbinic thesis advisor. Abe Aaroni was the quintessential teacher of Hebrew language. In his own life, teaching at Herzeliah Teacher's Institute in New York City, in the New York City public school system, at Thomas Jefferson High School and Jamaica High School (where, coincidentally, he was close friends with my aunt, Jean, *z"l*, who taught music there, and my wife's French teacher), and later in his life at HUC–JIR, he nurtured generations of students who love Hebrew. To this day, long after his retirement, many alumni still stay in touch with him, crediting him as the best teacher they ever had. I am honored to count myself among them. I dedicated this book to him, not only because of what he taught me and how he conveyed it, but mainly because he showed me what it is to be a teacher. His caring, warmth, and dedication to his students served as a most important model for all of us who aspire to teach others. May he experience continued good health so he can enjoy the rewards for the gifts he gave to so many.

I have also benefited greatly from the wonderful individuals associated with Jewish Lights Publishing. My friend Stuart M. Matlins, founder of Jewish Lights, has constantly encouraged me to share my own passion and teachings with as wide an audience of learners as possible. He has been a mentor who has helped me better understand how to engender a serious approach to Torah study through the written word. I have also been the beneficiary of the support and direction of Emily Wichland, the managing editor of Jewish Lights and a consummate professional. Emily's insights, vision, and prodding have made this book immeasurably better than it would have been without her help. The hand of Sally Freedman, who edited the book, may not be evident to the reader, but its presence its found on almost every page. Her structural suggestions helped create a manuscript that could best communicate the essential message that all of us can be serious students of Torah and find our own meaning in the text.

This book, *Hineini in Our Lives,* is more than an exercise in sharing textual insights and interpretations with the reader. It is an attempt to underscore how the biblical text calls to each of us, demanding that we respond out of our own life experiences. In so doing, not only will we learn about ourselves, but we will also be better able to hear the call of all those we encounter on our journeys— not only those whom we love, but also the nameless people whom we meet by chance. They may be able to give us more than directions on the road. Perhaps they will influence the direction of our lives.

Norman J. Cohen

Introduction

Reading through the Prism of Midrash— Making the Text Our Own

When we pray or when we recite liturgical texts, we remind ourselves of our relationship with God, and of God's nature, but we also experience the covenant anew. The process is both didactic and experiential.[1]

A primary example is the Passover Haggadah, in which we read: "Even if we were all wise, all persons of understanding, all knowledgeable of Torah, we would still be commanded to tell the story of the Exodus from Egypt." No matter the breadth or depth of our knowledge, it is incumbent on us to retell, to relive, the story of our journey from slavery to freedom. In retelling the story, the goal is for each of us to feel as though we ourselves actually had gone forth from Egypt.

THE SEARCH FOR MORE THAN THE *PSHAT*

For most Jews, the challenge to personalize our life stories is not carried over to our study of the Bible. Many of us, even the most committed, view the reading of the Bible as a dispassionate exercise. Our sole intent is to use our analytical skills—be they linguistic, literary, source-critical, or historical—to understand the conventional meaning of the text (in Hebrew, the *pshat*, the simple, more obvious meaning). We focus on the question of what any particular biblical verse or narrative meant for the time in which it was written.

However, the literal reading is not the only possible way to interpret the text. The mystics of the Middle Ages understood the Torah to be an inexhaustible well that contained many levels of potential meaning. These different levels of meaning, or modes of interpretation, were conventionally divided into four categories, described by the word *PaRDeS,* an acronym for *pshat* (literal), *remez* (allegorical), *drash* (midrashic), and *sod* (mystical). The *PaRDeS* (literally, a citrus orchard) came to be understood as a symbol of the place of speculation about the Torah's meaning.[2]

The Rabbis of old recognized that there were "seventy faces to the Torah,"[3] only the first of which was the *pshat.* They intuited that the text, any text, is multivocalic, that there are a multiplicity of meanings implicit within the text, and that all readers can find a voice that will touch them. The Rabbis also taught that "every word of Torah can be divided into seventy languages," that is, the number of nations they thought existed in the world.[4] The message is clear: There are as many interpretations of any given biblical verse as there are people in the world.

Although the biblical text may be finite, its re-creation, mediated by the process of interpretation, is infinite. Many meanings may resonate within each word, each letter of Torah, when engaged readers open themselves up to it in a significant way. The text truly comes alive when readers immerse themselves in the text. The process of finding new meaning in the text through the process of interpretation has been compared to the birthing of a child. Once the umbilical cord—the tie of the biblical text to a particular time, place, and set of authors—is severed, the text takes on a life of its own. It can grow, expand, and change as readers of every age interact with it.[5] Postmodern scholars describe this process as the "recontextualizing of the text." We find meaning in the text by reliving it, by filtering it through the prism of our own lives.

THE THREE LAYERS OF THE MIDRASHIC PROCESS

If it is to have any authenticity, the attempt to find contemporary meaning in the Bible must be grounded in the Bible itself. The term midrash comes from the Hebrew root *darash,* which means "to seek, search, or demand," meaning from the biblical text.[6] The starting point in our search for personal meaning is a close study of the Bible. It is incumbent on us to use all the knowledge we possess of the Bible—philological, literary, archeological, and theological—and the knowledge of the world of the Ancient Near East in which it was written to approximate what the biblical writer(s) intended in any given passage. Our task at the outset is to attend to the meaning of the biblical text in its context. We must first ask: What was the intent, the message of any particular biblical passage when it was written?

However, since we are the heirs not only to the Bible, which is called the Written Torah or the *Torah she-Bihtav,* but also to the Oral Torah of rabbinic teachings, the *Torah she-Ba'al Peh,* our second task as active students of Torah is to view the sacred stories of our past through the eyes of two millennia of interpreters and to benefit from their readings. The sages of the past viewed the biblical text against the backdrop of the issues of their day. As they interpreted the Bible, they were responding to the political, religious, and sociocultural conditions under which they lived—that is, the exigencies of their own life situations. Their midrashic interpretations incorporated their responses to the challenges that they faced living in *Eretz Yisrael* and the Diaspora under the Greeks, Romans, Parthians, Babylonians, Christians, and Muslims.

Since each generation of rabbinic interpreters came to Torah anew, finding the answers to the questions and challenges to Jewish survival that were particular to their time and place, multiple interpretations of any given passage were possible. The Midrash (the entire body of rabbinic midrashim) has been described as a cacophony of readings of the Bible that cannot and should not be harmonized.[7] There can always be "another interpretation," a *davar aher* (literally, "another word"), and many of these interpretations of the same biblical verse are contradictory. Yet, the Midrash typically does not attempt to smooth over the contradictions. Multiple interpretations merely provide the student of Torah with many voices from which to learn—voices that seem to argue with one another even across generations. New readers are beckoned to join in a dynamic conversation that has been conducted over two millennia, a conversation in which all strive to find their own meaning.

Therefore, it is not sufficient for us to read the interpretations attributed to the great teachers of past generations, though we can surely gain invaluable insights from them. Midrash, by definition, is the process of finding contemporary meaning in the biblical text. Therefore, the study of our sacred texts forces self-involvement. As contemporary readers, we are called on to immerse ourselves in the dialogue with Torah across the generations, a dialogue that is embedded in the religious consciousness of the community of Israel. When we ourselves become engaged with the text, new meanings are created that give voice to our very beings. In creating our own midrashim, which respond to our particular questions and dilemmas, we bring to the fore elements of ourselves that may not always be conscious.

This is the final stage in the process of creating contemporary midrash. After reading and studying the biblical text, and then seeing how the cumulative tradition interprets any given text, it is left to us to wrestle with the sacred stories of Torah. If we are grounded in the traditions of the past, then our modern readings will be built on a firm foundation, enabling them to become a new link in the chain of interpretation extending back to Sinai.

READING FOR MEANING

We as readers are not passive agents. Rather, we are active participants in the dynamic process of creating meaning through our encounter with the text. A text that is not pondered has no meaning.[8] We create the meaning as we experience the text from the vantage point of our lives.

In order for us to draw our own meanings from the biblical text, it is necessary for each of us as devoted and passionate readers first to read the text slowly, imbibing the power and potential meaning of every syntactical element—every word, phrase, and symbol. And since the biblical text is so terse, with few details provided to the reader, the inclusion or even absence of any element may be of great significance.[9] We must spend time with the biblical text, live with it, and allow the stories of our past to resonate within our very beings. If we run precipitously through the text, as if the object were to cover the entire text in a minimum amount of time, then we are destined to see only the *pshat*, the text's surface meaning. To be active readers is to become engaged with the text in its breadth and depth.

As we wrestle with every element of the text, we must be willing to ask every meaningful question about it that we can think of. The art of interpretation rests in a significant way on our ability to elicit and address all the problems, conflicts, and ambiguities inherent in each passage. By highlighting the philological, literary, theological, sociocultural, and historical concerns inherent in the texts we are reading, we automatically locate hooks on which new meanings can hang. Every question, every problem presents an opportunity to create new interpretations of this ancient text.

As we ask our questions, it behooves us to ask the most difficult questions about the text, which for us as modern readers are either questions of belief or humanistic questions about the characters and their lives. We must be able to see the text from within, placing ourselves inside the characters and the fabric of their lives and relationships. In so doing, we will come to realize that the biblical characters, who are portrayed in very human terms, are faced with situations and issues very much like our own. And in engaging with them through our immersion in the text, we can begin to struggle with our own life situations.

Every question about the biblical text gives us entrée into its meaning. The search for meaning often demands that we focus on one question, one textual problem, one narrative moment that enables us to discern the potential impact of the text on our lives. Rather than taking a scattershot approach to the words and images that make up an extended story, we may more easily see the relevance of the biblical characters' interaction by zeroing in on one moment with which we can identify. Of course, we should not lose sight of the larger picture. We can learn a great deal from the larger, extended narrative involving any particular character. For example, who Joseph is and how he changes over the extended story of his interaction with his brothers can speak to each one of us who has siblings (Genesis 37–50). Yet, in seeing the personalities in the Bible at crucial moments in their lives that are similar to our own, not only can we learn about them, but in the process we can gain insights into

ourselves. Filling in the details of such narrative moments by probing
the interaction of the characters, their feelings, and their concerns
enables us as modern readers to see the relevance of these ancient stories to our own lives.

Sometimes, the challenge is to see the narrative through the eyes
of characters whose voices we rarely hear. If, for instance, Sarah could
tell us how she felt when Abraham took Isaac on the road to Mt.
Moriah (Genesis 22), or Moses could share with us his anger at the
people when they complained to him about the lack of water at the
very moment of the death of his sister Miriam (Numbers 12), we
might be better able to tap into similar feelings we have had in our
own lives. Such biblical voices can remind us of who we are and how
we can become better people—better siblings, parents, spouses, children, lovers, and friends. This is especially important when it comes
to the female characters whose voices are often lost to us. They can
teach us—all of us, both men and women—about our essential
natures.

In the end we discover that when we study the biblical text,
what we are doing is not simply reading and analyzing the narrative,
learning about the characters and their lives. Rather, we find ourselves confronting our own baffling life dramas. Torah is a mirror:
When we gaze deeply into it, it reflects back to us our own personas,
ambivalences, struggles, and potential for growth. The challenge for
us as readers, therefore, is to experience the text, relive the story—in
essence, to become one with it. At that moment, when the sacred
story of our people's past melds with out own life stories, we will not
only be touched by Torah, but transformed by it.[10]

RESPONDING TO THE CALL:
OUR OWN PERSONAL *HINEINI*

Reading a sacred text demands self-reflection. No matter who we are
and or how much knowledge we bring to the moment of engagement
with Torah, meaning is created if we open ourselves up to it. Though
we all may be at different stages on the journey of Torah study, each
of us has the potential to find personal meaning in the text. And since
the text addresses each of us according to our individual capacities

and where we are in our lives, the biblical text may be read differently by us at different times in our lives and in different circumstances. As we change, so might the meaning of any given text for us.[11] It makes no difference whether we are rabbis, teachers, scholars, authors, theologians, students, or interested laypersons. The text beckons to each of us, calls to us to respond to it out of the depth of our beings. If we are open and ready, we can hear the call.

Part I

Fourteen Biblical Texts, Fourteen Opportunities for Meaning

1
Recognizing the Other

> Some time afterward, God put Abraham to the test. God
> said to him, "Abraham," and Abraham answered, "Here I
> am." And God said, "Take your son, your favored one,
> Isaac, whom you love, and go to the land of Moriah, and
> offer him there as a burnt offering on one of the heights
> that I will point out to you.
>
> *(Genesis 22:1–2)[1]*

Hineini (Here I am) is such a simple word, but it is perhaps the most
recognized word-symbol in the entire Bible. As it powerfully signifies
the willingness to respond within a relationship, it challenges all of us
to reflect on our relationships with our spouses, parents, children, siblings, lovers, and friends.

Therefore, it is surprising that it is not used until Abraham
responds to God's call in Genesis 22. Why don't the earlier universal
characters, such as Adam, Cain, and Noah, respond with the word
hineini when God speaks to each of them?[2] Are we to assume that
hineini was reserved for the Israelites as they relate to each other and
to God? That somehow *hineini* is used only within the covenantal
relationship between God and the people of Israel or among the
Israelites themselves?

Abraham does not respond in this manner in any of the previous stories in which he is called by God. Perhaps it is purposeful that
hineini is used at the denouement of Abraham's life, when he is
called to make the supreme sacrifice. *Hineini,* in part, has to do with

sacrificing for the other, and every time it appears it forces us to consider the nature of our relationships.

THE TEN TRIALS OF ABRAHAM

God's test in Genesis 22 is by no means Abraham's first. This episode is known as *Akeidat Yitzhak* (the Binding of Isaac), in which Abraham is asked to take Isaac, the son of his and Sarah's old age, and bring him to Moriah and offer him as a sacrifice on one of the mountains.[3] According to the rabbinic tradition,[4] God tested Abraham on nine previous occasions. Like all of us, Abraham experiences the call to Moriah in the context of his accumulated life experiences.

The ten tests or trials, which span much of Abraham's life, represent the stages of his growth, from infancy to later maturity, just as our life experiences are the markers of our life journey. With these trials, whether it was his being cast into the fiery furnace in his youth, leaving his father's house in Haran, battling the five most powerful Canaanite kings, circumcising himself and his son Ishmael, banishing Hagar and Ishmael into the desert, or binding his son Isaac,[5] God tested Abraham to see how firm his belief was and whether, as a worthy partner, he could fulfill all the responsibilities with which the Divine would charge him.[6] Similarly, we are tested by the experiences with which we are confronted in our lives; our response to each one can be seen as a measure of who we are and what we are made of.

Two of these events in Abraham's life journey stand out because they seem so similar. At the beginning of Abraham's story in Genesis 12, when he is living in Haran, God calls and commands him: "Go forth *(lech lecha)* from your native land and from your father's house to the land I will show you.... Abram took *(va-yikakh)* his wife Sarai and his brother's son Lot...and they set out for the land of Canaan" (Genesis 12:1–5). How striking that similar terms and expressions are used years later in our story of the *Akeidah,* when God commands him: "Take *(kakh)* your son...and go *(lech lecha)* to the land of Moriah, and offer him there on one of the mountains that I will point out to you" (Genesis 22:2). In each of these encounters with the Divine, which in essence frame Abraham's life, he is commanded to "take" one of his kin and set out on a journey ("go"), the end of which seems uncertain. In the beginning of his relationship with God he is told to set out for a land that God will show him (though we know he is heading to Canaan), while toward the end of his life he is pointed to a mountain that God will eventually identify. Abraham's compliance with God's command in Genesis 12 is the first step toward his covenantal relationship with the Divine, while his response to God's request to bring Isaac as a sacrifice in Genesis 22 represents the culmination of their relationship. Abraham never again speaks with God, though he lives for a considerable time after the *Akeidah.*

The two commandments of *lech lecha* are the bookends of Abraham's relationship with God, the core of his life experience, in which God seems to constantly test him. Although the phrase "God put Abraham to the test" *(nissa 'et Avraham)* is only used in the *Akeidah,* each time God called to Abraham, commanding him to act, must have felt like a test.[7] All of us, like the patriarch Abraham, have felt burdened and even tested when someone we love makes demands on us. In each instance, the question is whether we have the strength to respond affirmatively. This is the same question Abraham has to answer. Can he respond to the different challenges with which God confronts him? Can he say, *"Hineini,"* not only when God demands that he fulfill his role as patriarch of his people, but also when the Divine commands him to sacrifice his beloved son?[8] Can he carry out God's will and yet remain whole in his faith and person?[9]

OPPORTUNITIES FOR REFLECTION AND GROWTH

With each test, Abraham is given an opportunity to reflect on his relationship with God; what it means to stand in covenant with the one power in the universe and grasp the implications of that relationship for the future. This is especially true in the case of the *Akeidah,* which calls into question all the presumptions and promises of the past. Will Abraham be able to sacrifice Isaac, the very embodiment of his future, the promised greatness of his progeny,[10] his own immortality? His future and that of his people depend solely on Isaac's survival. God's command to sacrifice Isaac will help Abraham clarify the truth of his entire relationship with God.[11]

Every test is an opportunity for self-reflection, enabling each of us to think about who we are and the nature of our priorities and values. For Abraham, this opportunity is captured in the two key words used in this final trial, *lech lecha,* which epitomize each stage of his journey. Though used as an kind of emphatic, the words literally translated mean, "Go to yourself," impelling Abraham to come to know himself and what is important to him. So the test involves a journey inward.[12]

The Rabbis understand the test of the *Akeidah* as a moment of self-reflection on Abraham's part and read the opening words of Genesis 22 in this light. They interpret *Va-yehi akhar ha-devarim ha-eileh* (meaning "Some time afterwards," though literally, "And it was after these things") to mean that at that moment Abraham is mired in his own thoughts and musings (the word *devarim* can also mean "words") about himself and his relationship with God.[13] God's command to sacrifice Isaac is a chance for him to tap into the core of his being, to come to know his own heart.

In testing Abraham, God allows him to gain a clearer sense of himself and his character. Only through the struggle involved in responding to God's command to sacrifice Isaac can Abraham fully realize his own nature and potential. In responding to God's request, not only does Abraham plumb the depth of his being, but also he sees his potential translated into action.[14] As we struggle to understand Abraham's response to God's call, we can better understand our own responses to God's demands of us as well as those made by people we love.

TRUST BUILT OVER TIME

The *Akeidah* is clearly the most important moment of Abraham's life—the ultimate test of his nature and his faith. Yet, we need to remember that this is the last in a series of ten tests that span a good portion of Abraham's life and that he has heard God's call to action many times before. Abraham is not naive when he hears God's demand that he bring Isaac to the mountain as a sacrifice.

From the very first time the Divine appears to Abraham in Haran and asked him to leave behind his home, his family, and all that defined who he was, Abraham rises to each challenge and realizes in so doing the fulfillment of God's promises to him. God promises to protect him, to make his progeny into a great nation, and that they will inherit the Land of Canaan in perpetuity, and with every test comes the renewal of the promise and the guarantee that he and his family will survive. And just as Abraham fulfills his covenantal obligation by responding to God's demands, God, in turn, not only preserves Abraham's life, but allows him to flourish in the land of his people's destiny. Even in the face of his greatest personal pain prior to the *Akeidah*—Sarah's demand that he banish Hagar and his firstborn son, Ishmael, to the desert (Genesis 21),[15] God promises Abraham that Ishmael will not only survive, but become the father of a great nation (Genesis 21:13). Abraham is assured that the future is guaranteed, which enables him to harken to God's demand that he obey Sarah's request.

Abraham's relationship with God is forged over an entire lifetime, with trust built up gradually over time.[16] As a result, when God calls out Abraham's name, Abraham is ready to respond, *"Hineini"* (Here I am). His *hineini is* a response of recognition, based on his long-standing relationship with God and the trust they share. And so it is with each of us, and our relationship with everyone close to us. When one of them requests something of us, our impulse must be to respond out of the long-term commitment we share and the trust built up over time.

READINESS TO ACT REGARDLESS OF THE REQUEST

Abraham's response of *hineini* to God's call represents his readiness to act.[17] The Rabbis refer to this as *lashon zimmun,* an expression of readiness. Depending on the nature of the *hineini* response, the Rabbis characterize each as being a different kind of *lashon*—literally, language.[18] Here, Abraham knows exactly what he is doing; the *hineini* demonstrates his certainty about his relationship with God and how far he is willing to go as a result of it.[19] While Abraham surely has to have misgivings about God's impending request, having just been asked to banish Hagar and his firstborn son Ishmael to the desert, nevertheless, he does not hesitate to respond.

Abraham is "present" and willing to respond and act, even though he has no notion of what God's demand will be: All he hears is God uttering his name. In every previous test, Abraham has known from the very moment that God spoke to him exactly what God's request entailed. Even at the outset of his journey, when God asked him to leave his homeland and journey to the land of Canaan, Abraham knew what was being demanded of him: "Adonai said to Abraham: 'Go forth from your native land and from your father's house to the land I will show you'" (Genesis 12:1). But here in the *Akeidah*, toward the end of Abraham's covenantal journey, God merely calls out to him, "Abraham," and Abraham immediately indicates his readiness to act regardless of the nature of the demand by responding, *hineini*.

This is made abundantly clear in the following midrashic interpretation: "And [God] called him, 'Abraham'—the purpose of [God's] calling was to announce God's presence to him prior to demanding of him an enormous task. And Abraham understood and responded, *'Hineini'*—[meaning] 'Behold I am ready for anything that you will ask of me.'"[20] Abraham was willing to answer God's call whatever its nature.[21]

This is what *hineini* is all about—the initial willingness to respond to the other, the readiness

> This is what *hineini* is all about—the initial willingness to respond to the other, the readiness to act on the other's behalf no matter what is being asked. When trust has been built up and we have lived in a committed relationship over time, then each of us has to be ready to respond and act when the other, to whom we are committed, calls.
>
> [See Rabbi Harold Schulweis's "One *Hineini* Against Another," p. 163.]

to act on the other's behalf no matter what is being asked. When trust has been built up and we have lived in a committed relationship over time, then each of us has to be ready to respond and act when the other, to whom we are committed, calls. This is a direct challenge to each one of us. Do we have the ability to respond to the requests made of us when we don't know what they will entail? When we are called by an elderly parent or by our child, is our first impulse to respond positively with commitment? Or, feeling burdened, is our immediate reaction at best lukewarm, especially knowing that the outcome may be painful?

HINEINI—THE LANGUAGE OF HUMILITY

When Abraham responds to God's call with the word *hineini,* indicating his readiness to act, what he communicates is his recognition of God's place in his life and his understanding that God's demands on him are justified. Perhaps this is why the term *hineini* is understood as "the language of humility," *lashon 'anavah* in this case.[22]

Based on Abraham's use of the term *hineini* here, *'anavah* (humility) involves our ability to respond to the other. Realizing this, it is interesting that the word *'anavah* looks as if it comes from the Hebrew root *'anah,* which actually means "answer" or "respond." Being humble encompasses the willingness to limit our own activities to act on behalf of others, a willingness to forgo seeing ourselves as the focal point of the universe. But can we act on behalf of others in our lives even when it means placing an added burden on ourselves? In our biblical story, Abraham hears God's call and indicates his willingness to act, even though he intuits that in so doing he will be forced to sacrifice something of himself.

Abraham's *hineini* demonstrates his ability to give up something of himself because of his relationship with God, to set aside his own needs. This is seen most clearly when the Rabbis picture Abraham saying bluntly to God: "Master of the Universe, when You said to me, 'Take your son...,' I could have responded differently and I would have been justified. I, indeed, was tempted to say to You, 'Yesterday, You told me, "Through Isaac, you shall have offspring,"' still I restrained myself and did not argue with You...."[23]

Not only is Abraham willing to forfeit the promise of his future, which is embodied in Isaac,[24] but he is ready to sacrifice the son of his old age without an argument. We know that he loves Isaac. The biblical text tells us this directly, when God commands him: "Take your son, your favored son, whom you love" (Genesis 22:2). This is the first time that the word *love* is mentioned in the Bible. But it is no accident, since relationships of love are potentially fraught with sacrifice and pain.[25]

Hineini signals to us that we, like Abraham, must be willing to give up our personal hopes and needs, that which seems to be the most meaningful to us, for the sake of something or someone even more important.

After all that Abraham has endured in his life, and at the point when he and Sarah are blessed with a child in their advanced years, he nevertheless responds to God's call without any hesitancy whatsoever, *"Hineini"*—I am ready to make the ultimate sacrifice if necessary. This is emphasized by another play on the first words of our story: *Va-yehi akhar ha-devarim ha-eilah,* which literally means, "After these things." What are the "things" alluded to in the text? After all the things that Abraham has had to endure in his life, Abraham complies with God's demand unstintingly.[26] Abraham is the symbol of sacrifice, for he is essentially willing to give up himself. His life is the embodiment of recognition of the Divine in the world and closeness to God. His *hineini* here signifies total sacrifice, *korban*,[27] from the Hebrew root *k-r-v,* which means "drawing close." When Abraham, the believer but also the father, places his son, Isaac, on the sacrificial altar he has erected, he is forcing us to ask whether we, too, are willing to surrender ourselves totally for what we believe.

TRANSCENDING ONESELF THROUGH *HINEINI*

Yet, built into Abraham's *hineini* is the inherent irony that as he gives of himself to the Divine, he finds himself in the process. Abraham transcends the narrow confines of his own existence by offering himself through his son Isaac to the service of something greater. By placing Isaac on the altar, he is offering himself as a sacrifice, since Isaac embodies his future; nevertheless, in so doing, he transcends himself. How can we explain it? By giving up part of himself, he discovers more of his essential nature. But this is the very nature of Abraham's covenant with God, and the nature of the covenant in general. Abraham's relationship with God exemplifies an idealized form of all committed relationships.[28]

When we make room for the other in our lives—our spouses, parents, children, siblings, anyone for whom we care—when we are willing to forgo the fulfillment of our own needs in deference to theirs, we find that we grow as a result. By giving up something of ourselves, by limiting ourselves, we surprisingly find our lives enriched in countless ways.

But there is more. Our responsiveness to others, which is embodied in the utterance of *hineini,* enhances the entire human condition. We can heal our broken world—promoting *tikkun olam* (repair of the world)—when we are willing to see the world through the eyes of other people and respond to them with an open heart. Thus we can shape the future for our own descendants, transcending the confines of our own lives.

Through his willingness to respond to God's call, Abraham, too, guarantees the future for his children, the people of Israel. According to the rabbinic tradition, his *hineini* elicits an oath from God to protect his progeny in the future, which is based on God's words (in the mouth in the angel) in the *Akeidah* text: "By Myself I swear, the Lord declares: Because you have done this and have not withheld your son, your favored one, I will bestow My blessing upon you and make your descendants as numerous as the stars in heaven and the sands on the seashore" (Genesis 22:16–17). At the moment of the *Akeidah,* Abraham prays to God:

> Now each year on [the first day of Rosh ha-Shanah, the Day of Judgment], when Isaac's children are called to account before You, no matter how many accusers bring charges against them, listen in silence and pay them no heed, just as I kept silent [and did not express what was in my heart], but only said, *"Hineini."* In reply to Abraham's prayer, the Holy One, blessed be God, said, "Yes, I shall take note of what happened on this day [of the *Akeidah*]." Abraham said, "Swear unto me." And God swore at once, "By Myself have I sworn."[29]

Abraham's *hineini* transcends time and teaches us that our responses to other human beings can have a force that not only can affect our relationships and the world in which we live, but also can shape the world yet to unfold.

RESPONDING TO THE OTHER
ENHANCES GOD'S PRESENCE

When Abraham responds to God with *"Hineini,"* willingly restraining that voice in his heart that could have refused to sacrifice his beloved son, he elicits from God an expression of deep compassion and concern. God swears never to hold Abraham's children accountable in the future, promising to maintain silence in the face of their sinfulness.[30] As Abraham demonstrates his love for God and his faithfulness and devotion, so, too, will God respond to humankind. Abraham, known as "the friend of God,"[31] who out of his love for God faithfully leads Isaac to the altar,[32] prompts God to respond out of love and patience to his descendants.

Abraham's response to God enhances God's loving and compassionate presence in the world. Listen to the words of the tradition in this regard:

> The Holy One said to the ministering angels: "If I had listened to you when you implored me [not to create humankind], saying to me, "What is the human being that You are mindful of him?" would Abraham have had the opportunity to adorn My presence in My world?[33]

Through our actions, we human beings extend the Divine Presence. When each of us responds positively to others and to the perennial Other, those whose lives intertwine with ours, we, like Abraham our forebear, help them discern and fulfill the purpose of their lives. In the process, we reach our highest selves and make God's presence, that power in the universe that makes for wholeness and goodness, more evident in this imperfect world of ours.

2
Being Accessible to the Other

Abraham took the wood for the burnt offering and put it on his son Isaac. He took the firestone and the knife; and the two walked off together. Then Isaac said to his father Abraham, "Father." And he answered, "Here I am, my son." And he said, "Here are the firestone and the wood; but where is the sheep for the burnt offering?" And Abraham said, "God will see to the sheep for His offering, my son." And the two of them walked on together.

(Genesis 22:6–8)

When we respond to the other in our lives, those whom we love, we make God's presence a reality in this world. Therefore, it is not at all surprising that the word Abraham uses at the outset of the *Akeidah* in answering God's call is the very word he later says in response to his son, Isaac.

RESPONDING TO OTHER HUMAN BEINGS IS TANTAMOUNT TO RESPONDING TO THE DIVINE

The text in Genesis 22:6 emphasizes that Abraham and Isaac climb the mountain together *(va-yalchu shenayhem yakhdav),* Abraham carrying the flint and the knife, while Isaac carries the wood. Interestingly, the same phrase is repeated after the interchange between them. As father and son ascend Mt. Moriah together, Isaac calls out to his father and Abraham replies, *"Hineini."* Abraham responds *hineini* to both God and Isaac, underscoring the responsibility he feels toward both. When you and I hear the call of those whom we love, the other in our lives, and answer, *"Hineini,"* it is tantamount to responding to the call of the Divine. As Naomi Rosenblatt has written, "The spirit of this transcendent statement of accessibility resounds throughout human relationships: when an infant stirs in her cradle and its mother calls out, 'I'm here'; when a lover calls out in passion or in need, and the partner responds, 'Here I am'; or when a friend turns to us for a favor, large or small, the true friend responds, 'I am here for you.'"[1] Yet, we don't always realize that in responding to the other we are responding to God's presence.

Even as we respond to the needs of human beings whom we do not know well, we are also responding to the highest call in the universe and we experience potential redemption. Hearing their voices and responding, or truly seeing their faces, is the same as hearing God's voice and seeing God's face. This is precisely what Jacob says to Esau at their reunion years later (Genesis 33:10).

In this regard, the Rabbis tell the story of Rabbi Joshua ben Levi,[2] who, while strolling in the city of Safed near the cave in which Rabbi Shimon ben Yohai is buried, meets the prophet Elijah, whom they believe will announce the coming of the Messiah. Not wanting to miss this opportunity, Rabbi Joshua asks the prophet, "When will the Messiah come?"

"Go ask him yourself," is the prophet's reply.

"Where can I find him?" queries the Rabbi.

The prophet responds, "He's in the gate of the city of Rome."

The rabbi continues, "And how shall I recognize him?"

"He is sitting among the poor who are burdened with illness. All of them first untie the bandages over their wounds and then retie them, whereas he unties and reties each separately, saying to himself, 'Should I be wanted, that is, if the messianic age is at hand, I must not be delayed.'"[3]

A simple rabbinic tale, but one laden with profound meaning. For the Rabbis stress that in order to discern the messianic potential in the world, we must look directly at and see the other in our midst. By truly seeing others and their suffering, we can see and better understand God's redemptive presence in the world.

Abraham focuses his full attention on Isaac when he reciprocates Isaac's emphasis on their relationship: Isaac calls out, "Father," and Abraham responds in kind, "My son." The biblical text goes out of its way to underscore their relationship, which each of them recognizes: "Isaac said to *his father,* Abraham, '*My father,*' and in turn, Abraham answered: 'Here I am, *my son,*' and 'God will see to the sheep for an offering, *my son.*'" The repetition of the relational words is noted in several midrashim, all of which stress that the reason for the repeated emphasis on their relationship is to show that Abraham, the father, loves his son, Isaac, and is concerned about him.[4] Abraham responds to Isaac and seems to understand him as they journey together to Moriah.

Yet, does Abraham truly understood Isaac? Is he in touch with his son's feelings and emotions? Or does Abraham's response simply imply that he hears Isaac's call, but doesn't realize its depth? Perhaps Abraham, who is so self-involved, so bent on fulfilling God's command, can only say to his son, "Here I am," and nothing more. Note, in this regard, the Aramaic Targum (translation of the Bible) of Yonatan ben Uzziel, which simply translates the words *Hineini beni* (Here I am, my son) as "Here I am," leaving off the words "my son." By omitting the term "my son," this translation seems to imply that Abraham is not fully present for Isaac.

Do we not frequently act like Abraham, thinking that we are really there for those whom we love, especially our children, spending so-called "quality time" with them, while our thoughts are a million miles away? Our children need more from us, just as Isaac's call to his father demands a true response from Abraham. It involves more than simply questioning his father's presence.

[See Rabbi Laura Geller's "Bringing My Whole Self to God," p. 125.]

But let us be honest with ourselves. Do we not frequently act like Abraham, thinking that we are really there for those whom we love, especially our children, spending so-called "quality time" with them, while our thoughts are a million miles away? Our children need more from us, just as Isaac's call to his father demands a focused response from Abraham. It involves more than simply questioning his father's presence.[5]

THE CALL OF THE OTHER EMBODIES ESSENTIAL CHALLENGES

However, it may be that Abraham does indeed hear the depth of Isaac's call, and when he responds to him, this allows Isaac to verbalize his real concerns. After Abraham says, *"Hineini,"* Isaac asks, "Here is the firestone and the wood, but where is the sheep for the burnt offering?" Because he senses that his father is ready to truly hear him, Isaac voices his deepest concerns: What are you really going to do? Will there be a sheep for the slaughter? What is going to happen and what will become of me?

This is our test as well: Do we truly listen to the others in our lives? For only if we do will those individuals for whom we ostensibly care really open themselves and their inmost feelings to us.[6]

The essential questions embedded in Isaac's call to his father—Who are you? Where are you? And where is God in all of this?—are the very questions that must have been in Abraham's heart as well. But not until his son asks these questions during the three-day journey to the mountain is Abraham able to confront his own doubts and to understand what he feels and believes. When challenged in a very direct manner by Isaac, Abraham must come to grips with his relationship with God. He must see that his relationship with the Divine is built on trust, which has been developed over a lifetime filled with promises that have been made and kept by himself and God.[7] Now, convinced that God will somehow ensure Isaac's safety, and guarantee his survival and the continuity of the covenant, Abraham responds to Isaac's questioning: "God will see to the sheep for a burnt offering, my son." God will surely be there for you (and for me).

It is no different with each of us. Only when we are confronted by those whom we love—even by what seem at first blush to be the naive questions of our children when they are young—do we truly confront our own beliefs and are able to articulate them clearly and succinctly. Isaac's question enables his father to affirm for himself, as much as for his son, that there is an omnipotent force in the universe that will provide a means of redemption.

But there is more in Abraham's response. Not only does he respond to his son out of his understanding of God's will, but Isaac's call, which indicates his son's desire to know the truth, gives him the opportunity to communicate the whole truth to him. By a simple play on words, the Rabbis envision Abraham saying, "God will see to the burnt offering [and it is you], my son!" Since the word *"beni"* (my son) follows the phrase "the sheep for the burnt offering," the Rabbis infer that Isaac is the sheep. There may also be the additional play on the word *se* (sheep), which in Greek means *"you,"* thereby allowing the reading: *"You* are the burnt offering, my son."[8] Isaac's call and then his piercing question give Abraham the opening to tell his son the stark truth. At first, when Isaac calls out, "My father," he doesn't say another word, reluctant to reveal to Abraham what is truly on his mind. Perhaps he intuits that Abraham indeed intends to sacrifice him. In uttering the words "My father," Isaac may be testing Abraham: Will he still react to him *as his father?* But upon hearing Abraham's response, "Here I am, my son," Isaac knows that his father loves him and that he can never sacrifice him on his own. This opens the way for a real dialogue, and he asks Abraham about the sheep for the burnt offering, in order to understand what is propelling his father to take him to the mountain and bind him as a sacrifice.[9] When Isaac knows the truth—that both he and his father are subject to God's will—he is willing with a full heart to be the desired sacrifice. According to one rabbinic interpretation of the scene, Isaac then reassures his father of his willingness to follow Abraham's instructions: "My father, everything of which God has spoken to you I will do with joy and fullness of heart."[10]

THE TWO WALK TOGETHER:
RELATIONSHIP SOLIDIFIED

As father and son make the journey up the mountain, we see an essential change in Isaac. Having reached the foot of Mt. Moriah,

Abraham places the wood for the burnt offering on his son and he himself takes the firebrand and the slaughtering knife, the two of them setting off together. Isaac is already playing the role of the animal by carrying the wood on his back. However, contrary to the previous interpretation, perhaps it never dawns on Isaac that he will be the actual burnt offering. The Midrash always allows for even seemingly contradictory interpretations in order to emphasize different points. The text says, *va-yalchu shenayhem yakhdav* (the two of them walked together), both in their naiveté: Abraham trusting in his covenantal relationship with God and Isaac similarly trusting his father. Rashi, in his comment on Genesis 22:6, emphasizes that they are both naive: "Abraham, who knows he is going to slaughter his son, proceeds willingly and with joy, just as does Isaac, who senses nothing." They walk together in silence, perhaps oblivious to what lies ahead. According to this interpretation, Isaac proceeds on the road up the mountain lacking all knowledge of what is about to occur.[11] The Rabbis picture Abraham and Isaac walking hand in hand—indeed together—though this is because Abraham is holding his son's hand tightly, thinking that Isaac could run in fear should he intuit what is about to happen.[12]

Like Abraham, we who are blessed to be parents sometimes want to hold on to our children for as long as possible, shielding them from the painful truth not only about life but about ourselves. And we continue to do so, even when it is detrimental to them. What does it take for us to realize that our children need to hear more from us; that they need to learn from us the truth about the world? Perhaps it takes our children asking us pointed questions that force us to respond, as Isaac does when he asks his father, "Where is the sheep for the offering?"

Abraham not only assures his son that he is there for him, but also conveys to Isaac that God expects him to be the offering, so Isaac can become a full participant in the scene as it unfolds. Isaac, now the willing participant, is again described as walking together with his father to the top of the mountain: *va-yalchu shenayhem yakhdav.* Father and son walk on together, but this time with each knowing what is in store. Isaac proceeds not merely because he trusts his father, Abraham, but because he trusts in God as well. Abraham and

Isaac hold hands, both intent on seeing the test to completion.[13] They now are one,[14] both proceeding with a full heart, at ease, ready to do what God demands. Abraham is ready to sacrifice his son, and Isaac is ready to be the sacrifice, if need be.[15] Isaac is even portrayed in the Midrash as praising God with the words: "Blessed is God, who selected me this day as an offering before [the Divine]."[16]

As Abraham responds to his son, Isaac, assuring him of his presence and love, so, according to one midrashic interpretation, Isaac now is able to reach out to his father. Having heard the truth and reconciled himself to it, he places his hand on his father's head, calming him, consoling him, and assuring him that he understands that he is simply fulfilling God's command.[17] He knows that his father loves him and that this is not his own doing, but rather it is the Divine will and that both of them are subject to something greater than themselves. They stand together, knowing and sharing the truth, and ready to act.

3
Awakening to Relationship

Abraham built an altar; he laid him on the altar, on top of the wood. And Abraham picked up the knife to slay his son. Then an angel of the Lord called to him from heaven, "Abraham! Abraham!" And he answered, "Here I am." And he said, "Do not raise your hand against the boy or do anything to him. For now I know that you fear God, since you have not withheld your son, your favored one, from Me."

(Genesis 22:9–12)

The fateful moment has arrived and Abraham stands on the peak of Mt. Moriah with every intention to fulfill God's command to sacrifice his son. He has come so far on his journey and is not afraid to complete the test that God has given him. God calls him by name at first, and now, having built the altar, bound his son upon it, and raised the slaughtering knife, Abraham once again hears the call from heaven. But this time the call is different.

ABRAHAM IS IMMERSED IN THE TASK

When God initially calls to him, God calls out "Abraham" once, and Abraham responds, *"Hineini."* He responds to God, trusting in their long-standing relationship, though the task has not yet been spelled out. Now, at the denouement of the test, God has to call his name twice, since Abraham is so intent on doing as God has commanded

21

him. Acting for God, the angel cries out, "Abraham! Abraham!" and he again responds, "Here I am *(Hineini),*" signaling his willingness to take his son's life, as God has requested.[1] Engaged in carrying out God's will, he becomes so suffused with the love of God and the determination to fulfill the word of the Divine that, according to one midrashic tradition, he does not heed the call to desist even after hearing his name twice.[2] At that moment, the angel continues, "Do not raise your hand against the boy!" Abraham protests, "Then I will have come on this journey for no purpose!" Still bent on proving his fidelity, he pleads with the angel, "Okay, I won't touch him with my hands, but let me just take the knife and draw some blood. Please, let me do something!" But God's messenger insists, "Don't do anything to him; inflict not a blemish upon him." (There is a wonderful play here on the word *me'umah,* meaning simply "something" or "anything." The term *mum* means "blemish" and, therefore, the Rabbis read Genesis 22:12 as if the angel cries out, "Don't even inflict a blemish upon him"). However, Abraham would not yield to the angel: "God commanded me to take Isaac's life and you command me not to touch him; the words of the teacher and the words of the disciple—to whose words should I harken?[3]

The angel's double call of Abraham's name indicates the great urgency of the moment. Abraham, consumed with a passion for fulfilling God's command, is about to slaughter his son, Isaac, and the angel hastens to repeat his name in order to distract him.[4] Like a person crying out in great distress, the angel booms forth: "Abraham! Abraham! What are you doing? Stop! Do not touch the boy! Don't lay a hand on him!"[5]

THE AWAKENING OF ABRAHAM, THE FATHER

Though of course never tested like Abraham, are we not like Abraham in the determination that he shows? We, too, passionately devoted to our own callings, can be consumed by them, whether they be our careers, our religious convictions, or simply our need to please others in our lives. Such depth of commitment or of need can drive us to the point of being totally oblivious to individuals in our lives whom we ostensibly love and who love us. Like our biblical ancestor, we, too, can fail to hear the voices calling out to us.

Abraham is so consumed by the task at hand and so bent on demonstrating his unconditional fidelity to God that he does not hear his name when the angel calls out the first time. Yet, when his name "Abraham" rings out again, this time with even greater urgency, he is finally awakened out of his stupor, awakened to the reality of what he is about to do. And he responds, *"Hineini"* (Here I am). Abraham must be terrified at that moment,[6] terrified of himself and what he is capable of doing in the name of his belief. If only he could describe for us this moment of awakening, when he realizes that he would have taken his son's life had not the angel—or God—stayed his hand. Perhaps for the first time in his life, Abraham, the exemplar of the one who believes in God and is willing to sacrifice everything for that belief, is really fully present.

When the angel calls from heaven a second time, Abraham, the father, finally becomes aware of what he is about to do to his son. In a sense, there are two Abrahams on the mountain that day—Abraham, the believer, and Abraham, the father. The Abraham who is ready to sacrifice his son, whom he cherishes and who represents his future, is addressed by the angel's first call. However, Abraham, the father who loves his son, has to have been overcome with grief as he raises the slaughtering knife in response to God's command. According to the rabbinic tradition, tears gush from Abraham's eyes and fall on Isaac as Abraham raises his voice in anguish heavenward.[7] The tears that fall into Isaac's eyes are the cause of Isaac's impaired vision later in his life (Genesis 27:1). In effect, Isaac bears the scars of the *Akeidah* all his life. Yet, the angel, in calling Abraham a second time, seeks to touch the father in him, thereby preventing him from taking his son's life.

> Such depth of commitment or of need can drive us to the point of being totally oblivious to individuals in our lives whom we ostensibly love and who love us. Like our biblical ancestor, we, too, can fail to hear the voices calling out to us.
>
> [See Rabbi Richard Jacobs's "Being Accessible to the Other in Our Lives," p. 133.]

When God initially addresses Abraham at the outset of the *Akeidah,* God commands, "Take your son, your favored son, Isaac...And go to the land of Moriah, and offer him there...on one of the heights that I will point out to you" (Genesis 22:2). It seems that Abraham's challenge is to find the place about which God spoke. And when he arrives at Mt. Moriah, we read, "On the third day, he raised his eyes and saw the place *(ha-makom)* from afar" (Genesis 22:5). From the beginning, Abraham's quest is to find *ha-makom,* the place. The Rabbis, of course, stress that God is called *ha-Makom,* since God is ubiquitous; God is everywhere, in every place. Therefore, Abraham starts his journey to Moriah searching for God. However, in the process, Abraham finds his son.[8] Before the *Akeidah,* Abraham's life is focused mainly on his relationship with the Divine, on his responsibility as God's covenantal partner. Only after completing the journey to the mountain does Abraham recognize that what is truly important is his relationship with his son, Isaac. When his quest ends with finding his son, Abraham also finds God.

If only we, like Abraham, would learn that we can experience the greatest holiness in the world in those moments when we are truly there for our children, our spouses, those whom we love and who love us. When we are awakened to their importance in our lives and the blessing that comes through relationship, when we hear their call and see their faces, then we will see God's face.

A MIX OF RELIEF AND LOVE

The double call of the angel indicates that there are indeed different—perhaps even conflicting—feelings stirred at this moment of truth in Abraham's life. As mentioned, while Abraham, the believer, rejoices in fulfilling God's will, Abraham, the father, weeps in pain. To be sure, Abraham experiences a mix of emotions, and when he responds to the repeated call of his name, which prevents him from taking his son's life, he has to have felt a combination of relief, joy, and fulfillment, perhaps even anger and love.

The tradition emphasizes that the angel's—God's—double call indicates God's love for Abraham. It is referred to as *lashon hibbah,* the language of endearment.[9] It is only after Abraham indicates his willingness to respond to God's command, thereby passing the test, that God calls out his name twice—a clear sign of affection and love.[10] God now knows the depth of Abraham's commitment, even if God would never have allowed Abraham to take Isaac's life in the end.

An alternative interpretation sheds a different light on the angel calling out Abraham's name twice. According to this view, it is like two friends who are traveling together, when one sets off on his own, leaving his friend behind. The first is amazed and calls to the second, "My friend, my friend," in an attempt to call his friend back before he goes too far away. The second appears to have irritated his friend by setting out on his own, by "doing his own thing." So it is with God and Abraham. As God sees Abraham rushing to slaughter Isaac, God—the angel—cries out, "Abraham, Abraham," as if to say, "Wait, what are you doing? You've gone too far!"[11]

The angel's double call may also represent God's love and concern for Abraham (and Isaac?). God will not allow his partner in the covenant, with whom he has journeyed since Abraham's youth, to tread a path that will distance him from that which is holy. Abraham is indeed God's friend and God earnestly beckons him back. And upon hearing his name twice, Abraham responds, *"Hineini"* (Here I am. I haven't gone astray. I'm still very much with you in covenant).

THE MOMENT OF TRUE REVELATION

According to the Rabbis, when Abraham responds, *"Hineini,"* to the angel's double call, he uses *lashon ha-kodesh* (the holy language).[12] Ostensibly it means that he uses Hebrew, though the subtle implication is that Abraham's response itself embodies holiness. Perhaps when Abraham recognizes that the angel is calling to prevent him from taking his son's life and the parent in him responds affirmatively, this in itself is a holy act on his part. The point of the *Akeidah* is to affirm the sanctity of human life—God's intent from the very beginning.

We should ask why the angel calls out Abraham's name twice and not God. Why is God's voice heard directly when the command is uttered to bring Isaac up to the mountain as a sacrifice and now, when his life is to be spared, it is merely the angel who cries out? The rabbinic tradition is quick to point out that when Abraham stretches forth his hand to take the slaughtering knife with the intention of fulfilling what seems to be God's command for him to sacrifice Isaac, the angels in heaven weep aloud, crying out, "It is anathema [for Abraham to slay his own son]." This interpretation turns on a wonderful play on the biblical text cited from Isaiah 33:7: "Behold, their valiant ones *(areilam)* cried aloud *(huzah)*." Though the meaning of the term *areilam* is uncertain, it is understood as "angels," reading the Hebrew as *ereilim*. So the Rabbis say that the angels (as the angel mentioned here in Genesis 22:11) cry out. But there is an additional play on the word *huzah,* literally meaning "from without." They read it as *hizzah,* meaning "something outside [of acceptable bounds]." God could not have wanted Abraham to kill Isaac, for it would not be unacceptable![13] Therefore, the angel's call at the climactic moment embodies all that is right and holy. The angels, as an extension of God, give voice to God's true intent.

In some texts, the angels actually are pictured at this moment as challenging God and reminding God of the essential Divine Nature: "'Please, O God, You who are a compassionate and merciful ruler over all that You created...You who give life to everything...Have mercy and compassion on Abraham and on Isaac, his son, who have fulfilled Your command this day. Have You seen, O God, Isaac, the son of Abraham, Your servant, bound as an animal sacrifice on the altar? May Your mercy now be upon them.' At that moment, in response to the angels' plea, God appeared to Abraham and called to him from heaven...'Do not raise your hand against the boy or do anything to him.'"[14]

From this interpretation we deduce that the angel merely calls Abraham's name twice to get his attention and make him focus on what is about to be said. It indeed is the Divine who actually stays Abraham's hand by commanding powerfully, *"Al tishlakh yadcha el ha-na'ar v'al ta'as lo me'umah!"* (Do not raise your hand...or do anything!)[15] This is *lashon ha-kodesh,* holy language, words that embody the holy.

It is poignant to note in this regard that every time God speaks to Abraham, the verb used is *amar,* meaning "say," including God's initial remarks to Abraham in the *Akeidah:* "[God] *said* to him, 'Abraham'...and [God] *said* to him: 'Take your son....'" However, there is one exception, in which God "calls" to Abraham, using the Hebrew verb *kara (kuph, reish, heh)*. It is found at the climax of our story when the angel (God) *calls out, va-yikra,* to Abraham, preventing him from taking Isaac's life. But why is the verb *kara* (call) used here? Because it indicates a moment of true, complete revelation. According to the tradition, there is no true revelation from God if it is not preceded by a "calling"—the use of the verb *kara*.[16] The words that preserve Isaac's life are God's most authentic *dibbur* (communication, command) to Abraham. Can it be that when we ourselves feel compelled to act to save or enhance human life, we, too, hear a Divine call, however we would define "God"?

SPEAKING TO FUTURE GENERATIONS

God's second command to Abraham stands in sharp contrast to the first. At first, God seems to challenge Abraham to test the intensity of his belief. Just how far will he go to fulfill God's command to sacrifice his son? Now, in the guise of the angel, God addresses Abraham, Isaac's father, and demands that he desist from that very act of sacrifice, since it is not what God wants. The double call at the end of the story indicates that two Abrahams are present on the mountain that fateful day and struggle to discern and respond to God's words.

Abraham's challenge is our challenge. How do we respond out of the different facets of our nature as we attempt to infuse our lives with God's words? How do we balance our need to prove to ourselves and to others the depth of our faith and belief or our need to fulfill our highest personal aspirations with our commitment and responsibility to those we love? How can we be the fathers, mothers, spouses, siblings, children we should be when we are so caught up in our own agendas?

The message inherent in the double call to Abraham is a message for all of us, for all time. When the angel cries out to Abraham twice on Mt. Moriah, we, too, are addressed. The call reverberates across the generations because God is addressing both Abraham and all future generations at the same time,[17] challenging all of us as human beings, to examine with an open heart our priorities in life and the choices we make. If only we better understood the essence of God's call to us.

4
Response in the Everyday

When Isaac was old and his eyes were too dim to see, he called his older son Esau and said to him, "My son." He answered him, "Here I am." And he said, "I am old now, and I do not know how soon I may die. Take your gear, your quiver and bow, and go out into the open and hunt me some game. Then prepare a dish for me such as I like, and bring it to me to eat, so that I may give you my innermost blessing before I die."

(Genesis 27:1–4)

In studying Genesis 22, the *Akeidah,* we focused mainly on the pattern of God calling to Abraham by name and Abraham responding, *"Hineini,"* thereby affirming his willingness to do whatever God demands. Therefore, it is not at all surprising to us as readers that here in Chapter 27, Isaac now calls out his son Esau's name, and Esau answers, *"Hineini."* Just as God calls his chosen one—Abraham—so, too, does Isaac address Esau, his firstborn, who is now to be blessed.[1] Not only should we expect that the literary paradigm of the *Akeidah* would be repeated in subsequent narratives, but it is predictable that Isaac's actions later in his life would be affected by what transpired on Mt. Moriah. Undoubtedly, he has borne the trauma of that day throughout his life, and it has to have shaped his persona and the ways in which he relates to his own children.

Often in our own lives, how we were treated as children by our parents determines how we treat our progeny. We internalize the models with which we grew up and find it very difficult to break this seemingly endless cycle. Yet, if our parents mistreated us or deprived us of needed affection and love, we may go overboard in showering our own children with love in inappropriate or damaging ways. In some cases our own upbringing can make it impossible for us to view our children realistically; they can do no wrong in our eyes and we are oblivious to their faults, even to their essential natures.

THE *AKEIDAH'S* IMPACT ON ISAAC'S ABILITY TO SEE THE REAL ESAU

According to one thrust of the tradition, Isaac's willingness to obey his father during the *Akeidah* demonstrates Isaac's purity of heart and his essential goodness. He is so pure that he is oblivious to any kind of evil. Therefore, it never occurs to him that his own son Esau is evil and that his actions are an abomination, as the Rabbis emphasize in most rabbinic texts. He is seen as the embodiment of Israel's enemies.[2] Isaac is portrayed as being naive and his naiveté prevents him from realizing that Esau's response to his call is not sincere and that Esau does not deserve to receive his blessing more than Jacob.[3]

The biblical text tells us that "Isaac's eyes were too dim to see *(me-re'ot)*"—he simply cannot see the real Esau, his firstborn; this is one result of his experience on Mt. Moriah. Yet, a simple play on the Hebrew word, *me-re'ot,* which can literally be translated as "from [the act of] seeing," prompts the Rabbis to deduce that Isaac's inability to discern Esau's essential nature is due to what he "saw," or experienced at the climactic moment of the *Akeidah.* At the moment when his father raises the slaughtering knife to kill him, Isaac sees the *Shekhinah,* God's presence, on the mountain, and his eyes cannot bear the sight. In a sense, he is blinded by the brightness emanating from God.[4]

As we have already seen, some rabbinic interpretations of the *Akeidah* emphasize that Isaac carries the scars caused by his father's willingness to sacrifice him. One emphasized that it was Abraham's tears that blinded Isaac. In a similar midrash, the Rabbis relate that when Abraham binds him on the altar, the ministering angels begin to weep aloud, their tears dropping into Isaac's eyes as he looks heavenward for God's intervention. Those tears shed by the angels at the sight of Abraham about to take Isaac's life cause the impairment of Isaac's sight later in his life, as our text states, "When Isaac was old and his eyes were too dim to see."[5] Therefore, Isaac's response to Esau— both his desire to bless his son, which stands in contrast to his own father's treatment of him, and his inability to see Esau in realistic ways—was the result of what happened to him on Moriah.

Some traditions dispute the notion that Isaac is unable to see Esau as he truly is, noting that Isaac knows his son very well. According to these texts, Isaac wishes to bless Esau precisely because he is aware of Esau's weaknesses and misconduct. Isaac is angry about Esau's marriage to two Hittite women (which occurs in Genesis 26:34–35, immediately before Isaac's call to Esau), and hopes to change his errant ways by invoking God's blessings upon him.[6] Isaac does care for his eldest son and when he calls to him, he does so out of deep concern. He truly intends to bless him and thereby direct him to the right path.

Are we not occasionally like Isaac? We, too, go out of our way to compensate for our children's limitations and faults, in hopes of turning them around—lavishing them with unwarranted praise and gifts. Our impulse is to give more and more in the belief that our love and support will result in better behavior.

ISAAC TRULY LOVES ESAU FOR WHO HE IS

Although the rabbinic tradition generally views Esau in a negative light, the *pshat,* the simple surface reading of the biblical text, does not necessarily warrant such a conclusion, especially in our passage. The Bible indicates that Isaac's feelings for Esau are honest. Isaac favors his firstborn son because Esau cares for him and continually provides for the family. He knows in his heart that he can count on his son being there for him. Like all elderly parents, he needs the reassurance that he will not be alone in his old age. Perhaps this is a the result of his horrible memories of the experiences of the *Akeidah* and his own father's abandoning him. Isaac truly loves Esau and needs to demonstrate to him how much he means to him.[7]

Esau deserves nothing less, since he constantly nurtures his father, providing Isaac over the years with the tasty game that he loves.[8] Because he hunts food for the entire family, especially for his father, Esau plays a key role in Isaac's old age—he provides the sustenance that fuels his life.[9]

Is it any different in our families, when one child cares for and nurtures an elderly parent? The child who lives close by and literally feeds the parent usually is the one who initially is the object of the parent's love and blessings. Isaac depends on Esau for his nurturing and counts on him for his survival, so he wants to ensure Esau's happiness; so, too, our parents, who depend on us, invest in us and in our well-being.

In caring for our own parents as they grow old and infirm, what we give to them is a gift of self, over and over again. Isaac calls to Esau as he has done hundreds of times before, and commands him to take his quiver and bow and hunt the game that he loves, with the promise that he will give Esau his innermost blessing (literally, that his soul will bless him). The slaughtered animal that Esau brings resembles Esau: The animal's pelt reminds Isaac of his son, who, like the animal is "of the field" and is hairy all over (Genesis 25:25–27). The animal is a surrogate for Esau;[10] Esau gives [of] himself to his aged father, whom he loves. And Isaac can identify with Esau's selfless gift, since he, too, according to the rabbinic tradition, was willing to give himself as a sacrifice when God called in the *Akeidah*.[11] Isaac, bound on the altar on Mt. Moriah, is able to understand the significance of the animal offering that Esau brings to him.

Aren't we able to understand our own children's actions when we ourselves have acted in similar ways in our youth? If only we could admit to ourselves more often that our behavior was not very different from theirs!

THE CHALLENGE TO RESPOND TO EVERYDAY TASKS

Although Isaac, having experienced the *Akeidah,* is able to identify with Esau's self-sacrifice, the circumstances of each are quite different. Esau's challenge does not come on a mountaintop, at the high place, but rather in an everyday moment, with which every family is familiar. Our test of faith occurs in seemingly mundane situations, when an aging parent—our parent—who can no longer take care of himself totally, calls to us, as Isaac called to Esau. We, like Esau, are asked to go out shopping and prepare dinner for a parent who not so long ago was preparing dinner for us. Or perhaps the request is for us to take her to a doctor's appointment or to push him in a wheelchair to the park for an hour's outing. Whatever the circumstances, the challenge of this call is the same: Do we have the strength and the patience to respond as Esau did, *"Hineini"?*

When Isaac calls to him, we not only sense Esau's desire to be there for his father, but we also feel the burden he bears as the child who is the perpetual caregiver. This comes through poignantly in Esau's curt response to Isaac: Isaac calls *"beni," my son,* and Esau merely replies, *"Hineini."* Though Isaac calls to Esau with the familiar, "My son," Esau does not reciprocate by saying, *"Hineini avi,"* Here I am, *my father,* and the reason is clear. This is perhaps the hundredth time that Esau has been asked to do his father's bidding, and he naturally feels put upon. Isaac has always been dependent on him and Esau is tired of constantly being the one to supply the family with food. Any one of us upon whom it has fallen to care for our elderly parents understands Esau's feelings implicitly. It is the story of every family, and Esau's abbreviated response to Isaac of *"Hineini"* (leaving out the word *"avi,"* my father), which lacks the expected warmth and closeness, forces us to weigh our

> Any one of us upon whom it has fallen to care for our elderly parents understands Esau's feelings implicitly. It is the story of every family, and Esau's abbreviated response to Isaac of *"Hineini"* (leaving out the word *"avi,"* my father), which lacks the expected warmth and closeness, forces us to weigh our own feelings about our elderly parents.
>
> [See Phyllis Trible's "Beholding Esau," p. 169.]

own feelings about our elderly parents.[12] So, knowing ourselves, let us not be too harsh on Esau. As ambivalent, upset, and even angry as he may have felt as his father's caregiver, he nevertheless does respond positively, indicating his readiness to hunt for his father. When all is said and done, Esau does say, *"Hineini,"* and in so doing reveals to us his essential nature. He does love his father and wants to accord him the respect he deserves from a son. Of all the characters in the Bible, Esau is held up by the Rabbis as the model of *Kibbud Av* (honoring one's parents).[13] Not only does he go out to hunt for his father, but he prepares Isaac's favorite dish. Even though Esau's actions follow his father's request, the fact that he gives his father such pleasure underscores what is really at stake—the special honor he pays to Isaac, his aged and infirmed parent.[14] Esau helps all of us better understand the importance of giving to the other, regardless of our ambivalent feelings. We can and do frequently have mixed emotions about constantly responding to those who need us, but that need not paralyze us.

WE RESPOND TO CERTAIN INDIVIDUALS

Esau knows that his father loves him because of the care and feeding he provides, and that Isaac has special affection for his firstborn son (Genesis 25:28), an affection not shared by his mother. As a result, Esau responds to his father in ways that he can't respond to anyone else—neither his mother nor his brother, Jacob.

Esau will do anything to please Isaac. When he realizes how much it matters to his father that he and Jacob not marry women from the surrounding Canaanite tribes, Esau goes to Ishmael, Isaac's half-brother, and takes his daughter Mahalat as a wife. Though, as we noted, he had already married two Hittite women (Genesis 26:34), he takes an additional wife in hopes of maintaining his father's love, even after Isaac has blessed his brother, Jacob (Genesis 28:6–9).

So, when his father Isaac calls him directly, saying to him *(va-yomer ailav)* affectionately, "My son," Esau cannot respond in any way other than "saying to him *(va-yomer ailav), Hineini*"—I am ready and willing to do whatever you want and need. The seemingly superfluous word in the text, *ailav* (to him), underscores that both Isaac and Esau speak to and then respond to each other in special ways. Esau is able to be there for his father because of the manner in which Isaac treats him.

Are we any different from Esau? Doesn't our ability to respond to the other depend, at least in part, on the person calling us? It is impossible to respond to everyone who enters the orbit of our lives: We simply do not have the time and energy to do so. Yet, we cannot ignore the calls of people with whom we are particularly close and who have constantly responded to our needs. We know who they are and when they need us, and we must respond to them in an unqualified manner: "*Hineini*—Of course I will do what you want if I possibly can."

HINEINI—ECHOES OF REDEMPTION

The rabbinic tradition stresses that when we respond to another, even in a seemingly mundane context, giving something of ourselves in the process, it is tantamount to responding to the Divine. Sacrificing ourselves for the sake of the other is similar to offering a sacrifice to God.

The Rabbis argue that Isaac's call to Esau and Esau's providing his father with the game that he hunts take place on the first day of Passover.[15] Esau is called by his father to bring [something of] himself to him on the very day that Israel brings the paschal sacrifice to God, marking the moment of Israel's redemption, and as the angels in heaven sing praises to God. Esau's [self-] sacrifice embodies Israel's and all humanity's recognition of God and our obligation to respond to God's presence and God's call to us. Perhaps when Esau brings an animal sacrifice to his father at the time of redemption, Passover, he reminds us that Isaac is seen by the Rabbis as a willing self-sacrifice to God during the *Akeidah,* which, as we noted, they believe took place on the first day of Passover. Both father and son are perceived to be models of redemption for all of us: When we give of ourselves to the other in our lives—God or human beings—we bring the world closer to the fulfillment of the messianic hope embodied in Passover.

5

Unqualified Openness: The Challenge and the Risk

> Rebekah then took the best clothes of her elder son Esau, which were in the house, and had her younger son Jacob put them on; and she covered his hands and the hairless part of his neck with the skins of the kids. Then she put in the hands of her son Jacob the dish and the bread that she had prepared. He went to his father and said, "My father." And he said, "Here I am. Who are you, my son?" Jacob said to his father, "I am Esau, your firstborn; I have done as you have told me. Pray sit up and eat of my game, that you may give me your innermost blessing."
>
> *(Genesis 27:15–19)*

As soon as Esau leaves to hunt the game and prepare his father's food, we know that his mother, Rebekah, believing that Jacob should be the son to receive the blessing, prepares the dish Isaac loves, places animal skins on Jacob's hairless arms and neck, dresses him in Esau's clothes, and sends him into his father's tent (Genesis 27:5–17). Jacob, pretending to be Esau, calls to his father, *"Avi,"* (My father), and Isaac answers in kind, *"Hineni, mi ata beni"* (Here I am. Who are you, *my son?*) Unlike Esau, who responds to his father's call with some ambivalence, Isaac's response to Jacob shows his unqualified openness. Jacob calls out, "My father," and Isaac replies, "Here I am, ready to relate to you in every way, my son." Isaac is ready to fulfill his responsibility in his relationship with his son.

THE RISK OF SAYING *HINEINI*

As we encounter Isaac's response, we may compare it to the previous *hineini* replies we have seen. The syntax here stands out and requires some interpretation. Isaac does not merely say, *"Hineni beni"* (Here I am, my son), but he adds: *Mi ata* (Who are you)? What is the nature of Isaac's question and why is it inserted here?

Though later a seemingly confused Isaac blurts out that "The voice is the voice of Jacob, but the hands are the hands of Esau" and "Are you really my son, Esau?" (Genesis 27:21–22), it is hard to imagine that he could not tell his sons apart. Even if he were almost blind, he would have been able to compensate for his disability by listening more intently than a sighted person. "The voice [was indeed] the voice of Jacob!" If this is the case, then the question "Who are you, my son?" is not meant to communicate Isaac's confusion; rather, it is an intimation that he is about to be met by deception. Though he is open and ready for relationship no matter who is standing in front of him, his son Jacob is not ready to reciprocate. Rather than answering honestly and forthrightly, Jacob says, "I am your son, Esau, your firstborn."

Such is the risk of *hineini*. When we are willing to be vulnerable by being open and responsive, we can never be sure what kind of response we will receive in return. Even when we relate to someone whom we love and who ostensibly loves us in return, we can be hurt when our openness is met with the lack of a wholehearted response or, even worse, by lies and outright deceit. Like Isaac, we must be willing to pay this price for the possibility of establishing a meaningful relationship with another human being. Sometimes we, too, simply cannot recognize those ostensibly closest to us because of how they have responded to us.

RESPONDING TO ALL OUR CHILDREN

It is precisely because Isaac responds openly to Jacob's call as he feigns being Esau that we can learn about the nature of relationship from him, especially the relationship between parents and children. When Isaac says, "Here I am. Who are you, my son?" he may not know which of his sons is standing in front of him, but he is open to whomever it is. He first says, *"Hineni"* (I am here for you), and then he asks who is calling. It simply doesn't matter whether it is Jacob or Esau; he is there for both his sons.

This is our challenge, too, if we are blessed with more than one child or are a part of an extended, blended family. Many of us face this situation every day, and Isaac reaches across generations and forces us to confront ourselves and our feelings. Even though we may have somewhat different feelings for each of our children and stepchildren, are we able to respond to each in a meaningful way? Are we truly present for each one, recognizing their particular needs, and do we make ourselves available for each one? Isaac, for all that he suffered at the hands of his own father, is ready to say, *"Hineni"* to each of his sons.[1]

SIMPLY BEING PRESENT IS NOT SUFFICIENT

Yet, the real test is not only being there for our children, spending meaningful time with them, sharing with them, being sensitive to their needs, but being willing to challenge them to face themselves. Isaac does not simply respond, *"Hineni,"* when Jacob calls, but he goes on to say, *"Mi ata beni"* (Who are you, my son?). Isaac's question is neither simple nor naive. He has the insight and the strength to ask his son the difficult questions: Who are you really, my son? What are your values? Isaac asks Jacob to remove his disguise, his Esau-mask, and come to grips with his essential nature, his values, what drives him as a person.

> This is Isaac's focus: He indicates not only that he is there for Jacob, but that he loves him so much that he will even challenge him out of his love and concern.
>
> [See Alan Dershowitz's struggle with Jacob's deception in "Jacob's Tangled Web," p. 121]

Isaac challenges Jacob to grapple with who he is, and this is the crucial part of his response to his son. This is emphasized by the shortened vocalization pattern of the word *hineini* here, so that it is pronounced *hineni,* with the accent moving to the end of the phrase, *mi ata beni.* (The vowel under the first *nun* in the word *hineini* is a *segol,* which is shorter than a *tzaire* that is present when *hineini* stands alone.) This is Isaac's focus: He indicates not only that he is there for Jacob, but that he loves him so much that he will even challenge him out of his love and concern.

Isaac shows us what parenting is all about; what relationships entail. He is not afraid to challenge his child to be the best person he can be. Some of us, out of fear that we might lose the love and affection of the other in our lives, especially our children, shy away from demanding the highest and the best that lies within them. Though we know intellectually that a loving relationship means helping the other to the fullest extent possible, some of us are not secure enough emotionally in our love to challenge our child, our spouse, our sibling, our lover to come to grips with their shortcomings. In our story, Isaac teaches us what being a good parent is all about.

THE MOMENT OF SELF-REVELATION

Isaac, however, is not the only one to risk engaging with another. The moment when Jacob enters his father's tent and calls to him is equally as challenging. The Rabbis re-create this scene and specify just what it means for Jacob to reach out to his father. Rebekah, having prepared Jacob in every way, including protectively dressing him in Esau's clothes and the animal skins, accompanies her son to the *petah,* the opening of Isaac's tent. She turns to Jacob and says, "Until now, I have protected you and helped you, my son. Now, you must rely on your own merit and God's protection."[2]

When Jacob leaves the safety of his relationship with his mother and crosses the *petah,* the threshold into Isaac's place, it is as if he has been birthed into a new reality in his life. With his mother's assistance, he has passed through a liminal space, a space of change, and emerged a different person.[3] He leaves behind his youthfulness, in which he was content to dwell in his mother's tent, to be cared for and to remain unengaged with the outside world,[4] and he is pushed by Rebekah to relate to and care for his father. He figuratively leaves his mother's womb and enters the real world of engagement with others, which demands that he remove his protective "skins" and confront who he is at his core. And this is not easy.

According to one midrashic tradition, as Jacob enters Isaac's tent carrying the food that his mother has prepared, he faints dead away. At that moment, God has to send two of the ministering angels, Michael and Gabriel, each of whom grabs hold of one of Jacob's arms to bring him before his father.[5] Jacob loses all control, bowed by the burden of his deception, and begins to weep uncontrollably.[6] He is completely on his own and must now reach out to his father, who from the very beginning loved his brother Esau more (Genesis 25:28).

Though Jacob is frightened and reticent, he manages to call out, "My father." These words show Jacob's concern for his father, the tradition referring to them as *lashon tzeniut* (the language of modesty).[7] In calling out this one word, *Avi* (My father), he effectively announces his presence to his sight-impaired father, who cannot see him, yet all the while testing whether his father Isaac recognizes his voice. If he thinks that his father realizes that it is Jacob and not his brother, Esau, who stands before him, Jacob can abandon the plan that his mother had set in motion.[8] Jacob is learning how to maneuver in the world of appearances, illusions, but also of confrontation and revelation. He knows what is at stake and he tries to slowly make his father aware of who he is.

There is great irony here. Jacob assumes a disguise; he puts on a mask, impersonating Esau; and yet it is precisely at this point that his father comes to know him. Until now, Jacob is totally uninvolved; he is not engaged in the day-to-day responsibilities of the family at all. He is cared for by his parents and even by his brother. Yet, when his mother Rebekah urges him to take his brother's place and feed his father, he is ready to open himself to his father's knowing him. Engaging with Isaac, Jacob exposes himself for who he is; he is willing to risk all.[9]

Like Jacob, it is easier for each of us to hide behind the masks we've worn that prevent us from truly engaging with the other in our lives. It is simpler for us to remain in our own insular worlds, isolated but protected, lonely but safe. Why should we risk crossing the threshold to engage the other, when in allowing that other in our lives to really come to know us, we will have to deal with our own identities? Why not remain in the womb we've loved, rather than reaching out and exposing ourselves to the pain of rejection?

CALLING TO THE OTHER HELPS
US KNOW OURSELVES

When Isaac asks Jacob, "Who are you, my son?" it is not clear from Jacob's reply who he is at his core. His self-revelation is contained in the words: "I am Esau, your firstborn; I have done as you told me." From one perspective, Jacob is simply pretending to be Esau, and in so doing he completely understands Esau's nature. Esau, as Isaac's firstborn, continually does what his father wants; he has always done Isaac's bidding.[10] When his father asks him to "prepare a dish for me such as I like, and bring it to me to eat" (Genesis 27:3–4), Isaac knows that his son will respond positively, just as he has done in the past. Jacob assumes Esau's nature as well as wearing his clothing in an effort to fool his father.

However, as Jacob wears Esau's clothing and looks and feels like him, not only does he begin to take on his brother's role, but also he assumes his persona. In impersonating his brother, Jacob evolves in new and complex ways, embodying some of Esau's essential traits.[11] In one sense, when Jacob purchases the birthright from Esau, he becomes Esau.[12] Jacob imitates the other in his life, and, in so doing, he becomes him. Therefore, when he responds to Isaac, "I am Esau, your firstborn," he indeed is telling the truth.

Yet, we know that he remains essentially Jacob, no matter how much he resembles Esau. Even though he may be struggling with who he is, he cannot ignore the essence of his being. He is Jacob and he cannot run away from that. The Rabbis underscore this in one interpretation of what Jacob says to his father, *"Anochi Eisav bechorecha."* This is usually translated as, "I am Esau, your first-born." But since Hebrew has no punctuation and the verb *to be* is not expressed, it is possible to read the two sentences: "[It is] I. Esau [is] your firstborn."[13] In this interpretation, Jacob can be seen as revealing himself to his father, even as he is attempting to fool him and receive the blessing. Perhaps Jacob is really saying, "It is I, Jacob, the son to whom you have not shown your affection, but who deserves the blessing, though Esau is your firstborn!"

Jacob reveals himself as he speaks; his voice, his words, tell it all. Isaac surely recognizes Jacob's voice—Isaac says in response to Jacob's words, "The voice is the voice of Jacob" (Genesis 27:22). Isaac hears that it is Jacob, his younger son, who is bringing him his food. Jacob in effect emphasizes, "It is I, Jacob, bringing you your food who deserves the blessing, even though Esau is your firstborn son."[14] The word *Anochi* (It is I) is a powerful one because it echoes the first word that God speaks in giving the commandments on Mt. Sinai: *Anochi Adonai Eloheicha* (I am the Lord, Your God) (Exodus 20:2).[15] In using the word *Anochi,* Jacob indicates to his father that his identity and fate are bound up with those of their people; he, and not Esau, will stand in the line of patriarchs and matriarchs leading to the covenantal moment of the Jewish people.

Jacob reveals himself to Isaac in an even more direct way when, a little later in the interchange, Isaac asks him point blank, "Are you my very son Esau?" (Genesis 27:24). Jacob responds with the even shorter word *"Ani,"* (I am). This is the pure moment of Jacob's revelation of self to his father, and perhaps even to himself. It is as if he said, "I am [Jacob, not Esau]."[16] This authentic response is free of all role playing; it is the *Ani* of inner freedom and authentic self, disengaged from the perceptions of others.[17]

Jacob's entry into Isaac's tent signals his achieving full personhood: As he passes over the threshold he challenges each of us to understand that when we engage with the others in our lives, especially those with whom we are closest, we have the chance to discover ourselves. In reaching out to others and sharing with them, and thereby revealing to them our essential being, we come to know ourselves in the process. Jacob can truly say, *"Ani"* (I am [a human being created in God's image])—there is substance to my being, goodness in my soul. In feeding his father, he comes to see himself vis à vis others and all that relationship implies for the very first time.

6
Fulfilling Past Promises

Now [Jacob] heard that Laban's sons were saying: "Jacob has taken all that was our father's, and from that which was our father's he has built his wealth." Jacob also saw that Laban's manner toward him was not as it had been in the past. Then the Lord said to Jacob, "Return to the land of your fathers where you were born and I will be with you." Jacob had Rachel and Leah called to the field…and said to them, "…Your father has cheated me, changing my wages time and again. God, however, would not let him do me harm. If he said thus, 'The speckled shall be your wages,' then all the flocks would drop speckled young; and if he said thus, 'The streaked shall be your wages,' then all the flocks would drop streaked young. God has taken away your father's livestock and given them to me…And in the dream an angel of God said to me, 'Jacob!' 'Here I am,' I answered. And God said, 'Raise your eyes and see that all the he-goats which are mating with the flock are streaked, speckled, and mottled; for I have seen all that Laban has been doing to you. I am the God of Beth El, where you anointed a pillar and where you made a vow to Me. Now, arise and leave this land and return to your native land.'"

(Genesis 31:1–13)

Having stolen his brother's birthright and blessing, Jacob flees to Haran at his mother Rebekah's behest and his father Isaac's directive, journeying to his uncle Laban's house, with the intent of staying there while Esau's anger abates (Genesis 28:41–45). Twenty years go by and through his hard work and initiative, Jacob amasses a huge flock, becoming quite wealthy. Though he has agreed with Laban that he will only be entitled to the spotted goats (Genesis 30:25–34), God sees to it that his flocks increase tremendously, to the chagrin of Laban and his sons. Jacob becomes aware of the talk among Laban's sons and notices that Laban begins to treat him differently, and he conveys his concerns to his wives, Leah and Rachel, Laban's daughters.

EXPERIENCING GOD'S PRESENCE IN A DREAM

Worried about Laban's treatment of him and whether Laban would honor his promise that all the spotted goats—those streaked and speckled—would be given to him as his wages, Jacob has a dream about the goats mating in the flock that shows his concern and vulnerability. He envisions an angel of God addressing him, to which he replies, *"Hineini."* God is not revealed directly to Jacob; it is an angel who appears in a night vision, and the angel does not literally call out to him—the text does not use the verb *kara* (call), but rather Jacob recounts, *"va-yomer alay"* ([the angel] said to me). Jacob is afraid and concerned about his family's situation in Laban's house and God appears in the guise of the angel to assure him that Divine providence is at work. Jacob himself sees that the goats mating with the flock are all spotted, thus ensuring that there will be many streaked and speckled animals, all of which are rightfully his.

But at this very point in his dream, the angel appears, compelling him to realize that it is God's hand making this happen. The angel implores him, *"Sa na eynekha u'r'ey,"* literally, "Please raise your eyes and see." Jacob must open his eyes and see his vision of the mating goats, but, more important, he must fully grasp that God is with him, protecting him. The angel confirms what Jacob has known—that God has been with him ever since the revelation at Beth El, at the outset of his journey twenty years before. He knows that the God of his father, Isaac, promises then to protect him and that God would surely not allow Laban to injure him.[1] Jacob continues to benefit from God's providence, and everything that happens to him is the result of God's plan.

Although it is an angel who calls out to Jacob, urging him to realize the import of his dream about the mating goats, according to the tradition it is God who continues speaking.[2] God identifies the Divine Self as the God of Jacob's youth when he anointed a pillar at Beth El and, emphasizing that God is cognizant of how Laban has treated him, commands Jacob to return to his native land. God has seen all that has transpired in Laban's house, which indicates God's deep concern for the suffering that Jacob has experienced, just as God will see and respond to the plight of Jacob's progeny in Egypt in the future.[3] God evidences great compassion for Jacob, exactly at the moment that Jacob needs it.

Like our forebear Jacob, when each of us feels most vulnerable, we, too, need to feel the presence and support of the other in our lives. When the tradition describes God as responding to Jacob in a wholly compassionate tone,[4] we know that is exactly what the relationship demands. Whether we describe it as knowing that God loves us or that there is a force in the universe that makes for wholeness, or it is just the love and concern of our spouse, parent, lover, child, or sibling, the presence and response of the other sustains us when we need it most.

RETURNING TO THE PLACE OF POTENTIAL RELATIONSHIP

God witnesses Laban's mistreatment of Jacob and knows that if Jacob is to survive and flourish he must leave Haran and return to the land promised to his fathers and to him. In their encounter at Beth El, as Jacob departs for Haran, God actually promises to always be with Jacob, protect him on his journey, and ensure his safe return (Genesis 28:15). Now, when his future is in peril in Haran, God impels him to leave, thus enabling the Divine to fulfill the promise made twenty years before at Beth El to return him to his homeland.[5] According to the Rabbis—applying the words of Psalm 142:6 to Jacob, God was to be his "refuge," his "portion in the land of the living," and this could only mean in *Eretz Yisrael*.[6]

God's command to Jacob to return to the land of his fathers, the land of his birth, and God's assurance that God will be with him in covenant (Genesis 31:3) are powerfully reminiscent of God's demand of Abraham to leave Haran, the place of his birth and his father's home, and journey to Canaan. Only there will Abraham experience God's blessing. To be sure, the nature of the journeys is reversed—Abraham leaves his homeland to establish the covenant with God in the Land of Israel, the land of promise, while Jacob must return to his homeland in order to fulfill the covenant. Yet, both are tested in the same way: They must break established familial bonds and set off on an arduous journey with their families to forge a relationship with the Divine that will lead to fulfillment of the covenant.

The Rabbis point out that in all the years that Jacob dwelt in Laban's house, God never spoke one word to Jacob. Genesis 29–30, which records Jacob's twenty-year sojourn in Haran, does not mention God ever speaking with him. Suffering in Haran, Jacob remembers that God promised at Beth El to always protect him, and now he longs to hear God's voice and to know that God is still with him. God then reaches out to Jacob, assuring him that the Divine will be with him *if* he leaves Haran and Laban, and returns to the land on which the covenant will be fulfilled.[7] God would not countenance the *Shekhinah,* the Divine Presence, dwelling with Jacob outside the Land of Israel, in a place of impurity.[8] The fulfillment of God's covenantal promises to his fathers hinges on Jacob returning to the land that God promised to them,[9] so Jacob departs from Laban's house as quickly as he can.[10]

Perhaps the ability to be there for the persons who are significant in our lives depends in part on our proximity to them. If we live far from those we love—our parents, siblings, children—few opportunities present themselves to respond in ways that can solidify our relationships. In our world of great mobility, we all suffer from the limitations of geography. We long for those earlier days when families lived in circumscribed locations and parents, cousins, uncles and aunts, and grandparents were intimately involved in each other's lives. Unfortunately, we know what it is like to live in Haran, far removed from the potential and promise of *hineini* moments in our relationships. We, too, must heed the call to bridge the chasm created by geographic distances and find opportunities to journey to the places of our fathers and mothers, our sisters and brothers, our children, so that we can be with them, as Jacob could experience the fullness of God's presence in the Land of Israel.

FULFILLING PAST PROMISES

It is poignant that in Jacob's dream, God emphasizes that "I am the God of Beth El." In reminding us of Jacob's vision of the ladder reaching toward the heavens at the outset of his journey to Laban's house, God makes us grasp the importance of Jacob's dreams set apart by twenty years.[11] In Jacob's youthful encounter with the Divine, God promises to be with him and return him to the land of his birth. Now, twenty years later, in light of Laban's treatment of him, God must fulfill his part of the covenantal bargain. God will ensure that Jacob flourishes even in the wake of Laban's actions, and God will be with him as he returns to the land of his fathers. The dreams, both of which involve Jacob seeing God's angels, are the bookends of Jacob's personal journey, and they underscore the mutual obligations that both God and Jacob must fulfill.

By saying that the Divine is the God of Beth El, where Jacob anointed a pillar and made a vow to God, God commands Jacob to return to the land, to that very place of Beth El, in order to fulfill the vow made twenty years earlier. As he is about to depart, Jacob vows that if God protects him on his journey to Haran and ensures that he returns safely to the land of his fathers, then Adonai shall surely be his God and that he will set aside a tithe from all the abundance with which God will provide him (Genesis 28:20–22). It is as if God were saying to Jacob, "Twenty years ago you made a vow to me. It is time for you to fulfill it." God will not tolerate any delay.[12] After reminding Jacob of the vow he made at Beth El, God commands him to literally "Arise *(kum)* and leave this land." The word in Hebrew—*kum*—is derived from the same root as *kayyaim,* meaning "fulfill," as if to specify that the purpose of Jacob's return to the land is to sacrifice on the altar at Beth El, thus fulfilling the vow he made to offer a tithe to God.[13]

If Jacob is to inherit the mantle of leadership from his father, Isaac, he has to fulfill the vow he had made. He erects a pillar at Beth

El and anoints it, designating it as an abode of the Divine. Yet, it remains for him to sacrifice there, thereby truly transforming it into God's place—*Beit El,* the House of God.[14] Only by sacrificing animals from the flocks he has amassed in Haran under God's providence can he sanctify God's presence. How ironic! The struggle with Laban is all about the flocks they raised and tended, and what Jacob feels is due him after twenty years of hard work. And God has ensured that much of Laban's livestock becomes his (Genesis 31:9). Now, Jacob is reminded that he must fulfill the vow he made to give back to God a tithe of the very flocks he has gained. Jacob, with all his acquired wealth, can only fulfill his covenantal obligation to truly sanctify Beth El by giving of himself, thus recognizing the source of his bounty and being.[15]

THE CALL TO ALL GENERATIONS

The tradition emphasizes that when the angel/God speaks to Jacob in his dream, commanding him to return to the land and fulfill his vow by offering sacrifices at Beth El, the angel/God speaks not only to Jacob, but to all future generations.[16] The call to Jacob reaches across the generations to each of us, beckoning us to respond as Jacob did, *"Hineini."* We, too, must come to realize that we can only fully respond to the other in our own lives by giving of ourselves in the deepest ways. *Hineini* is not a perfunctory reply. Rather, it entails giving back to the other—whoever it may be—that which he/she gave to us. *Hineini* implies reciprocity in relationship. *Hineini* requires us to fulfill promises we have made.

Just as Jacob can only sanctify God's presence in this world by acknowledging through his self-

Just as Jacob can only sanctify God's presence in this world by acknowledging through his self-sacrifice what God has provided to him, so each of us can create a bit of holiness, *kedushah,* when we give a part of who we are to another.

[Note Reb Zalman Schachter-Shalomi's examples of giving to the other, p. 157.]

sacrifice what God has provided to him, so each of us can create a bit of holiness, *kedushah,* when we give a part of who we are to another. When we are blessed to have a special person in our lives who gives so much to us, let us remember that we are obligated to give in return. It is not a freewill offering. It is as if we ourselves, like Jacob, are commanded by God to reciprocate.[17] And in so doing, not only will we strengthen our relationships with those most precious to us, but we will enhance the Divine Presence in the world.

7

The Significant Ramifications of Our Response to Others

So his brothers were wrought up at him, and his father kept the matter in mind. One time, when his brothers had gone to pasture their father's flocks in Shechem, Israel said to Joseph, "Your brothers are pasturing at Shechem. Come, I will send you to them." He answered, "Here I am." And he said to him, "Go and see how your brothers are and how the flocks are faring, and bring me back word." So he sent him from the Valley of Hebron.

(Genesis 37:11–14)

To us as readers, the actions of both Jacob and Joseph seem totally puzzling. The text indicates clearly that Jacob knows how his other sons feel about their brother Joseph, the one who elevates himself above his brothers through his outlandish dreams of superiority (Genesis 37:5–11). What makes matters worse, Joseph frequently gossips behind their backs. He returns from the fields where they shepherd his father's sheep with tales about what they said about their father in order to ingratiate himself even more with Jacob.[1] So we must ask why Jacob risks sending Joseph, his beloved son, to Shechem, knowing the depth of his other sons' hatred of him?

Similarly, it seems much more reasonable for Joseph to refuse his father's request. Is he oblivious to the hatred his words and actions have engendered among his brothers? Is he so caught up in his dreams of grandeur that he cannot see the extent to which he has alienated them and isolated himself? Or does he realize that, away from his father's protective presence, his brothers will have him exactly where they want him—alone and vulnerable—yet for some reason he still responds, *"Hineini,"* I am ready to go, when his father calls?

WHY DOES JACOB SEND JOSEPH?

Our scene opens with Joseph's brothers shepherding their father's flocks in Shechem, in what today is considered the northern part of the West Bank. Jacob seems concerned about Joseph's brothers' safety: He asks Joseph to "see how his brothers are," literally in Hebrew, to see about their *shalom,* their welfare. And Jacob has every right to be concerned, since Shechem is the place where his sister Dinah was raped and her full brothers, Simon and Levi, slaughtered the men of the village (Genesis 34).[2] Jacob berated the brothers, warning, "You have brought trouble on me, making me hated among the inhabitants of the land.... My men are few in number, so if they unite against me and attack me, I and my house will be destroyed" (Genesis 34:30). Now, the brothers have chosen that very place for pasture, and Jacob probably has visions of the Shechemites attacking the brothers and avenging their deaths.[3]

But perhaps Jacob had another motivation in sending Joseph to Shechem to see his brothers. Surely, one of the most difficult things that parents have to confront is tension and animosity among their children. We who are blessed to be parents and all of us who have siblings well understand the pain we feel when relationships among children are severed. Jacob agonizes over the rift that has grown between Joseph and his brothers and does not want to see it widened. He still harbors a hope for family unity, as every parent does. So when Joseph's brothers go north to Shechem to find better grazing for the sheep, Jacob seizes the opportunity to effect a reconciliation between the dreamer and his hostile siblings.[4] Joseph has to confront his brothers on his own, away from the doting presence of his father, if they are ever going to repair their relationship. When Jacob commands his son to "go and see how your brothers are," see to their *shalom,* he wants Joseph to see and care about their welfare, about them, and perhaps thereby create greater *shalom* between them. We can identify with Jacob's hope for reconciliation between his sons. We, too, have seen families torn apart, and perhaps have experienced the pain firsthand. And, like Jacob, we hold out hope that our children, our brothers, or sisters, can come home again.

Jacob's plan is simple: that his other sons will appreciate Joseph's arrival with supplies and his concern for their welfare. This plan is embodied in his hope that Joseph will return to him safely with word of them.[5] In telling Joseph, "bring me back word," Jacob shares with us his prayer that Joseph's brothers' animus will dissipate and that all will work out well in the end.[6] Yet, Jacob cannot help but feel tremendously conflicted, even guilty, over what he has done. According to the Rabbis, Jacob later confesses that he was consumed with remorse upon hearing Joseph's *hineini*: "I knew that your brothers hated you, and yet you answered me, 'Here I am.'"[7] The recollection of his son's willingness to journey forth to Shechem is a constant source of pain during Joseph's long absence. Jacob also knows that Joseph must have been very anxious about his impending confrontation with his brothers and, as a way of assuaging his own guilt while assuring Joseph that it will be all right, Jacob accompanies Joseph part of the way. He goes as far as the Valley of Hebron before sending Joseph off on his fateful journey alone. The biblical commentators point out that Hebron is situated on a mountaintop. So if Jacob sent Joseph off from the valley below, Jacob must have accompanied him at the outset of his journey. This interpretation assumes that Jacob and his family have settled in Hebron.[8]

Jacob's ambivalence in sending Joseph to Shechem is evident in his choice of words. At the outset, Jacob says, "Come *(lekha)* and I will send you to them." *Lecha* literally means "Go," but it is different from the regular imperative *lech*. The added suffix denotes a courteous request: "Go, if you please." It is not a demand, since Jacob understands the dangerous nature of his request and that Joseph may hesitate to accept. However, when Joseph responds, *"Hineini,"* agreeing to undertake his father's mission, Jacob then uses the usual imperative form, "Go *(lech)* and see how your brothers are."[9] Had Joseph voiced fears about being attacked by his brothers, Jacob's ambivalence and guilt would have been magnified.[10]

Even though Joseph is willing to go to Shechem to see his brothers, perhaps Jacob knows in his heart of hearts that the brothers' hatred of Joseph cannot be eradicated. Jacob is sending Joseph on an impossible mission. Jacob's command to him to "see how your brothers are—see about their *shalom*—and bring back word *(davar)* to me" simply underscores Joseph's status in Jacob's eyes and why Joseph's brothers hated him. Joseph always "brings back evil reports" about his brothers to their father and they despise him so much that they cannot speak to him in peace, *dabro le-shalom* (Genesis 37:2–4).[11] Something terrible can/will would happen when the brothers meet, and perhaps Jacob knows that he will never see his beloved Joseph again. This interpretation is based on the fact that Jacob does not say that he will see Joseph again, but rather that Joseph will only "return word to him."[12]

Perhaps our parents, or even we, as parents, in a desperate attempt to effect some sort of rapprochement among our own children, so misassess what is possible that we cause even greater harm. In our eagerness to ensure that our sons and daughters get along with each other, we create scenarios that simply exacerbate the problems. We engineer meetings in Shechem, only to discover that Shechem is a place of greater pain, and even violence.

WHY DOES JOSEPH SAY *HINEINI?*

The mission on which Jacob sends his favorite son is indeed impossible. We can easily imagine that the brothers chose to graze the flocks in Shechem, a few days' journey from the family's home far to the south, precisely because they already harbor plans to rid themselves of the dreamer who has made their lives miserable.[13] And Joseph would have to be totally oblivious not to realize that his father's request is fraught with immense danger. It would have been absolutely understandable had Joseph objected when Jacob asked him to visit his brothers alone. We would have expected him to say, "How can I possibly go to Shechem? Are you crazy? They hate me!"[14]

But not only does Joseph not object in any way, he immediately responds to his father with the one word that indicates his wholehearted readiness to undertake the task—*hineini*. Joseph is totally prepared to journey to Shechem, even though he knows the depth of his brothers' hatred of him.[15] The simplicity of his *hineini* and his ability to be present for his father in an untenable personal situation—one in which most human beings would have been unable even to utter a word of response—is a challenge to every reader. How can Joseph respond so openly and forthrightly to his father's words when he knows what awaits him in the fields of Shechem? How can we respond when requests made of us are laden with possible pain, even danger?

Yet, Joseph cannot say "no" to Jacob, the only person who truly cares for him. Our desire and ability to respond often depend on who is calling us. The biblical text emphasizes that Joseph responds because it is Jacob who asks, when it states, *"Va-yomer* lo: *'Hineini,'"* "And Joseph responded *to him:* 'Here I am.'" If a request comes from someone we respect and/or love—our parent, spouse, child, beloved—we really feel that we have no choice but to say, *"Hineini."* We have to respond to them and, in so doing, reciprocate their love for us. But does it always happen that way? Do we indeed find the strength to act on the other's behalf in the face of all that burdens us, and the stress we feel, or worse, when we understand the clear risks entailed in responding to the other in our lives?

Joseph is able to summon the necessary inner strength to do exactly as his father requests,[16] and to treat Jacob with the honor and reverence due a parent from his or her child, no matter how difficult the circumstances and the threat to himself.[17] According to the Rabbis, this is a poignant example of *Kibbud Av* (honoring one's parents), from which all of us can learn.[18] Jacob could have responded to his son's unqualified willingness to do as he requested by saying, "I know well that your brothers are not only jealous of you but they hate you, and nevertheless you responded, *'Hineini!'"* And to this, Joseph might have replied, "Father, I know how they feel. Do you think I've been oblivious to their remarks, innuendoes, and looks? Yet, even if they were to harm me, I could not possibly refuse you. I love you."[19]

THE TASK WE ACCEPT IS OFTEN NOT THE TASK INTENDED

As dangerous as the journey to Shechem may be, when Joseph says, *"Hineini,"* he is bent on fulfilling the task that his father has given him:

to visit his brothers and report back to Jacob. As he leaves his father's tent, little does he know what is going to happen. As the story develops, he travels to Shechem and finds his brothers pasturing the flocks near Dothan. They throw him into the pit, where he languishes for three days. They finally sell him to an Ishmaelite caravan, which takes him down to Egypt and sells him to Potiphar, Pharaoh's courtier. Following an aborted seduction by Mrs. Potiphar, Joseph winds up in prison, where over time he interprets the dreams of Pharaoh's butler and baker.

He eventually interprets Pharaoh's dreams, and, as a result, rises to the position of viceroy of Egypt, where he is instrumental in the years of famine in Egypt. Joseph's family leaves Canaan to settle in Goshen, only for a new pharaoh to arise and enslave the Israelites, who then suffer in Egypt for four hundred years. Moses finally comes, effects the Ten Plagues, liberates his Israelite brothers and sisters, and leads them for forty years through the desert to Mt. Sinai and the Promised Land. And Joseph? All he expects is to be gone for a week at most! He has no notion that his journey to Shechem is to be a part of the journey of slavery and redemption of the Jewish people. Joseph's *hineini* shows a readiness to respond to a task whose implications and impact cannot be foreseen. His is the willingness to begin a journey that leads to the unknown.[20]

> And Joseph? All he expects is to be gone for a week at most! He has no notion that his journey to Shechem is to be a part of the journey of slavery and redemption of the Jewish people. Joseph's *hineini* shows a readiness to respond to a task whose implications and impact cannot be foreseen. His is the willingness to begin a journey that leads to the unknown.
>
> [Compare Joseph's *calling* here to that of Lawrence Kushner in *"Hineini: The Calling?"* p. 141.]

When Jacob asks Joseph to journey to his brothers, he is referred to in the biblical text not as Jacob, but rather as Israel. Perhaps the switch in names here is purposeful, indicating that by dispatching Joseph on his fateful mission, he is shaping the destiny of the people of Israel.[21] Israel is indeed destined to suffer under Egyptian slavery, which is predicted as early as God's revelation to Abraham in Genesis 15:13–14. Joseph's journey to Shechem, his sale into slavery, and his establishment in Egypt are part of the Divine plan,[22] set in motion years before. The Rabbis emphasize this by a very creative play on our biblical text, when it states that "[Jacob] sent [Joseph] from the Valley *(emek)* of Hebron." They interpret this to mean that since Hebron is situated on a mountaintop and not in a valley, the text should be understood figuratively. Jacob's sending Joseph on his journey is the fulfillment of the profound (deep—*amuk*) plan that God conveyed to Abraham in Genesis 15, who himself is referred to as *"Hevron* (Hebron)"—a contraction of the words *haver na'eh,* (the pleasant companion of God). The identification of Abraham with Hebron is solidified in the minds of the Rabbis because he is buried in Hebron (Genesis 25: 9).[23]

Joseph's journey to Shechem does not merely involve visiting his brothers. Rather, it is the first step in a four-hundred-year odyssey of slavery and freedom of the entire people. And our lives are no different from Joseph's. Our responses to the seemingly simple requests of the ones we love may have ramifications far beyond those we can ever imagine. Often we cannot see how our willingness to say *"Hineini"* to our parents, children, spouses, lovers, and friends can even change the world![24]

There is much that Joseph does not realize as he leaves his father's tent on his way to his fateful meeting with his brothers. He thinks that his trip northward will only be a matter of days. He cannot have known at that moment that the next time he would see his father's face would be twenty-two years later in Egypt, when Jacob would be very old and nearing the end of his life. At the moment Joseph departs for Shechem, there is even the possibility that he will never see his father again. How can he know that the chance to say *"Hineini,"* to respond to his father, Jacob, whom he loves, will occur again? Joseph teaches each of us that we have to cherish the opportunities to act on behalf of those who mean so much to us. Such opportunities do not last forever. We never know when they will be gone. Potential *hineini* opportunities are precious, and it behooves us to focus on this moment in the biblical text to realize how such opportunities can change our own life journeys.

8
Responding to the Other's Fears

> So Israel set out with all that was his and he came to Beer
> Sheba, where he offered sacrifices to the God of his father
> Isaac. God called to Israel in a night vision: "Jacob!
> Jacob!" He answered: "Here I am." And [God] said: "I am
> God, the God of your father. Fear not to go down to Egypt,
> for I will make you there into a great nation. I Myself will
> go down with you to Egypt, and I Myself will also bring
> you back; and Joseph's hand shall close your eyes."
>
> *(Genesis 46:1–4)*

For twenty-two years, Jacob mourns Joseph's death. No matter what
his other children say to him, he refuses to be comforted. He misses
his favorite son immensely, and constantly cries over the loss of his
precious Joseph (Genesis 37:34–35). So when his sons return from
Egypt—having gone there during the famine to buy grain for the family—with the news that Joseph is alive, Jacob's heart goes numb. He
cannot allow himself to believe them. What if it isn't true? How could
he ever continue living after his hopes had been so dashed? But when
Joseph's brothers recount all that Joseph said to them as well as
Joseph's exploits as viceroy of Egypt, it is as if Jacob were reborn. He
shouts out, "Joseph is alive! I must go down to Egypt and see him
before I die" (Genesis 45:26–28).

Jacob immediately sets out for Egypt with his entire family and all his possessions, but he first stops in Beer Sheba to offer sacrifices to God. But why does he delay his journey to see Joseph, whose absence has been so painful to him? Why stop in Beer Sheba at all?

When God calls out his name twice in a vision while he is sleeping in Beer Sheba, "Jacob, Jacob," we now understand that there are indeed two Jacobs present. There is a *meteg*, a vertical line dividing the two names of Jacob in the biblical text, which underscores the tension between Jacob's two sides, according to the Rabbis.[1] Jacob, the father who longs to see his missing son again, has started out on his journey of reunion. But there is another Jacob—Jacob, the patriarch of his people, who is referred to as "Israel." And this Jacob is conflicted over leaving his homeland, the Land of Israel. Jacob is fraught with conflict between his needs as a parent and his role as a leader of his people.[2] In this sense, we are like Jacob when we struggle over our responsibilities as members of a family, especially as parents, and our perceived obligations to others in our professional lives or as members of the larger community. We find it difficult, sometimes even painful, to balance our two sides.

We sense Jacob's intense personal conflict because he envisions God's call to him in a night vision, unlike his father Isaac and his grandfather Abraham, who never experienced Divine revelation at night. The night is a time of reflection, when all fears are expressed. Restless and concerned about leaving the land promised to his forebears, Jacob needs to hear God's call in order to overcome his deep-seated anxiety.

WHAT DOES JACOB HAVE TO FEAR?

But why is Jacob afraid to leave *Eretz Yisrael* for Egypt when in his youth he journeyed to Haran in northern Mesopotamia and God protected him? What does Jacob have to fear? He is going to see his long-lost favorite son, who is now the Egyptian viceroy, under whose protection he and his family can surely live.[3] He may have no intention of remaining in Egypt for very long.[4] All he wants to do is see Joseph one more time before he dies.

Nevertheless, Jacob seems reluctant to make this journey to Egypt. He stops at Beer Sheba, which is situated on the north-south road from Hebron, at a distance of only twenty-five miles, but we are not given a reason why. Perhaps Jacob stops there to worship because the journey to Egypt is especially arduous for someone of his age. For an elderly person who has gone through as much as Jacob has in his lifetime, to leave his home and homeland at this stage of life has to be difficult. Yet, God's telling him to "fear not to go down to Egypt" implies that Jacob's concerns run much deeper.[5]

There is much family baggage associated with Jacob's leaving the Land of Israel for Egypt. He must agonize over leaving this land that is a fundamental part of God's covenantal promise to Israel.[6] His father Isaac frequently reminded him of the promise that God made to his grandfather Abraham that his offspring would inherit the entire land in which they dwelt, from Egypt to the Euphrates River (Genesis 15:18). Abraham and Sarah went down to Egypt two generations before and experienced great personal trauma—Sarah's becoming part of the pharaoh's concubinage (Genesis 12:10–20). And even though they returned to Canaan with great wealth, they did not establish a foothold in the land. All they possessed was the Cave of Machpelah, purchased as a burial site.[7] To make matters worse, when his father Isaac implored God to allow him to go down to Egypt, God commanded him to remain in *Eretz Yisrael* (Genesis 26:2). How can Jacob refuse to obey an explicit Divine command, when such defiance could have severe spiritual consequences for the entire people?[8] Jacob has also heard of the prophecy that Abraham's offspring one day will be strangers in a foreign land and enslaved for four hundred years (Genesis 15:13). Jacob worries that if he leaves the land promised to Abraham, then this prophecy would begin with him and his children.[9]

How can Jacob forsake the promise and abandon the land of his father and grandfather, the land promised to his progeny as well, the land in which *Shekhinah,* God's presence, dwells?[10] He entertains several fears—the specter of his family journeying to Egypt, the place of idolatrous abomination, only to find his children and their offspring not eager to leave this land of plenty in order to reclaim the land promised to them. He envisions his people assimilating into life in Egypt and losing their unique identity as a nation.[11] And he would be responsible for these calamities because he took the first step in the journey, which would inevitably lead to the demise of his people.

JACOB ATTEMPTS TO OVERCOME HIS FEARS

Jacob fears leaving the Land of Israel, though he desperately wants to see his son Joseph again. He even thinks of asking Joseph to come to Canaan to visit him,[12] as impractical as that may have been. Summoning up as much strength as possible, Jacob sets out from Hebron, where he lives (Genesis 37:14), making his way to Egypt to be reunited with his son.

Unexpectedly, however, when Jacob reaches Beer Sheba, he stops to offer sacrifices to God. Since Beer Sheba is so close to Hebron, it is surely too early for a break in the journey.

Yet, Jacob feels compelled to stop at this southernmost city on the border of *Eretz Yisrael* en route to Egypt. His grandfather Abraham had lived in Beer Sheba for a time among the Philistines, even planting a tamarisk there and invoking God's name (Genesis 21:33–34). Just as Abraham left the land of promise for Egypt, Jacob, too, journeys southward. He stops in Beer Sheba at the site where his grandfather prayed to God for Divine protection and offers sacrifices. No mention is made of Jacob actually building an altar, so it is possible that he used the very altar Isaac had erected years before (Genesis 26:25).[13] Jacob returns to his father's place and invokes the "God of his father Isaac" prior to leaving the land promised to his forebears. Just as Isaac asked to leave the Holy Land by praying at Beer Sheba, Jacob offers sacrifices in the hope of receiving Divine guidance. In fact, some fifty years before, Jacob himself set out on his journey to Haran and Laban's house from the very same place—Beer Sheba. He remembers the vision he saw at Beth El, and God's promise to be with him wherever he went and to bring him back to the land of his fathers.[14] Jacob reflects on that journey away from *Eretz Yisrael* in his youth and remembers how God indeed protected him and ensured his safe return.

In leaving the land of the covenant, Jacob needs to have God's blessing and assurance that his children and perhaps their progeny will survive.[15] Even if the exile predicted in God's revelation to his grandfather were to begin with him, would God forever be with them and ultimately return them to their land? Unlike Abraham, however, who also went down to Egypt in a famine, but only had to care for himself, his wife, Sarah, and his nephew Lot, Jacob is concerned about the future of his large, extended family, numbering seventy.[16] Are we any different? Do we not often worry about how the choices we make on our life journeys will affect those about whom we care— the individuals who come along with us, sometimes against their will? Jacob went down to Egypt and he took his entire family with him.

GOD'S RESPONSE TO JACOB'S FEARS

Amid Jacob's fears for himself, his family, and their future as he embarks on the journey away from the Land of Israel, God appears to him in a night vision. Perhaps the Holy One appeared to him in the darkness of the night to assure him that the Divine Presence would be with him even in the darkness and the oppression of exile, which is likened to the night.[17] Just as God responds to Jacob when he is most vulnerable and needy, we, too, must try to be there for those whom we love in their greatest time of need. When they reach out to us for comfort and assurance, we must ask whether we are aware of their suffering and pain, and if we are ready to call out to them in love.

God calls to Jacob, uttering his name twice, and in so doing shows

*J*acob is concerned about the future of his large, extended family, numbering seventy. Are we any different? Do we not often worry about how the choices we make on our life journeys will affect those about whom we care—the individuals who come along with us, sometimes against their will? Jacob went down to Egypt and he took his entire family with him.

[Compare Rabbi Neil Gillman's reflections on his family's journey in light of Jacob's journey on p. 129.]

Jacob his love and concern for him. Unlike the double call to his grandfather Abraham at the climax of the *Akeidah*, when God hastens to get Abraham's attention, here the dual calling out of Jacob's name should be understood as a sign of God's love. The Rabbis label the double call here as *lashon hibbah* (language of endearment and caring).[18]

And in response, Jacob uses the word *hineini*. As Jacob sets out on the journey to be reunited with his own son Joseph, he stops at the altar of his forebears in Beer Sheba and prays to the God of Isaac, the God of the generations that preceded him. How ironic! After not having been particularly close to his father all his life, when seeking to reunite with his son, Jacob acknowledges his connection to his own father and underscores his role as patriarch of their family. Finally, he is no longer running away; he is willing to assume the responsibility that he has inherited from his forebear.[19]

Because Jacob acknowledges that he sees himself as the heir to his father's and grandfather's covenantal position, God immediately identifies the Divine Self as *"Anochi ha-El"* (I am the very God who was with your forebears and also assured each of them that I would protect them). (The phrase *Anochi ha-El* seems superfluous in our biblical text, and therefore open to interpretation.) To both Abraham (in Genesis 15:1) and Isaac (in Genesis 26:24), God has also said: *"Al tira"* (Don't fear).[20] God immediately responds to Jacob's needs—Jacob prays to the God of his father Isaac, and therefore God identifies the Divine Self as the "God of his father." So we must ask ourselves: When those we love reach out to us, are we sensitive to their needs? Do we hear exactly what they are saying to us and do we respond in an appropriate manner?

Jacob is concerned about the future because of the covenantal relationship between God and his people. He fears their being exiled from the Land of Israel. But God then assures him that the Divine Presence will be with them even in Egypt. When God says, "I will go down with you to Egypt," God does not simply promise them that they will eventually return, but rather that the Divine will actually accompany them in exile.[21] God will not only be with them in Egypt, *Mitzraim,* but in all *meitzarim* (narrow places)—all places in which Israel suffers.[22] God's Presence, the *Shekhinah,* suffers along with Israel in every place of persecution, thereby guaranteeing their eventual return to the Promised Land.[23]

When God promises, "I Myself will also bring you back," using the future tense and the doubling of the key verb *alah* (to bring up), it cannot be a simple reference to Jacob's return to Canaan. We know that Jacob dies in Egypt. Rather, it is understood as God's assurance that his descendants will eventually return to the Promised Land and that his remains will also be brought back and buried in the Land of Israel.[24] This would indeed be the fulfillment of the promise made to his grandfather Abraham, that in the future Abraham's progeny will be enslaved, but in the fourth generation, they will return to the land (Genesis 15:13–16). Jacob's journey to Egypt, therefore, is part of God's larger plan, in which Israel will ultimately mature and become a great nation. Egyptian bondage will be a blessing, since it will be the crucible in which the people of Israel become united.[25]

God also comforts Jacob by saying that Joseph will care for him in his old age and be present when he is lying on his deathbed. Joseph will indeed close his father's eyes when he dies, which is seen as the ultimate act of a devoted child.[26] The irony, of course is that when Jacob acts as a parent to Joseph, perhaps for the very first time, by journeying to Egypt to be with him, Joseph will then reciprocate.[27]

Here we approach the essential *hineini* in this story. As a result of the responsiveness of human beings to each other, God will respond to the people as a whole. It is as if God were saying, "I will go down with you to Egypt and guarantee your return to the Promised Land *if* Joseph closes your eyes, that is, cares for you."[28] When human beings act in this world, especially when they respond to each other, God's presence is realized. When we say *hineini* to the people in our lives, we call forth the power in the universe that makes for ultimate wholeness and peace.

How fitting, then, that this is the last revelation to Jacob in his lifetime, and to the patriarchs as a whole. As Jacob is about leave the land of his forebears, entering Egypt and all the uncertainty regarding Israel's future as a people, God appears to him in a night vision, assuring him that the Divine will always be with them in their struggle to survive the darkness and pain of exile. And why will they ultimately return to the land of Abraham? Because God's presence will be manifest in the way they live their lives, in the manner in which they care for each other.

9

The Reticence to Respond

An angel of the Lord appeared to [Moses] in a blazing fire out of a bush. He gazed, and there was a bush all aflame, yet the bush was not consumed. Moses said, "I must turn aside to look at this marvelous sight; why doesn't the bush burn up?" When the Lord saw that he had turned aside to look, God called to him out of the bush: "Moses! Moses!" He answered: "Here I am." And [God] said: "Do not come closer. Remove your sandals from your feet, for the place on which you stand is holy ground. I am," [God] said, "the God of your father, the God of Abraham, the God of Isaac, and the God of Jacob." And Moses hid his face, for he was afraid to look at God.

(Exodus 3:2–6)

Moses is tending to the sheep of his father-in-law, Jethro, having driven the flock into the wilderness, when he comes to Horeb, which the ancients referred to as "the mountain of God" (Exodus 3:1). Whether or not Horeb is related to Mt. Sinai,[1] calling Horeb "the mountain of God" indicates to each of us as readers that the experience about to unfold anticipates the revelation at Mt. Sinai.[2] This is the moment in which God calls to Moses and he responds, *"Hineini,"* which eventually will lead to the solidification of the covenant between God and the people of Israel.

WHY DOES GOD APPEAR IN THE BUSH?

This sense of narrative anticipation is heightened as God appears to Moses in the guise of an angel in a blazing fire in the midst of a bush, a *sneh*. Since this word is very similar to *Sinai* in Hebrew—they are made up of the same basic consonants—one cannot help but feel that it is a direct allusion. Strengthening this connection, the word *sneh* appears only one other time in the Torah, in Deuteronomy 33:16, where it also seems like a play on *Sinai*.[3] Moses comes to Horeb, where the Torah is ultimately going to be given to his descendants, and God appears in the form of fire, since Mt. Sinai is pictured as consumed by fire and smoke (Exodus 19:8). The Torah itself is called the "fiery law" when it is revealed to Moses on Sinai (Deuteronomy 33:2). Therefore, on Horeb God appears literally in "the heart of a fire," *b'labat aish*. Several midrashic traditions note the use here of the term *labat,* derived from *l'aiv* or *laivov,* meaning "heart," instead of the expected terms, *lahav* or *shalhevet,* meaning "flame."[4] In order to prepare Moses for the thunder, lightning, fire, and smoke of Sinai, so that he will not be afraid, God wants to give Moses *heart,*[5] courage, in anticipation of the revelation at Sinai.[6]

God appears to Moses in both places: at the summit of the mountain and in the lowliest of bushes in the wilderness.[7] God's presence is everywhere; no place is devoid of the *Shekhinah,* not even a thornbush.[8] Many midrashim picture God leaving the realm of the Most High and in effect lowering the Divine Self in order to speak to Moses from the midst of the bush.[9] Sometimes, the call of the Other comes from the most unlikely of places, when we least expect it. But if we open our hearts and minds, we may be lucky enough to realize that the *sneh,* the lowly bush, is Sinai. Sinai is all around us; God is always there for us, calling to us.

This is especially true when we ourselves are in pain. Here, Israel is suffering under Egyptian slavery and God descends from the high place, saying, "I have marked the plight of My people in Egypt.... I am mindful of their sufferings. I have come down to rescue them from the Egyptians" (Exodus 3:7–8). Just as Israel is forced to go down to Egypt *(Mitzraim),* to descend *(yarad)* into the abyss of pain and despair, so God will leave the high place and descend in order to share

Israel's pain *(tzarah)*. God reiterates over and over again, "I will be with [Israel] in distress *(b'tzarah)*."[10] The clear linguistic play on *Mitzraim* (Egypt) and *tzarah*, (pain and suffering) is powerful.

Not only will the Divine be there, witnessing Israel's suffering, but God actually suffers along with the people: "In all their troubles, [God] was troubled" (Isaiah 63:9). The Divine figuratively is found in the thornbush, an emblem of grief and distress, because God shares Israel's great suffering.[11] The Rabbis teach very poignantly in this regard: "[This is similar to] the case of twins: If one has pain, the other feels it…. When the people of Israel are in trouble, they will call upon God and "in all their affliction, [God] was afflicted." God says to Moses, "Do you not realize that I live in pain just as Israel lives in pain? Know from whence I speak—from the thornbush—that I am a partner in their trouble."[12] God's presence, the *Shekhinah*, ostensibly suffers in slavery with God's covenanted people.[13]

God, therefore, is pictured as being everywhere and with everyone, protecting not only the mighty, but also the lowly, the troubled, the frail, and those most vulnerable.[14] Do we in the deepest recesses of our hearts believe that God suffers along with us when we are in pain, thereby offering us comfort and hope? Or, to put it in different theological terms, are we convinced that there is a power in the universe that makes for wholeness, even when we experience our greatest anguish? Experiencing the pain of Egypt—*Mitzraim*—as we live in our narrow places—*meitzarim*—can we sense the presence of the Other, comforting us and sustaining us?

God's presence in exile with the people of Israel and suffering along with them guarantees that Israel will survive. Just as the thornbush is the lowliest of all of the trees God created, so, too, Israel is lowly and humble in Egypt. Yet, the thornbush burns but is not consumed. Likewise, Egypt will not be able to destroy Israel.[15] But there is more: Not only will Israel endure, but the covenant will eventually come to fruition. The very symbol of Egyptian slavery and the threat to Israel's existence, the fire of the bush, also symbolize the Torah that Israel will receive in this very place. Moses will return to this holy ground, to the *sneh*, to *Sinai,* with God's people, and Israel will receive God's commandments,[16] the sign of God's love.

God responds to Moses' greatest fears, showing him that neither he nor the people of Israel will be consumed in Egypt. Moses, who witnesses firsthand the power of Egypt, is afraid not only that the Egyptians will destroy Israel, but that he himself will be killed because he has taken the life of the Egyptian taskmaster. God reassures him that he and his people will survive and return to the Promised Land.[17]

SEEING AND BEING SEEN

God's appearance in the Burning Bush underscores the ubiquitous presence of the Divine. God is manifest everywhere, from the lowliest of plants to the highest mountain peak. Yet, Moses would never have appreciated the significance of the fire in the midst of the bush had he not turned aside to look at this marvelous sight. First he had first to gaze and see the bush aflame, and then he had the impulse to leave the path and take an even closer look.

According to one rabbinic tradition, Moses takes three steps off the road in the direction of the bush, while a second asserts that he actually does not move, but rather cranes his neck to see the bush burning. When God sees that Moses goes to the trouble to see, God believes that Moses is worthy of having God reveal the Divine presence to him.[18]

God reveals the Divine Self to Moses only after Moses goes to the trouble of seeing God. With a twist of his neck to open himself to God's presence, Moses reorients his entire

God's appearance in the Burning Bush underscores the ubiquitous presence of the Divine. God is manifest everywhere, from the lowliest of plants to the highest mountain peak. Yet, Moses would never have appreciated the significance of the fire in the midst of the bush had he not turned aside to look at this marvelous sight. First he had first to gaze and see the bush aflame, and then he had the impulse to leave the path and take an even closer look.

[See Rabbi Sandy Eisenberg Sasso's "*Hineini:* I Am Not Supposed to Be Here," p. 153.]

being. He is now ready to witness God's presence. When God sees that Moses has turned aside to see the bush, God knows that Moses is ready to hear and respond. It is not a matter of simply "seeing" in a physical sense, but rather understanding with one's total being. Moses opens his heart and mind, and understands and internalizes what he has experienced—the awesome presence of God, which is beyond explanation.

Moses teaches us that it is possible to experience the presence of the other—whether it is the Holy One of Being whose presence fills the earth or the significant other in our own lives—if we dare to open our eyes, truly see what is important, and then turn aside from the mundane path we tread every day to encounter it. It takes both our interest and our willingness to draw near to enable us to solidify our relationship with the one we love. And then it will only happen if we are lucky enough that the other truly sees us as well.

GOD CALLS MOSES' NAME TWICE

The miraculous sight of a bush burning, but not consumed, catches Moses' attention, and he turns aside to observe it more closely. Moses both marvels at it and is frightened at the same time. And when he hears God calling his name from the bush, he recoils. He cannot fathom that the Divine is addressing him directly. After all, who is Moses at this time but a simple shepherd wandering with his father-in-law's flock in the wilderness? A person with a speech impediment who has great difficulty communicating, as he describes himself to God: "I have never been a person of words.... I am slow of speech and slow of tongue" (Exodus 4:10). An Israelite who fled Egypt having killed one of the taskmasters and having been ostracized by his fellow Israelites (Exodus 2:11–14).

So when he hears his name booming forth from the Burning Bush, he is absolutely speechless. He is overwhelmed and cannot utter a word.[19] His reticence, his insecurity, his seeming lack of confidence are all clearly in evidence. God has to call out his name again before Moses responds, showing just how human he is. Are we any different when we are called on to undertake a difficult task, one that we feel ill-prepared to take on? Do we not manifest the same reticence as

Moses, when he hears the call of the Other and is overwhelmed? When, in response to God's charge to him, Moses exclaims, "Who am I that I should go to Pharaoh and free the Israelites from slavery (Exodus 3:11)?" does not each of us in our hearts recognize and understand Moses' fears and insecurities? We, too, feel like imposters who cannot countenance the possibility that anyone will believe us, trust us, or follow us. The call of the other can be frightening, and we know how Moses feels when he hides his face from God, afraid even to look.

According to the tradition, Moses never gets over his reticence when God calls him. Every time God reveals the Divine Self, God has to call out "Moses" twice before he replies.[20] The repetition can easily be heard as an exhortation,[21] and at first Moses is unable to speak. Yet, unlike Jonah, who flees when God reveals the Divine Self (Jonah 1:1–3), Moses does eventually respond, *"Hineini."* He recognizes God's presence, as his forebears did, and he responds just as they did.[22]

GOD IS SUPPORTIVE OF MOSES

From the outset, God recognizes Moses' reticence. Realizing that if the Divine voice had bellowed forth from the heavens, Moses would have feared even more, God does

So when he hears his name booming forth from the Burning Bush, he is absolutely speechless. He is overwhelmed and cannot utter a word. His reticence, his insecurity, his seeming lack of confidence are all clearly in evidence. God has to call out his name again before Moses responds, showing just how human he is. Are we any different, when we are called on to undertake a difficult task, one that we feel ill-prepared to take on? Do we not manifest the same reticence as Moses, when he hears the call of the Other and is overwhelmed?

[See Rabbi Lester Bronstein's struggle as well with God's call, "Double Call," p. 117]

not overpower Moses with a thunderous call, but rather entices him to come closer with the spectacle of the flame.[23] And when God talks to him following his *hineini*, God identifies the Divine Self first as "the God of his father." Invoking Moses' father, Amram, God is revealed in a gentle manner to Moses in order to allay his fears.[24]

God's attempt to comfort Moses by alluding to a relationship with Moses' father also places God's call to him in the context of the long covenantal history of Moses' people. He, like all those who came before him, including especially Abraham, Isaac, and Jacob, will survive and flourish because God will never abandon him. God will always be with him and the people of Israel, and God hears their cries and will redeem them (Exodus 3:7ff). God underscores the unbroken continuity of the generations and thereby forces Moses to see that God's call to him will lead to the redemption of his people.[25]

God's response to Moses forces each of us to consider how we speak to those we love when they are feeling vulnerable. What words or images can we use to ease their fear and reticence? How can we be reassuring when they are apprehensive about what we will convey to them? Though Moses hides his face and cannot look, he nevertheless is able to hear and internalize God's message. Are our partners, lovers, children, and friends truly able to hear us when we speak because we have taken pains to ease their concerns? Is ours a soothing parental voice that is calming and reassuring?

It is very difficult to find ourselves standing on holy ground. In most cases, we don't even know that the place in which we are situated is holy—that it is suffused with God's presence. But God commands Moses to remove his shoes so that he can be more aware of the ground upon which he is standing (Exodus 3:5). When we are conscious that we are on *admat kodesh*, as Moses was, and especially when we are standing in that place without shoes protecting us from the pebbles and the grains of sand under our feet,[26] we, like Moses, need the calming presence of those who love us.

10

The Difficulty of Discerning the Call

Young Samuel was in the service of the Lord under Eli. In those days, the word of the Lord was rare; prophecy was not widespread. One day, Eli was asleep in his usual place; his eyes had begun to fail and he could barely see. The lamp of God had not yet gone out, and Samuel was sleeping in the Temple of the Lord where the ark of God was. The Lord called out to Samuel, and he answered, "Here I am." He ran to Eli and said, "Here I am; you called me." But he replied, "I didn't call you; go back to sleep." So he went back and lay down. Again the Lord called, "Samuel." Samuel rose and went to Eli and said, "Here I am; you called me." But he replied, "I didn't call, my son; go back to sleep." Now Samuel had not yet experienced the Lord; the word of the Lord had not yet been revealed to him. The Lord called Samuel again, a third time, and he rose and went to Eli and said, "Here I am; you called me." Then Eli understood that the Lord was calling the boy. And Eli said to Samuel, "Go lie down. If you are called again, say, 'Speak, Lord, for Your servant is listening.'" And Samuel went to his place and lay down. The Lord came, and stood there, and God called as before, "Samuel, Samuel." And Samuel answered: "Speak, for Your servant is listening."

(1 Samuel 3:1–10)

For most of us, it is difficult to hear the call of the other in our lives. At times we are so caught up in the day-to-day demands on us that it is impossible to be open to the needs of those we love and who love us. At other times, we are not experienced enough or mature enough to discern what they are communicating to us. If this is the case with our spouses, significant others, children, parents, siblings, and friends, how much more difficult is it to perceive the call of the Divine and then to be able to respond to it?

CONFUSING THE SOURCE OF THE CALL

Before we can be fully aware of the other, whether it be God or our loved ones, we have to be awakened from our slumber. How can we truly see them and hear their call if we are ensconced in our own world? At times we need to be jarred out of our comfortable places, where we may feel safe, though oblivious to all that is around us. We may feel protected, but we are merely isolated.

Samuel is sleeping in his place in the Temple when God calls him. In those days, prophecy was not widespread, so even Eli, the priest at Shiloh (1 Samuel Chapter 1), thought that a person had actually called out when Samuel came running to him, having heard the call. Eli knows that no one else is in the sanctuary, but he cannot fathom that God actually has called his young servant.[1]

If Eli, who has spent his whole life serving God, cannot conceive that God has called, then Samuel surely is unable to understand what is happening. Samuel simply believes that Eli has called his name.[2] Like Samuel, we frequently make the same mistake: We think that it is the other people in our lives whose voices cry out, when, in fact, it is the Divine reaching out to us. Little do we know that when we think we are responding to those close to us, or even to the strangers we meet, we are actually responding to the highest call in the universe. God calls to us through people.

So when the biblical text tells us that Samuel served God in the Temple at Shiloh *lifney Eli,* literally "before Eli," meaning "under his tutelage," Samuel is serving both Eli and God at the same time.[3] He is in God's presence, standing before the *Shekhinah,* each time he serves Eli, the priest.[4] To respond to other human beings, to act on their behalf, is tantamount to responding to the Divine in the world. But it takes sensitivity, introspection, and understanding to come to this recognition.

EVERYONE CAN HEAR THE CALL

As a child placed in the service of the priests at Shiloh by his parents (1 Samuel 1: 24–28; 2:11), Samuel is young and inexperienced. He is not very familiar with the religious life of his people, let alone aware of God's revelation. He cannot be expected to recognize God's call to him.[5]

Though we are told that Samuel is sleeping in the Temple near the holy ark, this cannot be taken literally. As a Levite, who serves Eli, the priest, Samuel surely sleeps outside the Temple proper, in the court where the Levites are situated.[6] Yet, even though Samuel is relatively far from the *Kodesh ha-Kodashim* (the Holy of Holies)—the Inner Sanctum, whence God's voice would emanate—nevertheless Samuel hears something and is awakened.[7] This may be the reason why the biblical writer tells us that "Samuel was sleeping…where the ark of God was" (1 Samuel 3:3). Though he has no notion of Who is calling him, even lying outside the Temple proper, he is still able to hear a voice. We, like Samuel, may not be able to completely understand what we are experiencing, but we, too, may occasionally be aware of something totally Other, feel the holiness of a certain moment, of a particular place. Although we cannot discern exactly what it is, nor perhaps find the correct words to describe it, we know that something or someone Other is tugging at us.

In contrast to his disciple, Samuel, Eli does not hear the call himself. Though God's voice reverberates like thunder, it passes unheard by those who are not meant to hear it.[8] The call literally passes over him as it moves from the Holy of Holies to Samuel.[9] The contrast between Eli and his young servant in the biblical text cannot be more glaring: We are told that Eli is asleep in his usual place, while Samuel is pictured as sleeping in the Temple; Eli's eyes have begun to fail—he can barely see—while "the lamp of the Lord" is still burning, enabling Samuel to see; Eli is oblivious to God's call, but Samuel immediately hears it. It is abundantly clear that Eli will soon be replaced by his disciple, Samuel. Yet, even before his guiding light is extinguished—the Rabbis understand the phrase "The lamp of the Lord had not yet gone out" as referring to Eli[10]—Samuel's light had begun to shine. God always prepares a new leader for the people of Israel before the previous leader fades away. As Ecclesiastes 1:5 states, "The sun rises and the sun sets": before Eli's sun is extinguished, the sun of his servant, Samuel, rises.[11]

WE ALL NEED EXPERIENCE AND MENTORING

However, Samuel is dependent on Eli. Without his guidance and experience, Samuel can never gain a clear sense of who and why he is being called. Eli will have to teach him to "know God," the supreme Other in his life. Through Eli's mentoring, Samuel can come to discern both the prophetic call and how to respond to it as well as the obligations associated with it.[12] As Proverbs 9:9 underscores, "Teach a wise man and he will gain in wisdom," and Samuel is just such an individual. He intuits God's call to him, and with Eli's instruction, he comes to know the fullness of the Divine Presence.[13]

We are just like Samuel in many ways. When we are young and less experienced, we may have a sense of the importance of other people in our lives and even feel

We, like Samuel, may not be able to completely understand what we are experiencing, but we, too, may occasionally be aware of something totally Other, feel the holiness of a certain moment, of a particular place. Although we cannot discern exactly what it is, nor perhaps find the correct words to describe it, we know that something or someone Other is tugging at us.

[See Peter Ascher Pitzele's personal struggle to discern the call in "The Story of a Calling," p. 145.]

from time to time the awesome presence of something holy in our lives. Yet, in order to more fully understand what we are experiencing as we stand in relationship with the other—be it another human being who is important to us or God—we need role models who can guide us, teach us. Through the sharing of their own life experiences with us and by directing us in our quest through word and deed, our mentors and teachers help us grow as human beings in ways we could not without them. With the guidance of Eli, Samuel comes to recognize God's presence, to hear God's call to him.

But even with Eli's help, Samuel comes to know the Other slowly, in stages. When he hears the call the first time, he runs in great anticipation to Eli, thinking it is Eli who is calling him. It can only be Eli's voice that he hears; no one else is present. However, after being told that Eli has not called out to him, when he hears the call a second time, he does not run to his master. Unsure of what he has heard, he proceeds more cautiously to Eli's chamber, perhaps somewhat embarrassed after being told once that he was mistaken.[14] Samuel is beginning to realize that the call is coming from another source and he simply does not know how to respond. Samuel's inexperience comes through in the text "The word of the Lord had not yet been revealed to him," and his unease is palpable. We see it once more when, after hearing the third call, he gets up slowly before going to Eli. The phrase in 1 Samuel 3:8 is *Va-yakom va-yelekh*, literally, "he arose and went," which indicates the inchoate nature of his action. And then, when Eli finally indicates to him that it is God who is calling, Samuel still seems reticent. Eli instructs him to say, "Speak, Lord, for Your servant is listening," when he hears the call again. However, it is startling that when Samuel does hear God's voice calling out, "Samuel, Samuel," he simply says, "Speak, for Your servant is listening." He does not follow Eli's instructions fully, of all things omitting God's name. Does he not say, "Speak, *Lord*," because he is still unsure that God is actually calling him,[15] or is he so awestruck, hearing God's call for the very first time, that he is afraid to address God directly by name?[16]

Samuel reminds all of us how difficult it is to truly hear, see, and meet the other in our lives. When we finally do experience a moment of recognition and engagement, we sometimes are so overwhelmed that we cannot find the right words to express what we are thinking and feeling. As we are overcome with emotion, both elation and fear at the same time, words may seem impossible.

GOD AND ELI ARE SUPPORTIVE OF SAMUEL: MAKING HEARING THE CALL EASIER

Eli understands Samuel's uneasiness upon hearing the call, the source of which he cannot discern; therefore, as his mentor, Eli attempts to be as supportive as possible. So when Samuel comes to him the second time, and Eli sees how reticent he is, Eli affectionately calls him "my son." In this soft and loving way, Eli tries to calm and assure his disciple that though he may be upset by the strange call, everything will be all right.[17]

The other, too, sometimes senses our difficulty and tries to make our moment of meeting that other easier. According to the Rabbis, God senses Samuel's unease and, in order not to frighten him further, calls out to him in the voice of a human being.[18] In fact, they surmise that God actually speaks to Samuel in Eli's voice. Not only does this indicate to Samuel that God is calling him because he has faithfully served Eli, but hearing Eli's voice will be a source of assurance to Samuel.[19]

To ensure that Samuel will be able to sense the Divine Presence, not merely hear a disembodied voice, God stands directly in front of Samuel. God actually comes and makes the Divine Presence known to Samuel as a way of assuring and comforting him. Unlike Moses, who has to move toward the Divine if he wants to be aware of God's nearness, Samuel does not have to move. God is there for him. And God calls out his name twice, as one would call a friend of long standing. God's calling out to him, "Samuel, Samuel," is an expression of endearment and intimacy.[20] God surely knows how Samuel is feeling, never having experienced such a moment, and God reaches out in a way that will enable him to hear and respond.[21]

GOD REACHES OUT TO ALL OF US

When God calls out Samuel's name twice, the Divine is calling out not only to Samuel, but also to every potential "Samuel" in every generation. The Rabbis believed that each generation will have a leader like Samuel who is able to hear God's call, respond, and galvanize the people.[22] So when the call of "Samuel, Samuel" comes forth from the Holy of Holies, it echoes across the generations, addressing all of us. Every one of us has the ability to hear the call of the Divine in the world; to discern the presence of the Holy in our world.[23]

And when we hear and respond to the Other in the world, God is miraculously present for us. In our responding to the call, we affirm the Other's existence. In the moment when we say *"Hineini,"* God reciprocates by saying, "Here I am" to us (1 Samuel 3:11).[24]

11
Fabricating the Call

After the death of Saul—David had already returned from defeating the Amalekites—David stayed two days in Ziklag. On the third day, behold, a man came from Saul's camp with his clothes rent and earth on his head; and as he approached David, he flung himself to the ground and bowed low. David said to him, "Where are you coming from?" He answered, "I have just escaped from the camp of Israel." "What happened?" asked David. "Tell me!" And he told him how the troops had fled the battlefield, and that, moreover many of the troops had fallen and died; also that Saul and his son Jonathan were dead. "How do you know," David asked the young man, "that Saul and his son Jonathan are dead?" The young man who brought him the news answered, "I happened to be on Mt. Gilboa, and I saw Saul leaning on his spear, and the chariots and horsemen were closing in on him. He looked around and saw me, and he called to me. When I responded, *'Here I am,'* he asked me, 'Who are you?' And I told him that I was an Amalekite. Then he said to me, 'Stand over me, and finish me off, for I am in agony and am barely alive.' So I stood over him and finished him off, for I knew that he would never rise from where he was lying. Then I took the crown from his head and the amulet from his arm, and I have brought them here to my lord." David took hold of his clothes and rent them, and so did all the men with him. They lamented and wept, and they fasted

until evening for Saul and his son Jonathan, and for the soldiers of the Lord and the House of Israel who had fallen by
the sword. David said to the young man who had brought
him the news, "Where are you from?" He replied, "I am the
son of a resident alien, an Amalekite." "How did you dare,"
David said to him, "to lift your hand and kill the Lord's
anointed?" Thereupon, David called one of the young men
and said to him, "Come over and strike him!" He struck
him down and he died. And David said to him, "Your blood
be on your own head! Your own mouth testified against you
when you said, 'I put the Lord's anointed to death.'"

(2 Samuel 1:1–16)

We, as readers, are immediately struck by the literary nature of this
passage, when we read that David has just returned from annihilating
the Amalekites,[1] while contrary to God's command, Saul previously
spared Agag, the Amalekite king, and the best of their possessions. As
a result, God rejects Saul as the king of Israel (1 Samuel 15:24–31).
This contrast between Saul and David is then played out in our story
with Saul being killed by the Amalekite, who, in turn, is killed by David
for slaying God's anointed leader. These narrative connections suggest
that our story about the Amalekite young man killing Saul never really
happened. It may simply have been fabricated by the biblical writer(s)
to make a point about the legitimate succession of David to the throne
of Israel. We are further led to question whether the events described
here ever actually occurred because the account of Saul's death in the
previous chapter—1 Samuel 31—is totally different. There, it is
reported that Saul actually takes his own life, having been severely
wounded by the Philistines, after his own arms-bearers refuse his
request to finish him off. He fears that the enemy will make a mockery
of him (1 Samuel 31:1–4). So we are left with the question: Is our story
of Saul's call to the Amalekite to take his life fact or fiction?

FABRICATING FOR ONE'S OWN PURPOSES

Some biblical scholars are convinced that the Amalekite's story rings
true. They argue that the lad would never have admitted that he

intentionally took the life of the king of Israel—technically making him guilty of murder—when he could have merely reported that he had found Saul lying dead on the battlefield.[2] From this perspective, our story simply fills in the gaps of the first version in 1 Samuel 31, in which Saul asks someone to put him out of his misery. It seems that its truthfulness is attested to by none other than David, who believes the Amalekite's account, since he immediately proceeds to mourn Saul's death.[3]

However, the more recent scholarly consensus is that our story is a fabrication, and that the first account of Saul's death at the end of 1 Samuel as authentic.[4] Not only does the story reported by the Amalekite to David contradict the version in 1 Samuel 31, but when the story of Saul's death is recalled later in 1 Chronicles, there is absolutely no mention of the Amalekite lad. The author of 1 Chronicles—traditionally thought to have been Ezra—who frequently repeats accounts of events related in 2 Samuel, must have believed that the Amalekite's story was false.[5]

The messenger's story is clearly the ruse of a shrewd schemer. Seeing King Saul lying dead on Mt. Gilboa, he seizes the opportunity to benefit himself. He appears in David's camp as a bedraggled, tragic figure, adorned with the signs of mourning—a bearer of great grief.[6] He prostrates himself before David, recognizing him as Saul's successor. Then he begins to test David's reactions by cautiously sharing his report: At first he spells out the bare facts of the losses on the battlefield and the news that Saul and Jonathan have died. But when David presses him for more information—"How do you know that [they] have died?"—he elaborates on how he came to take the king's life on his request. Like every good liar, the Amalekite lad knows the importance of providing details to make his story believable.[7] Perhaps even he believes it, just as any of us who spin some kind of fabrication can become convinced of the truthfulness of our own stories. The line between truth and fiction can become blurred and we ourselves are not totally conscious of the details we have created.

According to his story, not only is the Amalekite able to kill the king, but he succeeds in stripping him of the symbols of his royalty—the crown and the amulet—and then rushes off to Ziklag to the awaiting claimant to the throne. He imagines himself in a sense single-handedly crowning David as the new king, providing him with the accouterments of royalty.[8] He fully expects that David, who for so long has aspired to replace Saul as king, will be overjoyed at the news he brings. But lo and behold, David does not respond as the Amalekite expects. David does not celebrate, nor does he embrace the messenger in gratitude. David grieves along with his entire entourage for both Saul and his beloved Jonathan, but then he immediately sets about questioning the young man.

He already knows the messenger's identity from the interchange he described between himself and Saul, but David reveals his doubt when he asks the lad a second time, "Where are you from?"[9] The question is really accusatory: "If you live in the land of the Amalekites, how is it that you just happened to be on the battlefront among the Israelites?"[10] David can't believe that an Amalekite has conversed with Saul, and then is bringing him the crown and amulet, since the Amalekites are the Israelites' sworn enemy. And whereas before the lad identified himself as an Amalekite, now he changes his story a bit, claiming that his father is a resident alien who has converted to the Israelite religion.[11] But David then reasons that if he is indeed an Israelite now, how could he not have been afraid to murder the king, God's anointed?

We, like the Amalekite messenger, must be ready to face the same question: "Where are you coming from?" Those to whom we convey our stories may unexpectedly challenge us as to who we really are and how truthful we ourselves have been. David's question, which he asks twice, jumps off the biblical page and echoes in each of us: *Ei mizeh ata?* Where are you coming from? What is your baggage? Have you been telling the truth?

THE CALL NEVER OCCURRED

The lack of veracity of the Amalekite's report is indicated by the triple repetition of the phrase describing him: "the lad who was telling him [the news]." The redundant labeling clearly calls attention to what he is telling David and raises the question of whether it is a fabrication.[12] The first time the description is used by David occurs when he begins to press the lad concerning how he knew that Saul and Jonathan have been killed. It is in response to David's interrogation that the Amalekite appears to have concocted the interchange with Saul.

The lad tells David that he just happened to be *(nikro nikraiti)* on Mt. Gilboa and saw that Saul was severely injured, and that the Philistine soldiers were approaching. The Hebrew root of *nikro nikraiti*, meaning "I happened to be [there]," is *karoh,* which is very similar to *karah,* meaning "call." So when, in the Amalekite's story, Saul calls *(va-yikra)* to him, it raises the possibility that the call never occurred, just as the Amalekite lad's presence on Mt. Gilboa, in the midst of the battle between Israel and the Philistines at the moment when Saul is mortally wounded, seems impossible. We should note that the Hebrew root, *karoh,* is used in the core biblical passage defining the Amalekites—Deuteronomy 25:18. In this text, the Amalekites "just happen upon" the Israelites on their journey to Canaan and attack the weakest group who are tagging along from behind. Not only are they not to be trusted, but they must be killed—as is the Amalekite lad in our story.[13]

The Amalekite describes Saul's calling out to him directly for help and his response of *"Hineini,"* which is immediately followed by the king's questioning of him: *"Mi ata* (Who are you)?" Just as Isaac confronts Jacob pretending to be Esau when he responds, *"Hineini,"* to his father,[14] Saul challenges the lad to know himself. Each of us must respond to the same question in our lives, especially in the ways we relate to those whom we encounter. When we say, *"Hineini,"* when we claim to be present for the other in our lives, are we making a genuine attempt to respond? Or are we merely responding based on our own needs and agenda?

Who is this Amalekite messenger and what is his personal agenda? Why does he concoct this story of responding to the king's plea to end his life and then bring the symbols of royalty to David? From the beginning, the biblical writer alerts us to the Amalekite's purpose, when he describes his appearance before David with the words, "Behold *(hinei),* a man came from Saul's camp." The word *hinei,* translated as "behold" or "look," urges not only David and his soldiers to "see" the Amalekite for who he is, but the reader as well. We are impelled to ask, "Who is this man who came from Saul's camp?" Is there a word of truth to his response of *hineini* to Saul?[15] We, like David, have to open our eyes.

WHAT PROMPTS THE FABRICATION?

We can figure out several reasons why the Amalekite fabricates the story he relates to David. First, it is a means of self-aggrandizement. The image of the king of Israel calling to him directly and then continuing the conversation with him is surely a way of elevating himself in David's eyes as well as his own. The text says, "[The king] called *to me*," and "He asked *me*." We do not find the direct reference to the individual in every *hineini* call. And when he claims that Saul said to him, "Stand over me [and finish me off]," he shows his desire to gain in stature. Saul's words are a graphic representation of the Amalekite's need to make himself feel more imposing than he is and more important: He towers over the king of Israel.

Similarly, by claiming to have killed Saul, David's rival, and bringing the crown and the royal insignia to him, the Amalekite probably hopes to ingratiate himself with David. Having come upon the king's body by chance on the battlefield, he sees an opportunity to be rewarded by David for killing his archenemy, and perhaps even to overcome his marginal status as a *ger toshav,* a resident alien, by helping to establish David as king of Israel.[16]

Another possible motivation for the messenger's actions is that he is compelled to fabricate the story of Saul's calling him and his willingness to respond. Having been a

The Amalekite describes Saul's calling out to him directly for help and his response of *"Hineini,"* which is immediately followed by the king's questioning of him: *"Mi ata* (Who are you)?" Just as Isaac confronts Jacob pretending to be Esau when he responds, *"Hineini"* to his father, Saul challenges the lad to know himself. Each of us must respond to the same question in our lives, especially in the ways we relate to those whom we encounter.

[See Phyllis Trible's "Beholding Esau," p. 169.]

scavenger on the battlefield and having confiscated the royal crown and insignia, he brings the symbols of royalty to David in an effort to capitalize on his greed. But he has to couch the objects in the context of a story that could also explain why he of all people had come to possess them.

Whether it is because he needs to feel more important than he is or to ingratiate himself in the new king's eyes, or even to justify his own questionable actions, the lowly Amalekite messenger acts out of less than honorable motives. Yet, if we are honest with ourselves, we can identify with his actions: At one time or another, we all have fallen prey to the same kind of ignoble motivations. We, too, have concocted stories or "enhanced" their details in order to place ourselves in a better light in the eyes of those we love. When we read about the Amalekite's claim to have heard the king's call and to have responded to it, even if the tale is far from the truth, we must confront the storyteller in each of us!

THE PRICE ONE PAYS FOR A LIE

Though the messenger expects to gain in stature and to be handsomely rewarded for his efforts by David, he experiences the opposite. When we manipulate the truth, we suffer personally in the end. Instead of being elevated, the Amalekite remains a *na'ar*, an immature young man, in David's eyes. David refers to him as a *na'ar* over and over again, which stands in tension with the first description of him by the biblical writer, who says, "a [grown] man, an *ish*, came from Saul's camp." The contrast underscores the fate of the Amalekite in the end. And, ironically, it is one of David's young attendants, a *na'ar*, who eventually kills the Amalekite. Just as he claimed that Saul "called out" to him, so, too, David "calls out" to one of the *ne'arim* to strike him down as his punishment. This is a dramatic example of measure for measure: The *na'ar* who killed Saul is killed by a *na'ar* in David's camp.

But the Amalekite's fate is sealed by his own lie. Had he not claimed to have killed the king, he would not have been killed. And even though he didn't kill Saul, he became known as the slayer of the king of Israel.[17] As David emphasizes, the Amalekite's own mouth testifies against him: He, himself, reveals the lies he has told. So it is with each human being: The seeds we sow through what may seem to be small manipulations of the truth eventually rise up to bring us down. If each of us were always conscious of how we embellish our stories, perhaps we would avoid the fate of the Amalekite lad who claimed to have spoken with the king of Israel.

12
The Ever-Present Other

> I responded to those who did not ask; I was present to
> those who did not seek Me. I said, "Here I am, here I am,"
> to a nation that did not invoke My name. I constantly
> spread out My hands to a disloyal people, who walk the
> way that is not good, following their own designs.
>
> *(Isaiah 65:1–2)*

Following the defeat of Judea by the Babylonians, the destruction of
the Temple, and the exile of the people in 586 B.C.E., Israel's lament
is poignantly described in the Book of Isaiah.[1] The Israelites are pictured as feeling that God has rejected them because of their sins, has
hidden from them, and is totally oblivious to their continuous suffering and pain.

PROJECTING OUR OWN GUILT ONTO THE OTHER

The complaint of the people to God reaches a crescendo at the end of
Chapter 64, when the prophet pictures them as saying:

> No one calls Your name, rousing himself to cling to You. For
> You have hidden Your face from us, and made us melt
> because of our iniquities. But now, O Lord, You are our Father,
> we are all the work of Your hands. Be not implacably angry, O
> Lord; do not remember our iniquities forever. Behold, look
> down upon Your people, upon all of us.... Zion has become a

desert, Jerusalem a desolation…. All that was dear to us has been ruined. At such things will You restrain Yourself, O Lord, will You stand quietly by and let us [cause us to] suffer so heavily?

(Isaiah 64:6–11)

The people of Israel cry out in anguish, chastising God for remaining silent in the face of their suffering. Their complaint is focused on two key words at the end: "Will You stand quietly by *(tehesheh)* and let us suffer *(t'aneinu)*?" When they need God to address them, to call out to them, they perceive the Divine as being totally withdrawn and silent. Though they feel that God has caused or at least allowed them to suffer *('anah)*, they hope that God will answer *('anah)* their pleas. How ironic it is that the words in Hebrew for "suffer" and "answer" are homonyms.

They are no different from their forebears in the desert who complained bitterly, claiming that God had taken them out of the fleshpots of Egypt to die of starvation. They rail against God when their food runs out instead of recognizing that God has the power to save them. They should implore God to be compassionate, when all they can do is murmur against the Lord and quarrel.[2] So, too, the Judeans who later suffer exile. As a result of their vulnerability, they blame God for their harsh circumstances.[3]

They fail to internalize that their suffering is due to their sins and not God's indifference. If there is to be a return to the land and a restoration of their autonomy, then complaint against God has to be replaced by an acceptance of responsibility for what they have done. The people's rebelliousness and sinfulness are the cause of their suffering, not the quiescence of the Divine.[4] They cannot see that God had always been there for them. If only they opened their eyes, they would realize that they created the distance between themselves and the Divine.

So it is with each of us. When we feel distant from the other in our lives or when there appears to be an insurmountable chasm between us and the other, we blame it all on that person. Whether it be our spouse, child, parent, sibling, lover or friend, in our view it is often they who are the cause of our pain, isolation, or anguish.

Projecting responsibility for the rift onto the other is so much easier
than accepting our own culpability. The irony, of course, is that by
doing so, we are placing all the power in their hands and denying ourselves the power to change our relationship with them. By default,
they control the relationship.

THE OTHER IS PRESENT AND ACCESSIBLE

The people indeed lament the destruction of the Temple at the hands
of the Babylonians and their exile from the land, and they complain
bitterly about God's indifference to them in Chapters 63–64 in the
Book of Isaiah. Yet, God does not stand by quietly. At the outset of
Chapter 65, God seems to respond directly to their claims, reminding
the people of Divine Omnipresence.[5]

Even though Israel has distanced itself from God, Isaiah por-
trays God as always close at hand, ready to be encountered.[6] Isaiah
stresses over and over again that God has implored the people to
"seek *(darash)* the Lord when [God] can be found; invoke *(karah)*
[God] while [God] is near" (Isaiah 55:6).[7] Time after time, God sends
prophets to their ancestors, urging them also to seek out *(darash)* the
Divine.

And it does not matter the kind of situation in which Israel is
ensconced. The *Shekhinah,* God's Presence, can even be found suffering along with Israel in times and places of persecution and exile.[8]
God is present in all circumstances, as our text makes abundantly
clear: "I am present to those who do not seek *(darash)* Me. I say,
'Here I am,' to a nation that does not invoke *(karah)* My name." In
essence, God is ever-present to all human beings. The Rabbis even
claim that God is present for those non-Israelites who are worthy. For
example, our verses from Isaiah 65 are applied to Rahab, the harlot
of Jericho who encounters the spies, and Ruth, the Moabite and
ancestress of King David.[9]

God is not silent, hidden from those who seek the Divine. God
is not merely a passive presence. On the contrary, God is understood
as actively making the Divine Presence available and accessible. The
Divine continually calls to us, encouraging us to seek God. Perhaps
we should translate our verse portraying God as saying to Israel, "I

was ready to be sought *(nidrashti)*; I was ready to be found *(nimtzeti)*." Indeed, God offers the Divine Self to each Israelite, only to be rejected.[10] Just as God calls out their forebears, "Find Me; search for Me," so, too, God reaches out to every Israelite suffering the pain and hardship of exile in the days of Isaiah.

God calls out continually to the people through the prophets. Every day, prophets like Isaiah communicate God's word to the people of Israel, underscoring their responsibility to respond to the God of the universe with whom they are covenanted.[11] The description of God as "constantly spreading out [the Divine's] hands to a disloyal people" is understood by some traditional commentators as meaning that God sends the prophets to reach out to the people.[12] They, however, do not understand that the prophets bear God's words, nor do they recognize God's presence.

Just like the Israelites of old, we, too, often do not recognize that we can gain a sense of God's presence and God's expectations of us through our contact with other human beings. If only we could see clearly that the individuals in our lives testify to God's presence in the world and point us in the direction in which we must journey, we would gain a sense of fulfillment in our lives.

If we are to sense God's presence, we cannot be passive. Just as God actively reaches out to us, we, too, must actively pursue the Divine, to seek out the Holy in our world. In our passage, the prophet pictures God imploring us to "seek, ask, invoke, and respond" by intentionally using these active verbs.

> Just like the Israelites of old, we, too, often do not recognize that we can gain a sense of God's presence and God's expectations of us through our contact with other human beings. If only we could see clearly that the individuals in our lives testify to God's presence in the world and point us in the direction in which we must journey, we would gain a sense of fulfillment in our lives.
>
> [See Rabbi Sandy Eisenberg Sasso's story, which embodies the struggle to be aware of God's presence in our encounter with other human beings, p. 153.]

The same is true in all our relationships. To find meaning as we relate to the others in our lives—those in our nuclear families and those outside—we must work at it. Our relationships will not be fulfilling if we remain passive partners, waiting for the other to act.

THE CONTINUAL, REPEATED CALL TO US

God is always there for Israel, God's covenanted partner, even though Israel does not call out to the Divine. How ironic! We have clearly seen that the word *hineini* is used as a reply to a call by the other. In its essence it is a word of response. However, here, God cries out, *"Hineini"* twice, even though Israel does not call to God at all. The passage asserts that Israel indeed "did not invoke [call] God's name," emphasizing that God has the capacity to be present and engaged even when human beings do not recognize the Divine Presence in the world. To "call the other" is to identify with the other.[13] Yet, even if Israel does not want to be "called by God's name," does not want to be identified as God's partner, does not acknowledge their relationship, God nevertheless is still present for them.

God was present in the past, even when Israel sinned. God's double cry of *"hineini"* has been interpreted to mean that God was present for Israel not only following the Babylonian exile, but for our earlier ancestors as well: "'*Hineini*' (I am here for you), waiting for you to seek Me, just as I was present in the past, even when your forebears rejected Me. It was I who was present at the rock when they drew water after fleeing Egypt; it was I who gave them manna to ensure their survival in the aridity of the desert of their lives; and I am here for each of you."[14]

The double call of *hineini* (Here I am) not only indicates God's presence and reaching out to the people of Israel, but also symbolizes God's readiness to accept the people and their repentance. God calls out to each Israelite, "Here I am, *Shuvu ailai*—return to Me—and if you do, here I am, ready to embrace you."[15] God will hear us if we cry out; God will respond to our prayers.[16] God may be frustrated by Israel's inability to seek God's presence, and perhaps the double *hineini* should be understood as God having to call out twice because Israel does not respond. In addition, how can we be sure that God's patience is infinite? Perhaps there will come a time when the Divine will no longer be responsive to Israel's pleas. In one passage, the Rabbis voice this fear by offering the following parable:

> A caravan was traveling on the road. At nightfall, it reached a rest stop and the proprietor said, "Come in because there are wild beasts and robbers on the road at night. The travelers replied, "We're not accustomed to staying at a rest stop." After they left, it became very dark and they became afraid. They returned to the rest stop and begged the proprietor to open up for them. He said, "It is not our custom to open up for travelers at this hour of the night. When I offered you lodging, you refused. Now, I cannot open up for you." So, the Holy One said to Israel: "Seek the Lord when God is found" (Isaiah 55:6), but none of you attempted to repent.... So, when [Israel] was delivered into the hands of the other nations, they cried, "Why, O Lord, do You stand from afar?" The Holy One replied, "When I requested of you, you did not accept. Now that you beg of Me, I will not heed you."[17]

However, the overwhelming sense of the rabbinic tradition is that God is always there for us, willing to take us back into the sheltering presence of the Divine. But is that true of the others in our lives? Do they have the capacity to wait forever until we can return to them? Will they always wait with open arms to receive us? Like the travelers on the road, we may find that the rest stop does not remain open to us forever.

EXTENDING ONESELF AS FAR AS ONE CAN

Unlike human beings, God is always reaching out to us, beckoning us closer. God is pictured in our passage as extending the Divine hands to Israel, no matter how far they have strayed. It is ironic that it is usually we human beings who spread out our hands to the Divine in a prayerful gesture. Isaiah himself pictures Israel raising their hands to God in supplication.[18] While it usually is human beings who reach out to the Divine, here God is willing to go so far as to reach out and implore Israel to return. Though the people of Israel do not extend their hands to the Divine, God is constantly reaching out to the people of Israel, begging them to respond.[19]

God's outstretched hands are a sign to the people of Israel. It is as if in raising the Divine hands God is both indicating to them where the Divine Presence can be found and motioning to them to come close.[20] God signals to them that if they draw near, the Divine will embrace them.[21]

It is also incumbent on us to extend ourselves as far as we can toward the other in our lives. If we truly love and care for another human being, we must reach out and draw that person in. We, too, cannot sit by passively waiting for our significant others to grasp the importance of our relationships. We must signal to those we love that we care about them and want to bridge the chasm that has separated us.

God signals to the people of Israel that the Divine still loves them and wants to have them as partners in covenant. But for that to happen, the people need to understand that they have to walk on the path of righteousness. They cannot continue to be an *am sorer,* a rebellious, disloyal people, treading an evil path. Rather, God spreads forth the Divine hands, pointing to the path of righteousness,[22] from which they have turned *(sur),* beckoning them to find the way back.[23] In so doing, God motions to each of us to find our path back to the other, who awaits us with open arms.

13
The Ultimate Call

Cry with full throat, without restraint; raise your voice like a
ram's horn. Declare to My people their transgression, to the
House of Jacob their sin. To be sure, they seek Me daily,
eager to learn My ways. Like a nation that does what is right,
that has not abandoned the laws of its God, they ask Me for
the right way, they are eager for the nearness of God: "Why
when we fasted, did You not see? When we starved our bodies, did You pay no heed?" Because on your fast day you see
to your business and oppress all your laborers. Because you
fast in strife and contention, and you strike with a wicked
fist. Your fasting today is not such as to make your voice
heard on high. Is such the fast I desire, a day for men to starve
their bodies? Is it bowing the head like a bulrush and lying in
sackcloth and ashes? Do you call that a fast, a day when the
Lord is favorable? No, this is the fast I desire: to unlock the
fetters of wickedness, and untie the cords of the yoke, to let
the oppressed go free; to break off the yoke. It is to share
your bread with the hungry, and to take the wretched poor
into your house; when you see the naked, to clothe him, and
not to ignore your own kin. Then shall your light burst
through like the dawn and your healing spring up quickly;
your righteousness shall march before you, the Presence of
the Lord shall be your rear guard. Then, when you call, the
Lord will answer; when you cry, [God] will say: "Here I am."

(Isaiah 58:1–9)

Chapter 58 is often referred to as Isaiah's "Yom Kippur sermon," since it is traditionally read as the prophetic portion *(Haftarah)* on Yom Kippur morning and challenges the efficacy of Israel's fast. To be sure, there were a number of days designated as fast days, especially following the defeat at the hands of the Babylonians in 586 B.C.E. and the destruction of the Temple, and the prophet could have been referring to any of these.[1] In his critique of their fasts, Isaiah calls into question the integrity of their religious behavior.

DELUDING OURSELVES AS WE SEARCH FOR THE OTHER

The people of Israel are pictured as seeking God daily. They are eager to learn of God's ways, they desire to observe the laws, and they crave nearness to God. God emphasizes their ongoing quest for the Divine, in saying, "They seek Me daily." And the people see themselves as righteous, or at least make themselves out to be such.[2]

But they are entirely unaware that their conduct is displeasing to God. While they think that they are scrupulous in their efforts to follow God's ways through the oracles of priest and prophet, and to worship God, starving their bodies and covering themselves with sackcloth and ashes on fast days, it is only *as if* they were truly righteous.[3] One Aramaic translation of the Bible stresses this point: "They seek My teaching daily as if they wished to know My ways which are correct, as if they were a people that acted virtuously."[4] That is, they can fast all they want, but their acts are not genuine and complete because they are not performed with a full heart. The people of Israel are not fully invested in living righteously.[5] Their fasts are merely an attempt to draw God's attention to them and to their plight. They themselves said, "Why, when we fasted, did You not see [us]?" The people are totally concentrated on themselves and their own needs.[6] They are self-absorbed.

Are we not often like Isaiah's contemporaries? Do we not think of ourselves as devoted and righteous, as we seek God's presence through our prayers and rituals? Even in our relationships with the others in our lives, do we not frequently see ourselves as reaching out to them, responding to them, when our actions are merely driven by our own personal agendas? Can we admit to ourselves that at times our actions are selfish; that we are motivated by what serves us well in the end rather than acting wholeheartedly for the other?

And we, like our Israelite ancestors, may need someone to confront us, forcing us to see the truth about who we are. God commands the prophet to "cry out with a full throat without restraint, to raise [his] voice like a ram's horn" in order to awaken the people of Israel to the truth. They do not recognize their sinfulness, which stems from their being totally caught up in themselves.[7]

Although in a sense their fasts involve sacrifice, they need to learn that their actions must constitute self-sacrifice that benefits other human beings. The irony is that instead of depriving themselves of food and nourishment for the sake of their relationship with the Divine, they are asked to give up something of themselves for the others in their lives. God challenges them directly in this regard: "No, this is the fast I desire," meaning, you should indeed sacrifice of yourself, but it must involve compassion and kindness to those less fortunate in society.[8] As our text emphasizes, our challenge is to "unlock the fetters of wickedness and untie the cords of the yoke." However, we must unlock not only the fetters that bind the oppressed in society, those who suffer in their lives, but our own fetters as well. We must undo ties that insulate us and prevent us from reaching out to others; and that is often very difficult. How can we overturn long-held patterns of behavior that cut us off from our higher selves, denying us the opportunity to truly fulfill God's words?[9]

WHEN WE REACH OUT TO OTHERS, GOD WILL RESPOND TO US

The prophet, in calling for the people to respond to the needs of the downtrodden members of the community, asserts a view of life that grew out of the Israel's experience of being liberated from Egyptian bondage. It is the paradigm of God's promise to Israel—that the Divine would ensure their liberation as a people, nurture them through the aridity of the desert, and ultimately guarantee their survival as a free people on their own land—that fuels the prophet's demand that they do the same for those in need among them.[10] In demanding that the Israelites of his day "let the oppressed go free" and "break off every yoke," Isaiah harkens back to God's very acts in the Exodus: "I the Lord am Your God who brought you out from the land of the Egyptians to be their slaves no more, who broke the bars of your yoke and made you walk erect" (Leviticus 26:13).

In modeling ourselves after the Divine, not only must we, too, help break the yoke of subservience that treats human beings as beasts of burden, but we are obligated to nurture those less fortunate than we. Undoing "the fetters of wickedness" is only the first step; we must then sustain those who are hungry with our own bread and bring the needy into our own houses.[11]

Our obligation extends to all those in the wider community who are in need. All poor and oppressed individuals should be our concern. Yet, the prophet emphasizes that we have a primary responsibility to take care of our own kin and fellow Jews. We simply cannot ignore those closest to us.[12] Similarly, each of us needs to hear the call of the others in our lives. As Isaiah underscores, we cannot ignore our own family members, those who mean so much to us. And it is often easier to hear and respond to the faceless needy, people whom we will never meet, rather than reaching out to our parents, children, spouses, siblings, and partners, since our relationships can carry so much baggage. Their needs are camouflaged by layers of shared experiences and defensiveness.

> As Isaiah underscores, we cannot ignore our own family members, those who mean so much to us. And it is often easier to hear and respond to the faceless needy, people whom we will never meet, rather than reaching out to our parents, children, spouses, siblings, and partners, since our relationships can carry so much baggage.
>
> [See Rabbi Richard Jacobs's comments about Abraham in this regard, p. 133.]

But when we hear their calls and act righteously, we experience a sense of reward and fulfillment in our lives. When we truly give of ourselves to others, when our goodness is evident, we experience God's presence in our lives. Isaiah asserts: "[When] your righteousness shall march before you, the Presence of the Lord shall be your rear guard."

GOD'S ULTIMATE RESPONSE TO US

We are told by the prophet that God does not even notice Israel's fasts, though the people are eager to draw near to the Divine. God demands that the prophet call out *(k'ra)* to them, declaring their transgressions, even in the face of their ritual supplications. However, God will indeed recognize their fasts when and only when these ritual acts are accompanied by deeds of righteousness directed toward other human beings.[13] It is then that they will call out to God *(tikra)* and God will not only hear their prayers, but will respond to them—when God will say, *"Hineini."*

We, too, will only sense the presence of the others in our lives—whether that be God or others whom we love—when we are truly there for them, when our actions show our deep concern for them. It is only when we respond to them in the fullness of our beings that they will help us grow and find fulfillment.

God will respond to Israel with *hineini,* indicating that the Divine Presence will ensure their survival, as well as their prosperity. According to Isaiah, if they live righteous lives, their "light will burst forth," which is understood by some of the classical commentators as indicating that they will find meaning and success.[14] Their well-being depends on how they treat other human beings, which in turn will affect their relationship with the Divine and God's presence in their lives. When they respond to the needs of others, their needs will be fulfilled by the Divine.[15]

The commentators emphasize that their ability to sacrifice for others, especially those who are oppressed and needy, will eventually lead to their own salvation. Ultimately, God will respond to their call by saying, *"Hineini,"* (I am here for you and will redeem you).[16] Just as God promised Moses at the Burning Bush, "Since you have taken the pains to search for Me, to see My Presence, I, therefore, will reveal Myself to you and redeem your people [from Egypt]," so, too, will God answer and redeem the Israelites in Isaiah's day.[17] According to the prophet, their righteousness will ensure their return from exile. Isaiah said, "Your righteousness shall march before you." God will bring Israel healing, and the people shall once again experience the fullness of the covenant as they live in the Land of Israel.[18]

As it was with Isaiah's contemporaries, so it can be for us. Like them, we are immersed in our own darkness—the pain of illness, the loss of a job, distance from those whom we love, feelings of isolation; we, too, know hopelessness that can overwhelm and suffocate us. Yet, Isaiah reaches across the generations, calling out to us like the blast of a ram's horn, signaling to us that not only can we survive, but we can even flourish once again. If only we can set aside our selfish concerns and sacrifice for others, we can move beyond our own pain and then experience healing and wholeness. We will see the light burst forth like the dawn, as it breaks through the darkness of our own lives.

And in the end, it turns out to be our own light that illuminates the world. Our lives can be made better and the world can move closer to a messianic time of healing and redemption, if only we realize that our sacrifices should not merely involve the giving up of food on a fast day, but rather the giving of self to the other in our lives every hour of every day that we live.

14

The Ultimate Response

Awake, awake, O Zion! Clothe yourself in splendor; put on your robes of majesty, Jerusalem, holy city! For the uncircumcised and unclean shall never enter you again. Arise, shake off the dust, sit [on your throne], Jerusalem! Loose the bonds from your neck, O captive one, fair Zion! For thus said the Lord: You were sold for no price, and shall be redeemed without money. For thus said the Lord God: Of old, My people went down to Egypt to sojourn there; but Assyria has robbed them, giving nothing in return. What therefore do I gain here? declares the Lord. For My people has been carried off for nothing, their rulers howl—declares the Lord—and constantly, unceasingly, My name is reviled. Assuredly [they shall learn] on that day that *I, the One who promised, am here.*

(Isaiah 52:1–6)

The prophet Isaiah describes God as recounting the history of Israel—it has suffered in exile at the hands of the Egyptians, the Assyrians, and now the Babylonians. However, the people's suffering and persecution, in which Israel is described as being bound and captive, will not last forever.

SUFFERING AND ALONE:
CUT OFF FROM THE OTHER

The people of Israel suffer the ignominy of exile because of their sins. Isaiah cries out, "You were sold [into slavery] for naught.... You were carried off for nothing. You put your stock in worthless things, you worshiped objects of no value, and as result, you languish in a place that is not your own."[1] We, too, are sometimes cut off from the other who gives our life meaning, isolated from the very individuals who are most important to us because we hurt them through our own actions. We suffer most, just as our Israelite forebears, when we alienate the others in our lives.

And while the Israelites cry out in lament, wailing over their condition, their tormentors howl in glee. The term *yeheililu* in v. 5 is ambiguous, and perhaps intentionally so.[2] It can mean "howl," "wail," or "lament," but also "praise" and "cry out for joy."[3] The root of the verb *yeheililu,* which seems to be *halel,* could also be *chalel,* which means "to profane."[4] These persecutors of Israel revile and profane God's name in the world. As long as Israel is exiled, God suffers too. But God's suffering is not the result of the boasts of the foreign rulers who have carried the people of Israel into exile. God's name is reviled because the people themselves do not truly know God's name as indicated by their sinful actions. No wonder that God does not respond when Israel cries out to the Divine to be redeemed. God will not answer Israel's prayers.[5]

Yet, the Divine, like Israel, God's partner in covenant, feels totally cut off and exiled. God laments the fact that the people of Israel are enslaved in Egypt and are persecuted by the Assyrians, and that God has nothing to gain through exile in Babylonia. According to the Rabbis, there are four things that God regrets, one of them being having caused the exile of the people of Israel.[6]

We, like God and Israel, feel the pain when we are cut off from those whom we love. There is almost nothing more painful than being separated from the other in our lives, whose mere presence gives our lives such meaning and vitality. Each of us, too, cries out, "What can I possibly gain being here [in a place where I am estranged from the one who is my partner in life]?" But the God of Israel cannot suffer for long. God cannot allow the Divine Name to be slandered or reviled, and the Divine's impatience is felt when God says, "What therefore do I gain here?"[7]

RECOGNIZING THE ENDURING
PRESENCE OF THE OTHER

God cannot suffer the exile of the people of Israel and ultimately the moment will arrive when the prophet will call to them to awaken from the deep sleep and pain of exile.[8] Comparing the exilic experience to wallowing in the dust, Isaiah urges the people of Israel to shake off the dust and arise, thereby regaining their stature.[9] The fetters that have held them captive are to be loosened, and in their place the people must clothe themselves in strength and majestic garments, signs of the renewal of their status as God's covenanted partner. Israel is once again invested with the strength that comes from relationship with God, relationship with the other.[10]

On that day, Israel will recognize the Divine Presence in the world. God stresses that the Divine Presence has been there, unchanged, waiting for Israel to return, when God says, "I, the One who spoke *(ha-medabber)*, that is, promised, am here." *"Hineini"* (I am here, ready to fulfill the promise I have made to redeem you).[11] All the people of Israel have to do is to come to know God's name, to reestablish their relationship with the Divine Other in their lives,[12] and God will bring tidings of the impending redemption. Just as God had spoken of the possibility of redemption in the past, so now God will herald the fulfillment of the Divine word, as Isaiah described: "How welcome...are the footsteps of the herald, announcing shalom, bringing good tidings, anticipating victory, and telling Zion, 'Your God is Ruler'" (Isaiah 52:7). This is the messianic vision that will be fulfilled on that day, *ba-yom ha-hu*, when the darkness of the night of oppression will be transformed into the light of day of deliverance.[13]

God's *hineini* on that day is a response to the very question uttered by the Divine, "What therefore do I gain here?" God's inability to suffer the exile of the people of Israel is the guarantee that God will eventually assert the powerful Divine presence and redeem them.[14] It is as if the words of Isaiah should be read as saying, "I am the One who now speaks *(ha-medabber),* saying to you Israel, *'Hineini'* (I am here)." Though hurt by the people of Israel's sinfulness, God is now ready to restore their covenanted relationship because they have come to recognize the Divine.

God's *hineini* here is a challenge to all of us to think about how we act within our own relationships. When the other in our lives finally responds to us, are we able to open ourselves, perhaps after being hurt by that very person before? Do we have the capacity to bridge the gap that has existed between us and our parent, spouse, lover, sibling, or child, even when we have not been the cause of it? Can we forgive and rekindle these relationships?

KNOWING THE OTHER IN OUR LIVES

The Israelites' knowing God's name symbolizes the renewal of their intimate, covenantal relationship with the Divine. When in exile, isolated and cut off from God, it is impossible for them to know God. When they pray to God, God does not respond.[15] Yet, at the time of the ultimate redemption, God will respond to their calls, since Israel now will truly know the name of the Divine.[16]

Knowing the name of the other in our lives, whether that "other" be God or those whom we love, is an expression of intimacy and closeness. Each of us strives for this in all our important relationships, because knowing the other in

God's *hineini* here is a challenge to all of us to think about how we act within our own relationships. When the other in our lives finally responds to us, are we able to open ourselves, perhaps after being hurt by that very person before? Do we have the capacity to close up the distance that has existed between us and our parent, spouse, lover, sibling, or child, even when we have not been the cause of it? Can we forgive and rekindle these relationships?

[See Reb Zalman Schachter-Shalomi's poignant words about forgiving the other and responding, p. 157.]

deep ways and sharing with the other our essential self helps us grow and gives us real pleasure. But achieving that kind of knowledge is difficult. Each person must risk exposing him/herself and being vulnerable, confident that we will not be hurt by the other when we open ourselves totally. If this occurs, then we will come to experience the blessing of totally sharing with another human being, just as God rejoiced in returning to Israel: "Your watchmen raise their voices, as one they shout for joy; for every eye shall behold the Lord's return to Zion" (Isaiah 52:8).

But when the people of Israel are redeemed, the entire world will witness it and come to recognize God's presence, as Isaiah states, "The Lord will comfort [God's] people, will redeem Jerusalem. The Lord will bare [the Divine] arm in the sight of all the nations, and the very ends of the earth shall see the victory of our God."[17] Like the Israelites of old, when we come to know intimately the others in our lives, living relationships shaped by our ability to say *"Hineini,"* those who witness this will realize what is demanded of them in their own relationships. They will understand that they, too, are capable of creating intimate, deep relationships with the others in their lives, relationships that can infuse their lives with meaning and help shape who they can become.

This is the prophet's messianic vision. On the day when God says *"Hineini"* to the people of Israel, and to all creation, we human beings will recognize that what brought this about was our ability to know God's name, to discern God's presence in the world, and to embrace it. Furthermore, we will understand that the journey from the slavery of Egypt, Assyria, and Babylonia, from the narrow and confining places in our lives in which we feel isolated and alone, to God's place, is contingent on our ability to say *"Hineini"*—to God, to our loved ones, and to the myriad other human beings we encounter in our life journeys. Simply put: God's presence in the world is synonymous with *hineini.*[18]

Part II

Personal Stories: Making *Hineini* Come Alive

Our encounter with the fourteen biblical vignettes, built on the response to the other with the word *hineini*—whether the other be God or those people who are close to us—shows us the power of the sacred text to reshape our lives. We know that we can make these sacred stories our own if we are willing to hear their call to us.

What follows are eleven powerful personal anecdotes by individuals who have heard the biblical text beckon them to respond—individuals who have heard both the call implicit in the text and the call of the other in their lives. Their *hineini* responses reflect the influence that the Bible can have in all our lives. Whether it be Neil Gillman's response to Jacob's journey to Egypt in Genesis 46; Peter Pitzele's story of struggle to discern the call, as did Samuel in 1 Samuel 3; or Zalman Schachter-Shalomi's response to the pain of colleagues as prismed through Isaiah's moment of calling, we cannot help but feel how the text shaped their lives.

When we as readers can identify with characters in the text, we sense the power inherent in their stories. As Alan Dershowitz struggles with Jacob's deception of his father in Genesis 27, Lester Bronstein reflects on Moses' insecurity and conflicts in Exodus 3, and Sandy Eisenberg Sasso understands God's presence even when Israel does not respond in Isaiah 65, we learn that the struggles of characters in the Bible can teach us much about our own natures.

However, to open ourselves to the stories of biblical personages, we need to see them as human beings, possessing the ambivalence and the range of feelings that we all do. Richard Jacobs probes Abraham's and Isaac's feelings in the *Akeidah* in Genesis 22; Laura Geller identifies with Abraham in the same narrative; and Phyllis Trible feels Esau's pain in Genesis 27. As a result, we as readers find our way into the text. It is incumbent on us to hear the different voices in the text, as Harold Schulweis demonstrates when he discerns the different calls of the Divine to Abraham in the *Akeidah*.

But the challenge for us is also to find our own unique voice, our own way of responding to the call and to the text, and we see this clearly in Lawrence Kushner's "*Hineini:* The Calling?"

Come and imbibe the power of these eleven offerings of the heart, gifts of self that will show us our own way into Torah. As we hear the *hineini* of each of these gifted teachers, let us begin the search to find our own voices in the text.

Rabbi Lester Bronstein is rabbi of Bet Am Shalom Synagogue in White Plains, New York. He is a member of Beged Kefet, a Jewish musical *tzedakah* collective, and lectures on the topic of Rabbinics at the Hebrew Union College School of Sacred Music.

Double Call

Rabbi Lester Bronstein

My Jewish "birth sign," if you will, is the Burning bush. That's what Jews were reading in the cycle of weekly readings of the Torah on that dark winter week when I was born, fifty years ago.

Most people would see this as a positive omen. "See," they would say, "you get a call from God and you respond. It fits you perfectly."

But the omen cuts two ways. Yes, the bush is God's wake-up call to Moses and Israel, and perhaps a wake-up to God's dormant self as well. But that call is hardly beloved, hardly yearned for. It is much like an alarm clock that finds the sleeper hiding from the day ahead. He keeps punching the snooze button, and the alarm returns with its persistent demand.

"Moshe, wake up."

"No."

"Moshe! Wake up, I say."

"How did you find me here?"

"I've just awakened myself."

"How so?"

"I have heard the cry of My people."

"God, I heard that cry years ago. That's why I vanished into obscurity."

117

"I've emerged from my own obscurity, Moshe, and now I call on you to do the same."

"I am less than capable."

"You'll do fine, Moshe. Besides, I'll get help for you."

Teachers and friends urged me to be a rabbi. In high school, people would jokingly refer to me as "rabbi," and my own rabbi hinted at such a future course in the Confirmation blessing he gave me. In college I began to gear myself toward rabbinical school, largely because of the expectations of those I admired.

In truth, I wanted to write pop music and be a folk singer. Who knows what I really wanted to do? Dutifully I applied to rabbinical school. I had fallen in love with Jewish life, but not with the idea of bringing it to others. I seriously considered making *aliyah*. I certainly did not want to spend my life in the narrow slot of an obscure suburban synagogue pulpit, hammering away at what seemed like the dull tasks of the American rabbinate for the rest of my days.

But I was rejected by the rabbinical school. It was traumatic. It was, in fact, the first call from the Burning bush.

It took me a number of years, and much studying, and much time teaching children and parents, and much time watching and learning from mentors old and young, to realize that the call from the bush is not to go and "be" or "do" something, but to "pursue" something, with no guarantee of success in the conventional sense.

I had to get far away from the original experience of rejection before I could find the strength to try again. I had to fall in love and get married. Ironically, I had to spend seven years working in a suburban synagogue, performing many of the slog-it-out tasks that rabbis do, but without any of the recognition or satisfaction (or remuneration!) that a bona fide rabbi receives. I had to work very hard, in relative obscurity, with no apparent reason to believe that my life would ever move beyond that point. Looking back, it was one of the most pleasant and peaceful times in my life. Call this "Moses in Midian."

The second call was not really a "call" at all. It consisted of a long trudge through urban snow. After several hours of walking through a city closed down by a blizzard, I simply arrived at my destination, took off my coat and boots, and came to the conclusion that it was time to get on with my life. The Jews needed another rabbi. There were too few people doing the work of shaping Jewish lives. I was needed, not to make a stupendous breakthrough and lead my people to salvation, but merely to perform the modest task of helping the Jews to stay alive for one more generation.

I swallowed what little pride remained from years before. I applied again. Again I was rejected.

Call this "Moses spurned by Pharaoh and Israelites alike."

Eventually I got in, in a most undramatic fashion. Years passed. I got through. Then I went back to the work I had been doing before, though now as a very different person.

A generation has passed. I serve in a suburban synagogue pulpit. I hammer away at the often dull tasks of the American rabbinate. I will probably spend the rest of my days in that same narrow slot.

Call this "Moses on the forty-year trek through the wilderness."

But I am well aware of the sacredness of the work. The Burning bush is visible—more or less—behind every mundane detail. Each phone call, each funeral, each bar mitzvah rehearsal, each committee meeting is a reiteration of the original double call. God's humble, burning face appears as a congregant in a hospital bed, fighting for his life after escaping a terrorist's conflagration. Then it makes itself known as a Down's syndrome child struggling to learn three verses of the Torah. Later, it will be in the voice of a black man who wants to become a Jew and call himself "Amichai," "my people."

Moses must have known what was in store for him when he resisted the call of his name and forced God to pronounce it a second time. He must have foreseen the frustration of doing God's work rather than his own. So it is for rabbis. If we were to tell ourselves the truth, we would say that we saw what was coming all along. But for some reason we want to do that work, though we know that we're spending our lives working for someone else, someone more demanding than any earthly supervisor.

My own post–Burning bush experience cannot be so different from that of other rabbis in middle age. People call us to serve on boards, to chair committees, to spearhead projects. We assume that we're being called because the really good people have already declined. They're too busy with the truly important stuff. They're absorbed in their own creative work—work that we ourselves would like to be doing, but we can't because we're stuck with this committee, this project. We're stuck because we said, "Yes." We almost always say, "Yes." We say, "*Hineini* (I'm here)," though under our breath we say, "Please, no, not me again!" That's why we get the double call ("Moshe, Moshe"). The voice calls once. It hears us whisper, "Not me again!" The voice calls a second time. "Fine," we answer. "I'll do what you say." Then the voice goes away. We are left once more with the task of determining on our own what it was that we were called to do. We wonder if we ever got the answer right, even once.

We look back after a number of years have passed. We see that we've actually made something of a difference. People remember. They thank us. They tell us that we were present for them at exactly the moment that mattered—that everything is different because of the role we played, way back when.

We feel that so little of our "own" work got done. Few of our "own" dreams were pursued. Too many double calls, too many "yeses." But deep within, we know that we got the answer right. The answer was *hineini*.

Even "not me again!" is a hidden form of *hineini*.

ALAN DERSHOWITZ is a noted lawyer and leading defender of individual rights. He is the author of several best-sellers including *The Case for Israel, Supreme Injustice, The Genesis of Justice, Chutzpah, Reversal of Fortune, Reasonable Doubts,* and *The Best Defense,* as well as *The Vanishing American Jew, The Abuse Excuse,* and *The Advocate's Devil.* A professor at Harvard Law School, he is also a newspaper columnist and a frequent guest on television and radio programs, and he lectures widely on Jewish issues.

Jacob's Tangled Web

Alan Dershowitz

As a young yeshiva student, I was shocked to read about Jacob's deception of his blind father Isaac. It sounded to me as if the Bible were suggesting that the ends justified the means, even if the means were as ignoble as deceiving a blind father and cheating (for the second time) a less intelligent brother. After all, Jacob manages to get his father's primary blessing and to use it to good purpose. I remember my rabbis struggling mightily to justify Jacob's trickery. They pointed out that God had prophesied to their mother Rebekah that "the elder shall be the servant to the younger" (Genesis 25:23) and thus Jacob is merely carrying out God's will. Moreover, Jacob is far better suited to the task of leadership. Some rabbis argued that Isaac isn't really deceived, since he makes it clear that he suspects that the person standing before him is not really Esau. But even if that were so, it would not mitigate Jacob's guilt. No, I was not persuaded by my rabbis.

What Jacob had done was wrong. I knew I could never do that

to my father. Indeed, when my father once asked me how I enjoyed school, on a day that I had cut classes to go to a Brooklyn Dodgers baseball game, I immediately broke down and confessed my sin. There was nothing that would justify lying to my father, even putting down my brother. So I had to figure out for myself what the message of this perplexing story was supposed to be.

This became clear a few weeks later when we read further into the text of the Jacob narrative. Although Jacob succeeds in the short run in securing his father's blessing, in the long run, his life is filled with deceptions directed against him by his own sons, as well as by other family members. The biblical narrative goes out of its way to show that Jacob's deceptions against others are turned back against him—over and over again. Indeed, the deceptions inflicted on Jacob are strikingly symmetrical with those he inflicted upon his father and brother, except that they are much worse. First he's deceived by his father-in-law, who plays bait and switch with his daughters. A midrash elaborates on the poetic justice. When he awakes on the morning after his wedding night and sees that he has slept with Leah, he reproaches her, saying, "O thou deceiver, daughter of a deceiver, why didst thou answer me when I called Rachel's name?" Leah responds, "Is there a teacher without a pupil? I but profited by thy instruction. When thy father called thee Esau, didst thou not say, Here am I? So did you call me and I answered you."

Later in his life Jacob is deceived with a vengeance by his own children. They persuade him that his youngest son, Joseph, has been eaten by a wild beast. The means employed to deceive Jacob are strikingly similar to the means Jacob employed to deceive his father. Just as Jacob masqueraded beneath the fur of a goatskin, Jacob's sons kill a "hairy goat" and dip Joseph's coat in its blood. What goes around comes around. Centuries later, Sir Walter Scott was to use a phrase that could well have characterized the life of Jacob: "Oh, what a tangled web we weave when first we practice to deceive!"

Once I understood the real lesson of the Jacob story, I was determined to live by it. But I was also determined to become a criminal defense lawyer. Can a criminal defense lawyer, who represents mostly guilty clients, be true to his task of providing a zealous defense without sometimes being deceptive? This is a question that every honest lawyer confronts throughout his or her career. There is an answer. The answer lies in the secular analog to Halakhah, Jewish law. There are rules within the legal profession that provide for the use of deception in certain situations but not in others. For example, it is acceptable for the police to tell a suspect in a criminal case that his codefendant has pointed the finger of guilt at him, even if that is not true. But it is not acceptable for a lawyer to tell a direct lie to a judge or a jury.

Early in my career I confronted this problem in a murder case. I was representing, on a pro bono basis, a young member of the Jewish Defense League who was accused of making a bomb that had been planted in an office building and had killed a young woman. My client had provided information to the police about this case after being promised that he would not be prosecuted for it and that he would not be called as a witness against the others who planted the bomb. But the policeman with whom he made the deal falsely denied making any such promise. Unbeknownst to the policeman, my client had surreptitiously recorded several of his conversations with the policeman, but not the one including the critical promise. The only way I could get the policeman to tell the truth about having made the promise was to mislead him into believing that the promise was recorded on tape (without expressly saying so). Could I use that deceptive tactic in order to get at the truth? I checked the rules of legal ethics and found no answer. I checked with colleagues and they were divided. Finally I decided that since there was no rule prohibiting the temporary use of deception to elicit the truth, I would employ the tactic. It worked. The policeman admitted that he had made the promise. But the trial judge criticized me for what I had done. We submitted an appeal, and the appellate court went out of its way to commend me for having gotten to the truth. I have never been completely comfortable with what I did, though I continue to believe that it was the right thing.

The Jacob narrative is designed to show that ethical problems are often not resolvable by black-and-white rules. There are many gray areas that require judgment calls. Remember that there were no formal rules in the Book of Genesis. Codification would have to await the revelation at Sinai and the Book of Exodus. The Book of

Genesis is about fallible human beings struggling to do the right thing and to respond to the needs of the other in the absence of a formal legal system. It continues to provide guidance in a world in which the legal system still contains significant gaps and in which *hineini* responses can be very complicated.

RABBI LAURA GELLER, the third woman to be ordained in the Reform movement, is the first woman to become senior rabbi of a major metropolitan congregation, Temple Emanuel of Beverly Hills. She is an authority on women's spirituality and the Jewish tradition.

Bringing My Whole Self to God

Rabbi Laura Geller

I've struggled with the story of the *Akeidah* for many years. It has always made me angry. When I was younger, I identified with Isaac. Why did he go along with his father so passively? Didn't he sense what was about to happen? I, too, knew what it felt like to be pulled along by someone else's agenda, not really clear what was right for me. At other times I identified with Sarah. Silent, unable to change the course of events, her heart breaking as she realizes what her husband has done. The sobbing sounds of the shofar come from her, articulating her rage and her despair.

I've been Isaac and I've been Sarah in the story, but Abraham? How could he sacrifice Isaac, a part of himself? How could anyone sacrifice his own child?

Impossible. And yet, I remember the night when I was hosting the first meeting of a new Jewish Women's Faculty Group in my home. It was 7:30; the discussion had begun over dinner. I was very focused on the potential of this group to make a difference in the Jewish life of the university where I served as rabbi. In the middle of my opening remarks, my six-year-old son wandered into the living room. "Mom, am I going to get to have supper tonight?"

"Abraham, Abraham! What are you doing? You are so focused on God's work that you forgot about supper for your son."

125

It turns out that it is not so impossible to be Abraham. It is, in fact, quite possible to be so bound up in responding to what I understand as serving God that I don't see the dangers of the path I have chosen, that I have been willing to sacrifice a part of myself.

Being the rabbi of a large congregation means that I have to juggle many balls simultaneously. There are hundreds of children in our three schools who require attention; there are b'nai mitzvah who need to be trained, congregants who want to learn Torah. There are sermons to write, classes to prepare, programs to plan, eulogies to deliver, mourners to comfort, sick people to be visited...the work literally never ends. Every dimension of the work is a challenge and a blessing. It is a privilege to be with people at important moments in their lives, moments of celebration and moments of loss. It is a gift beyond words to officiate at a *b'rit* and then a bar mitzvah of a child whose parents stood with me under the chuppah. It is a profound experience to be next to a woman chanting from Torah for the first time when I still have vivid memories of her floating in the mikvah at her conversion. It is a privilege, a gift, a profound experience to serve God in all these ways, to bring people closer to Torah and to help them find meaning in their life. And it is a challenge, because there is never quite enough time to prepare or to reflect. There is never quite enough time for my own family. And, surprisingly, there is never quite enough time to cultivate my own relationship with God.

Like Abraham, I get up early in the morning to serve God. Like Abraham, sometimes I am not clear on what the offering is that I am supposed to lay before God. Like Abraham, in the middle of any of these ways I serve God, it is hard for God to really get my attention.

"Abraham!" the angel called. But Abraham was too busy with God's work to hear that something was missing. "Abraham!" the angel called again. Only then did Abraham stop and notice that in his preoccupation to serve God, he wasn't really present.

Neither was I.

The angel who called me came in the form of the Spirituality Institute for Rabbis, a two-year program of study and spiritual practice designed to help rabbis deepen their own relationship with God. With wonderful teachers and courageous colleagues, I was challenged to discover a Jewish spiritual life separate from my role as rabbi.

Instead of focusing on how to lead prayer for other people, I was asked to pay attention to my own personal prayer. The Institute met four times over the two years, in weeklong retreats, and in the months between retreats we studied Jewish texts with a study partner, often over the phone. Much of the retreats were silent; we would meditate, then pray together, then eat in silence, then meditate some more, then eat in silence, and then learn together. I had never spent any time in silence before. I had never meditated before.

It took a day or two for the conversations in my head to quiet down, but when they did, I discovered an ability to pay attention that I had never noticed before. Eating in silence helped me notice the way food looks on a plate, the distinct smell of a particular fruit, the mixture of tastes that come in a meal, and, most important, the incredible blessing of abundance in my life. I had never really noticed. And in the quiet of the silence, as I listened to the sound of my own breathing, I could hear the name of God: YHVH. I could feel the divinity that flows through me and connects me to other people. I could hear that angel call. And I began to respond, *"Hineini."*

"Hineini"—responded not as rabbi, but as a human being longing to be connected to the Deep Structure of the Universe that we call God. *"Hineini"*—in responding, I recognized that *Adonai Echad* means that there is only God, and responding to the Oneness means bringing my whole self—all the roles I play as well as the person behind the roles—to God.

What Abraham learned on the mountain is that God doesn't want us to sacrifice a part of ourselves in order to serve God. God wants us to pay attention, to be present, to bring the fullness of our selves into our relationship with God. When Abraham looked up and saw the ram caught in the thicket, he saw a different path, a different way to serve God. And so he named the place *Adonai yireh* (YHVH sees), *b'har Adonai yayra'eh* (on the mountain of YHVH is the ability to see).

I am still the rabbi of a large congregation. But I do the work a little differently now. When I lead services I spend more time facing the ark than I used to, time when I concentrate on my own prayer, not on the congregation. I struggle with regular meditation, most often at home, but sometimes I even go into the sanctuary in the afternoon for my own private *Minchah* (the afternoon service) meditation. I work with members of my congregation to empower them to lead services and offer *d'vrei Torah,* so I can sometimes be a prayer in the congregation instead of a prayer leader. Some Friday nights I stay home, making Shabbas with my family instead of my congregation. And I meet regularly with a spiritual director, a woman trained to help people pay attention to the ways they experience God working in their lives. We meet monthly, pray together, and listen together to the ways I feel God's presence in my life. This spiritual work has helped me be a more focused teacher, a more empathetic counselor, and a more committed community activist. Perhaps even more important, it has helped me be more present to my family.

"Laura! Laura!" the angel calls. *"Hineini,"* I try to respond. "I am here now, though I know it is easy to get distracted." *"Hineini,"* I want to respond—not just as a rabbi, but also as a mother, a wife, a daughter, a friend. *"Hineini,"* I respond. "Here I am."

The view from the mountain of YHVH gives us the ability to see clearly. We can't stay on the mountain all the time. It is easy to lose the clarity of that vision. That's why we need angels in our life who challenge us to pay attention and who help us climb back up, again and again.

RABBI NEIL GILLMAN is professor of Jewish philosophy at the Jewish Theological Seminary in New York, where he has also served as chair of the Department of Jewish philosophy and dean of the Rabbinical School. He is author of *Sacred Fragments: Recovering Theology for the Modern Jew,* winner of the National Jewish Book Award; *The Death of Death: Resurrection and Immortality in Jewish Thought* (Jewish Lights), a finalist for the National Jewish Book Award and a *Publishers Weekly* "Best Book of the Year"; *The Way Into Encountering God in Judaism* (Jewish Lights); and *The Jewish Approach to God: A Brief Introduction for Christians* (Jewish Lights).

Parallel Life Journeys

Rabbi Neil Gillman

I knew only one of my grandparents.

My maternal grandmother, Dvora Gardner, came to Canada from Rumania in 1887 as a young woman in her twenties. She subsequently married my grandfather, who died in 1933 shortly before I was born. I inherited his name. My paternal grandparents died in Montreal during my early childhood. I have only the faintest memories of them.

But my maternal grandmother, who died in 1956 in her ninety-eighth year when I was a twenty-three-year-old rabbinical student, was a major figure in my life. She was a matriarchal woman who filled the room and dominated her family and just about anyone else she knew. She was recognized as the mother of the Quebec Jewish community. She lived in a large house, cared for by a maiden aunt, a block away from my childhood home. Throughout my Quebec years,

I spent about as much time in her house as I did in my parents'. Shabbat and Yom Tov meals regularly took place around her table and, in between, hours of conversation, stories about the "old country," about her early years raising a family of nine children (and burying three of them) in this outpost of primitive, anti-Semitic, French-speaking Catholicism, about the history of the Quebec Jewish community (18 families when she arrived, over 135 families during my years there, and now dying away), supporting her husband as he built up his business—folk wisdom, all delivered in her delightful mix of English, French, and Yiddish. I was the crown of her old age, the beloved grandchild, named after her late husband, upon whom she showered unqualified affection. I was her pride and joy.

What I could never understand was why and how she left Rumania in 1887, traveled by train across half of Europe, a young single woman, accompanied by an infant niece she was charged to bring with her to the New World.

For this young woman to abandon everything that was familiar to her—her birthplace, her home, her family, her native culture—and travel to some unknown, foreign land seemed then and still seems to me to be beyond belief. From where did she draw the courage, the initiative, the sheer determination to take this step and to carry it out? Where was her fear of the unknown? And from where did she draw the strength to raise a family and deal with her new life in Quebec—the financial insecurity, the primitive living conditions, the anti-Semitism, the death of her three children, the new languages? Was she responding to some unvoiced call?

Today, some decades later, I do not recall ever asking her those questions. I was too immature while she was alive to appreciate what that move entailed. I'm not even clear that it had anything to do with her Jewishness, which was intuitive, primitive, unlearned, but deeply embedded. Her God was an intimate buddy, but she would never have assumed that God had anything to do with her move. Her home was kosher, of course, which in those days, entailed *kashering* her meat and baking her own bread. By the time I came around, she could no longer walk to synagogue and she would never drive on Shabbat. (On the High Holy Days, she moved into the synagogue for the duration.) But every Shabbat morning, she went through the service alone at home, and I still own her well-worn siddur as testimony to that. She was proud that I was studying to be a rabbi, but her pride was mingled with a healthy suspicion of rabbis, stemming undoubtedly from her years of dealing with them.

I've often contrasted my own life experience with hers. I was born and raised in Quebec City, the heart of French Canada. I left Quebec City in 1950 to study at McGill University in Montreal and never returned. After graduating from McGill, I entered rabbinical school at the Jewish Theological Seminary in New York, and I have remained in New York ever since. My mother was also born in Quebec. My father came to Canada from Russia as a young boy. He met my mother when they were both working for my maternal grandfather, who owned a men's clothing factory in Quebec. They remained there until my father's retirement in 1972, when they moved to Montreal, where they spent their last years. As a child, I was the only student in my class who began in kindergarten and graduated high school without changing schools. I lived in only two houses in Quebec, with one family for three of my four McGill years, and, since my marriage, in three Manhattan apartments, all within a four-block area. I entered the Seminary as a student in 1954 and have never left. How boring!

But over a decade ago, I visited a maternal aunt shortly before her death. In contrast to my mother, she had "escaped" (her word) from Quebec by marrying a young Orthodox rabbi who served a congregation in Flatbush where she raised her four children. She began to talk of her childhood in Quebec and asked what it was like for me to grow up there. "Quite different than growing up in Flatbush," she laughed.

Then came the following: "I've never said this to you but I have always marveled at the fact that coming out of a small backward town as you did, without much of a Jewish education, you came to New York, studied at one of the great institutions of Jewish learning where you are now a 'renowned' (again her word) professor of Jewish studies. That my kids, growing up in Flatbush, a great Jewish community, studying in the best *yeshivot*, achieved similar positions is no surprise. But that you accomplished all of this is astonishing. Do you appreciate that? Where in the world did you get the courage to take those steps?"

She left me speechless. No, I didn't appreciate that at all. It seemed to be the most natural process in the world. What unvoiced call did I respond to? Where was my fear of the unknown? Did God play a role? I would never have claimed that then. There had been no opportunity for any kind of Jewish studies in Quebec, nor would I have been interested in pursuing them then. I began to take Judaism seriously late in my years at McGill, but in those days, McGill offered no courses in Jewish studies, and my theological commitments were vague and unformed. I simply became convinced that I had to become a serious Jew, and that meant moving to New York, becoming a rabbi, and pursuing advanced Jewish studies. I became convinced that this is what I had to do in order to be what I most wanted to be. Somehow, I felt, I would handle whatever came my way. The rest is history. Possibly it was that same conviction that drove my grandmother out of Rumania to the New World.

Did I connect my own life's journey with my grandmother's? Not at all. But in retrospect, though I had no formal Jewish education, what I did bring with me into rabbinical school was a different kind of Jewish learning, what educators today call "experiential learning," a familiarity with the tastes, sights, sounds, and smells of Jewish life. All of these I now associate with her. She too had little Jewish book learning, but I vividly recall walking into her home on Friday afternoons and literally smelling Shabbat in the air. I treasure the memory of her lighting Shabbat candles—a massive enterprise, for there was always one candle for every child and for each of her eight grandchildren—and the Passover seders that we celebrated around her table. To this day, I use my grandfather's olive wood etrog box, made in Palestine.

So maybe in ways that I never imagined, my journey was very much modeled on hers after all.

RABBI RICHARD JACOBS has been the senior rabbi of Westchester Reform Temple in Scarsdale, New York, since 1991. From 1980 to 1986, Jacobs was a dancer and choreographer with the Avodah Dance Ensemble. He serves on the board of ARZA/World Union; the Commission of Identity and Renewal of UJA–Federation of New York; and Synagogue 2000, where he is also a program fellow. He served on the international board of the New Israel Fund from 1992 to 2001 and is now the cochair of the NIF's Rabbinical Council and also serves as chairman of the Grants Committee of the NIF Joint Venture Pluralism. Jacobs is married to Susan K. Freedman and is the father of Aaron, David, and Sarah Jacobs.

Being Accessible to the Other in Our Lives

Rabbi Richard Jacobs

In the Binding of Isaac, the word *hineini* is uttered just three times, but this word contains the essence of what it means to be a religious person. *Hineini* can teach us about the very essence of relationship—about our relationships not only with God but also with other human beings.

Remember who the biblical Abraham is—he is the most important person on God's earth. God chose him to chart a new religious path, to be the prototype of what it means to be a religious person. God tells Abraham to take his son to Mt. Moriah and offer him up as a burnt sacrifice. Abraham thinks being religious means following whatever God asks of him. He gets up early the next morning and wakes his son Isaac, and the two set out on their three-day journey.

As they walk on their journey, Isaac is confused and scared, but his father presses onward, hardly noticing the fear and pain on the little boy's face. Finally, overwhelmed, Isaac calls out to his father, *"Avi,"* my father, and Abraham answers him, saying, *"Hineini."* Abraham says the word, but is he anywhere near his son at that moment?

I wonder if the father of the Jewish people has any idea who his son is. Abraham is too consumed with his holy work to truly notice the fragile little boy. He can't see or doesn't want to see that little Isaac is not the bold, confident man that he is. Isaac is timid, unsure of himself. I wonder why.

Maybe you saw the recent study that "fathers spend an average of seven minutes per day relating to each of their children. By and large, men spend more time showering and shaving than they do talking to their kids" (Matthew McKay, Ph.D., *Being a Man: A Guide to the New Masculinity* [Oakland, Calif.: New Harbinger Publications, 1993]).

Al Chet She'chatanu, for the sin that we have committed. I wonder how much time Abraham spent talking to Isaac. I'd like to think that I do a lot better, but my three children might tell a different story. "Dad, are you coming to my little league game this week?" Or "Dad, can we shoot some hoops now, or do you have to get back to the temple?" As a pulpit rabbi and a father and husband, I perform an endless balancing act, one that shortchanges my family more often than my congregation.

We are all like Abraham; each of us is so involved in our outside worlds—our careers, our interests, or our principles—that we do not or cannot see that our child or spouse or parent is bound up on the altar.

Charles Francis Adams, son of John Quincy Adams as well as a nineteenth-century political figure himself, kept a diary. One day he entered in it, "Went fishing with my son today—day wasted." His son also kept a diary. On that same day he noted, "Went fishing with my father—the most wonderful day of my life." How many of us kid ourselves when our loved ones call out to us and we say *"Hineini"* without ever looking up, without ever really listening? *Hineini* is a word we say too often and rarely mean.

The traditional commentators came up with three possible ages for Isaac at the time of the *Akeidah*—37, 13, and 5. It seems obvious that Isaac couldn't have been 5; otherwise how could he have "schlepped" the wood up the mountain? And he couldn't have been too old; otherwise, he would have punched Abraham long before the angel appeared! So it seems 13 is the most believable age, the age of uncertainty and passivity; an age laden with significance as a rite of passage.

And to think that for their B'nai Mitzvah our children only have to read Torah and say prayers! Thirteen is an age when our fathers and mothers loom in mythic proportions, larger than life; they are people we love and trust.

Just because Isaac is 13, however, doesn't fully explain his willingness to follow his father to Mt. Moriah. Why does Isaac go along with Abraham? Perhaps, it is not simply obedience but rather Isaac's delight at the prospect of spending three days alone with his "super-achieving dad" that causes him to overlook some of the journey's peculiarity. Isaac is the son of an incredibly busy and important father. Abraham is usually off rescuing some persecuted kin or trying to turn his religious vision into a full-fledged religion. So when Abraham awakens Isaac early that morning, is it any wonder that Isaac goes along with him?

How many Abrahams are reading these words? How many incredibly busy and important dads and moms identify with Abraham? How many of our young Isaacs are dying to have us wake them up one morning to spend three whole days together? I'm not suggesting that we take our children up a mountain and pretend to offer them as sacrifices. We can use our imaginations to plan less traumatic outings.

Our Isaacs desperately want us around more. We Abrahams are often busy with very important things: earning a living, healing the sick, teaching the young, defending the rights of others.

Sometimes we are even busy unwinding from our pressure-filled lives. We modern-day Abrahams might be sickened by Abraham's willingness to make Isaac pay the ultimate price, but let us not kid ourselves about the sacrifices we force upon our own Isaacs.

Our Genesis text asks each of us to examine the balance in our lives, including, or even especially, those of us who serve as rabbis. Hopefully our ancient narrative can wake us up before it is too late.

A great obstacle to learning to be present for others is the frantic pace of most of our lives. Back in 1971 at the Princeton Theological Seminary, two psychologists conducted a provocative study. They asked a certain number of seminarians to walk over to another building on campus and give a short talk on their motives for studying religion. They asked other students to go across campus to another building and give a short talk about biblical texts that teach caring for others. Along the way, the psychologists planted an actor who was slumped over, coughing and groaning. The experimenters further complicated the test by telling some of the students that they were late for their speaking appointment, while others were told they had ample time. They wanted to see what determined whether or not the students would stop and respond to the man in need.

And what did the psychologists discover? They found that, contrary to expectation, the content of the speech assigned to the students made no difference at all in the way they responded. What mattered most was whether or not the students were in a hurry. Of those who were told they were late, only 10 stopped to help the ailing man. But of those told they were early, 60 stopped to help. In effect, those whose time was short didn't feel they had the space in their lives for another complication. They didn't feel they could afford to say *"Hineini"* to this stranger in need.

I am certain that the reason many of us do not say *"Hineini"* to those who depend on us is that we are just too busy. I'm not suggesting that we quit our jobs, sell our homes, and move to rural Vermont, although I for one have given that some thought. Yet, there has got to be a way to strike a better balance in our lives. Believe me, the guy who needs to heed these words most is the one writing them.

Learning to say *"Hineini"* is about letting go of preconceived ideas and gently bringing ourselves into the presence of what is—not what we imagine or remember or desire. To truly be present requires conscious, sustained effort and attention, and a willingness to be authentic, awake, attuned.

Have you noticed that men and women have been socialized to communicate quite differently? Men call their partners when there is some information they need to relate or receive: "Hi, I'm coming in on the 5:54 train." Or, "Can you pick up Brittany from karate?"

Women call their partners just to check in: "How's your day going?" "Fine," he says trying to figure out the real purpose of her call until he realizes there is no information to relay. I have to say that when my wife and I were first married I just didn't get the check-in call. These were not calls borne of endless leisure, but rather of relationship. I guess you could say the check-in call is a kind of modern *hineini*. Learning to take such calls requires some major stretching for some of us; making such calls, even more. There is not, however, only one way to say *"Hineini"* to our loved ones and mean it. But it's got to be said plenty, or the relationship is going to wither.

Our spouses and our children need to hear us say *"Hineini"* more, and so do most of our parents. Sometimes parents have a very different idea about how their grown children should say, *"Hineini."* "I guess you've been so busy lately you didn't have time to call," they say. Or, "I can't believe you're not bringing the kids to visit us in Florida this year." Or "You're making a barbecue for all your neighbors? Oh, Dad and I will probably just grab a bite at the diner, but you enjoy, really." And then, when their health declines, *hineini* takes on greater urgency.

Some of us say a kind of *hineini* all day long at our jobs or in our communal activities but forget how to say it the moment we come home. Is this because our workplaces are more interesting or more emotionally rewarding than our home? In the workplace, we often feel more appreciated. Sometimes we experience greater self-esteem or more camaraderie than we do at home. For many men and women, the workplace is an escape from unwashed dishes, unresolved quarrels, crying tots, testy adolescents, and unresponsive mates. We are paid to say *"Hineini"* to our clients and colleagues. But what happens with our families?

Cataloguing the many ways we fail to say *"Hineini"* to our loved ones is a good first step toward addressing the problem, but we also need some strategies to do better. One spiritual strategy is known by the name of Shabbat. What if we tried to slow down our frantic pace for even one day? Isn't the point of Shabbat to slow down, eat meals together, and spend time with our families so that we might remember how to say *"Hineini"* to them?

Another spiritual strategy is to take some time in the middle of our hectic weekdays to stop ourselves before we do things like wolf down a sandwich at our desk. What if at such moments we just took a moment to stop and say a blessing, notice the food, and actually taste it.

For some of us, slowing down and finding some silence in our days can help us come into the present moments of life and stay there. Calming some of the chatter that fills and overfills our daily lives can be one strategy to learn to be present, to learn to say *"Hineini."*

Saying *"Hineini"* to God while ignoring the call of those we love is not the true path either. Responding to those we love with a true *hineini* is to ultimately be in God's presence, the eternal Thou. Martin Buber's I and Thou philosophy is based on a moment when Buber failed to say *"Hineini"* to one of his students.

Buber, the towering giant of modern Jewish philosophy, had just finished his morning studies and was still absorbed in his own thoughts when a young man knocked on the door of his study. Buber was known as a wise counselor to many young, seeking souls. Buber did not know Mehe, the young man at the door; nonetheless, he invited Mehe to come in. Buber was far from rude to the man. He listened politely to Mehe, but Buber's mind and heart were very far from the conversation. Buber failed to discern the urgency of Mehe's visit.

Two months later, one of Mehe's friends came to see Buber and told him of Mehe's death and what the young man had hoped his talk with Buber would be. Mehe had come to Buber not casually, not for a chat but for a decision. The decision was one of life and death.

Buber was devastated by this revelation. This young man had come to him out of burning need, but Buber was too absorbed in his own thoughts and in his own world to truly notice. Buber's life was changed forever by this encounter. Buber's life and philosophy were permanently redirected because of how he had failed to respond. He wrote his new philosophy of religious living in a book called *I and Thou*. There was no point to Buber's brilliant academic writing or teaching if he failed to be truly present for the people around him.

Both Buber's philosophy and the Binding of Isaac narrative teach us that to be truly present for our family and friends is at the very same time to be truly present for God. When we respond to those we love, we respond to the highest call.

Recently the long-time cantor of a liberal synagogue died. At his extended and emotional funeral, congregant after congregant gave testimony as to how the cantor was present for them at the most critical moments of their lives. The cantor's son, the last one to speak, said, "While my father was there for all of you throughout your lives, he wasn't there for me. I'm here to mourn the man who died and the man who never lived in my life."

You don't have to be a cantor or a rabbi to be devastated by this story. The cantor said *"Hineini"* to everyone...except his family.

There are a lot of people waiting for each of us to say *"Hineini."* What are we waiting for?

LAWRENCE KUSHNER is the Emanu-El scholar-in-residence at Congregation Emanu-El of San Francisco, where he devotes his full energies to teaching and writing. Prior to this, he was rabbi-in-residence at Hebrew Union College–Jewish Institute of Religion in New York, where he taught spirituality and mysticism and mentored rabbinical students. He presently serves as an adjunct member of the faculty. Before that, he was the rabbi of Congregation Beth El in Sudbury, Massachusetts, for twenty-eight years. Kushner is widely regarded as one of the most creative religious writers in America and is highly sought after as a lecturer and teacher. Through his lectures, articles, and thirteen books, he has helped shape the contemporary agenda for personal and institutional spiritual renewal.

Hineini: The Calling?

Lawrence Kushner

Everybody always wants to know: "Whatever made you decide to become a rabbi anyway?" It's certainly well-meaning. But, even in its innocence, the question somehow comes off sounding like "When was your soul taken over by the Lord?" or "When did you have your first psychotic break?" (One of my rabbinic students replies, "...for the chicks and the money.")

Me? I decided to become a rabbi when I was in the ninth grade. My own personal epiphany was ordinary, even banal. There were neither Divine voices nor heavenly lights, just an annual communitywide Friday evening service. I was sitting with my family at Temple Emanu-El in Oak Park, Michigan, a suburb of Detroit, where the four area congregations and their leaders had gathered to celebrate Reform Judaism. I looked at the seven or eight rabbis assembled on the *bima* as if they were in a lineup. Most of them I already knew from my involvement in the temple's youth group, and one I would subsequently know as a professor. It dawned on me that here were a group of men (in those days it was only men) who earned their living, who were actually paid to help people try to make sense out of the holiest moments of their lives. It struck me then (and it still strikes me now, forty years later) that surely there could be no more gratifying or important way for a person to earn a living. I turned to my parents and said, "I'm going to be a rabbi." They pay you to be a mensch; what a great deal.

In those days there was no notion that graduate rabbinical students should first spend some time "living out in the world" before entering rabbinical school. Indeed, four decades ago, the Hebrew Union College–Jewish Institute of Religion even had a joint undergraduate program with the University of Cincinnati. By taking graduate rabbinical courses over their four undergraduate years, students could earn the equivalent of one year of graduate credit. This also meant that you could become a full-fledged rabbinical student at the age of eighteen.

As it turned out, my last day at home in Detroit, before catching the Baltimore & Ohio sleeper down to Cincinnati, was Yom Kippur. For some reason (an educated guess would be terror in the family over my impending departure), we arrived very late at the temple for the concluding service. My father and I dropped off my mother and younger brother (who is now also a rabbi—my mother once called it "her specialty"). Because we were late, there were no parking spaces in the lot or anywhere for blocks around. So, by the time my dad and I managed to find a parking space and return to the temple, the main floor of the sanctuary was already full. Ushers suggested we try the balcony.

When we climbed the stairs at the back of the hall, the ushers there were not much more encouraging. They told us that there might be one or two seats left in the very last rows. Now the main sanctuary of the old Woodward and Gladstone building of Temple Beth El in Detroit was an ornate cathedral of a hall with ten huge stained-glass windows, plush red carpeting, elaborate murals, hundred-bulb chandeliers, and rich mahogany wood paneling. And the balcony was very high. I had never been up there before (nor have I ever been there since).

When my father and I made our way up the steep aisle to the back of the balcony, we saw that only two open seats remained in the entire room. And those were in the far corner of the last row. People had to stand up as we slowly made our way in front of them. I feared for a moment that I might lose my balance and fall. But, at least, we had seats—even if they were the worst seats in the house.

By the time we sat down, the service was already more than half over. To my surprise, I found myself looking down on the chandeliers and the heads of, literally, thousands of people. The rabbi was half a city block away and, in the light from the ark, he looked very, very puny. Indeed, the most vivid memory I have is of how far away he was, how small he looked, and, yes, how trivial he appeared—a tiny thumb of a man, dressed in a funny black costume, walking back and forth between the congregation and an ornate closet full of light. (It struck me even then that this might not have been an accident.)

That was the first and perhaps the most important lesson I learned about being a rabbi. But it was not the last. Rabbi Jerome Malino, his memory is a blessing, one of the great ones of the last generation, offered the following teaching when he must have been at least eighty years old: A student asked him what he was going to do with his approaching retirement. He thought for a moment and, with a kind smile, said, "I am going to continue my preparation for the rabbinate." The learning, it goes on forever.

PETER ASCHER PITZELE, PH.D., has been a professor of literature at Harvard University and the director of psychodrama services at Four Winds Hospital. He has blended his knowledge of literature with the improvisational methods of psychodrama to develop Bibliodrama, a way of looking at biblical stories through interactive and improvisational role playing. For fourteen years he has taught at the Jewish Theological Seminary's Rabbinic Training Institute. Peter is the author of numerous articles and two books: *Our Fathers' Wells, A Personal Encounter with the Myths of Genesis,* and *Scripture Windows: Towards a Practice of Bibliodrama,* which was runner-up for the best book in Jewish Education in 1998. His first novel, *Perfect Beauty,* is in production.

The Story of a Calling

Peter Ascher Pitzele

In the spring of 1969, I was twenty-eight years old. I was just finishing my doctorate in English literature at Harvard and I had recently accepted an appointment to the English Department as an assistant professor. Despite these outward signs of success, I was a deeply self-estranged young man. I had recently separated from my wife; I was living alone in a college dormitory where I was a tutor; and I was variously licking my wounds, gathering the courage to begin dating again, putting the final touches on a Ph.D. thesis in which I felt neither interest nor pride, and wondering whether I really wanted to keep climbing the academic ladder, the scaling of which had already cost me much time and trouble. I had been getting to know the faculty of the English Department at Harvard during my graduate years, and while they were clearly men and women of extraordinary knowledge, the community of academics did not appeal to me. I did not believe I belonged there, though it was by no means clear in what other community and in what other profession I might find my way.

On a particular Saturday night in March I was on my way back to my room from a morose and solitary dinner when I passed the college bulletin board and saw an announcement for the performance of a play to be put on that evening: Richard Wilbur's *Witch of Endor.* Having nothing better to do, I decided to go. Whether the performance was good or bad I cannot remember, but keen young scholar that I was, I understood that Wilbur had based his play on material he found in the Bible, and I was curious to know how he had transformed his sources. To satisfy my curiosity, I needed to find a Bible.

Today, more than thirty years later, I am never more than arm's reach from a Bible—several for that matter. In those days I did not possess a copy, and at 9:30 when I left the little theater, it was not so obvious where I could find one. I tried the undergraduate library, but got lost in the maze of its stacks. I went to the Main Reading Room, found a Bible in the Reference Room, and located the first Book of Samuel, in which the story of Saul begins, when the librarian announced that the library was closing. No, I could not check the Bible out; it belonged permanently in the Reference Room. Frustrated and made more impatient by my frustration, I thought to find a Bible in Memorial Church across Harvard Yard. Churches, I reasoned, must have Bibles, and for some reason I thought that an ardent soul could gain access to a church at any time night or day. It was locked.

I had been born in New York to Jewish parents, but both were so completely assimilated that they actually steered me away from any of those doors that would have led me into a Jewish world, so it never occurred to me that there might be a synagogue in Cambridge or a rabbi who might satisfy my curiosity about Saul. Thus cut off, I stood in the middle of Harvard Yard perplexed and oddly challenged. I can still remember casting my eyes to the night sky as if I might catch sight there of the Almighty's smile as God toyed with me. When, after all, had I ever wanted to read the supposedly Holy Book and why on the one occasion that I did, was God making it so difficult for me to find one?

I should say at this point that though I was deeply immersed in academia—I was what was called in those days a "close reader" of texts and as my Ph.D. thesis on Ben Jonson might have told you, I was also acquainted with the history and philosophical traditions of the English Renaissance—I was emphatically not a godless young man. In fact, I had had a powerful insight when I was a boy of fourteen that had left me persuaded of the reality of the Divine. That experience never translated into a practice; I never attended church; I never sat in meditation; and for reasons already given I had never set foot in a synagogue. Nonetheless, I was convinced by my spiritual revelation, modest as it was, that all religions stemmed from the same source and were only figured differently according to history and culture. God was One and I found that creed expressed not in the *Sh'ma*, which of course I did not know yet, but in the poetry of William Wordsworth; his sense was mine that

Tumult and peace, the darkness and the light—
Were all like workings of one mind, the features
Of the same face, blossoms upon one tree;
Characters of the great Apocalypse,
The types and symbols of Eternity,
Of first, and last, and midst, and without end.

In retrospect, I can see how on that night in March of 1969 my quest for a Bible was a kind of upwelling from that older experience in which I had received a deeper knowing. For fourteen years I had been looking for what could follow from my epiphany as a boy.

So, stymied in my quest for a Bible, I went out of the Yard and onto the thoroughfare of Massachusetts Avenue. Across the street I saw that the Pangloss Book Store still had a light on, but as I reached the door I read a sign on it saying the store was closed. I knocked—pounded perhaps—on the portal until it was opened by a young woman who referred me to the hours embossed on the glass and informed me that she was just about to shut off the lights. "Please," I said to her, "I am looking for a Bible. Do you have one you can sell me?" In Cambridge in 1969, if a young man pounded on the closing doors of a used book store on a Saturday night it might plausibly be for a copy of Aldous Huxley's *Doors of Perception* or for Thomas

Dequincy's *Confessions of an English Opium Eater,* but not for holy writ.

The young woman stepped aside with a weary sigh and let me in. She went to consult the shelves. Unfortunately, she told me as I waited at the counter, they had only a single volume of a five-volume limited edition of the Hebrew Bible. "What does it contain?" I asked. She read the contents and Lo! it contained the books of Samuel, I and II. I bought the book and took it back to my room, where I opened a bottle of wine and began to read, slowly, closely, verse by verse, line by line.

I started at the very beginning of the story of Samuel, reading of his birth, of the fate of the Ark, of Samuel's tenure as a judge, and of the cry of Israel to have a king. Deeply familiar as I had become with the cadences of Renaissance prose, I fell under the spell of the King James Version. Steeped as I had been in the history plays of Shakespeare, the history of this first king of Israel hit me with the force of a primal myth. I read on until I came to the passage where Samuel takes Saul up to a high place for his anointing. I felt, as if for the first time, the power and the depth of this mythic story of Samuel and Saul; I saw in it a template for stories that would be echoed and reprised in countless texts. This place to which Saul came: Was it not like the Top of Speculation to which Adam is brought by the angel Michael in Milton's *Paradise Lost?* Is it not like that very peak in the Alps where Wordsworth had his revelation in *The Prelude?* In a flash I saw that the great tradition of English literature formed a body of commentary, allusion, and reference to the Bible. And how could it not, since all the great writers had absorbed the Bible—its words, its characters, its scenes, its values—as their minds were formed? But why had none of my teachers ever led me to see this simple, cardinal fact? Why hadn't I been taught the Bible as a primary text? Why was it not at the center where it belonged? In that moment alone in my room, I was possessed—and I mean this quite literally—by a deep desire to learn the Bible and to teach it, for it seemed foolish to teach literature and not to teach the source out of which so much literature flowed.

I looked up from reading and, feeling myself in the grip of this desire to teach the Bible, I asked myself an odd question: What kind of a person has this kind of love for the Bible? For it seemed to me the desire I felt was more than a literary thing; there was a passion in me I had been missing all through my years in graduate school. And the answer that came back to me was: "Well, maybe I'm supposed to be a priest."

It would require too long an autobiographical digression to supply the necessary context for this moment—the moment of epiphany I experienced as a boy was not the only time I had been stirred with a sense of connection to spiritual truth; it's just that the stirrings had never crystallized into a sense of purpose. I can see now that the young man who was seated in his reading chair with an empty bottle of wine at his elbow and a recently bought copy of the Book of Samuel open on his lap was a young man profoundly longing for a vocation. Into that longing this insight about the singular importance of the Bible and this tentative, bemused sense of his possible identity—a priest? Me?—hit him with the force of a revelation. In a dawning awe at the prospect, I half-whispered the phrase, "O my God": it was the expression of my astonishment.

And it was as if these words, a mere cliché, the ejaculation of my surprise, were overheard by some infinitely distant and infinitely present deity who said "Yes" to my words; it was as if God were saying to me, "You called?"

In response to that response, I responded, reflexively, half-aloud, "O my God" again and this time as if to say with wonder, "You are here?" And again the "Yes" came back, this time with tenderness as if to say, "Of course, my dear one, I have always been here."

I began to weep. I said again, "O my God," and this time with a sense of gratitude for that presence. Again I felt a response, a "Yes," delivered with tenderness, a kind of maternal welcome.

A deeper "O my God" spilled out of me as if, with my head bowed, I made a pact with God to serve for having been welcomed. The "Yes" came back again now like a king who accepts the fealty of a knight.

"O my God," I said, grateful and overflowing with the sense of having found my place at last. "Yes, you are here," the voice said to me. "You are here where you have always wished to be."

"O my God," I said again and again, each time sensing a reply, and each reply was different, alive, intimate, surprising. It became between us a kind of murmuring flow, a call and response, and, at a certain point, overloaded with bliss or perhaps made one with the distant other who had become so close, I passed out.

I came to my senses to find that I was lying flat on my back with arms outstretched on the floor of my room, and my face was absolutely wet with tears. I had no sense of how much time had passed. Slowly I got to my feet, picked up the Bible where it had fallen to the floor, and stood at the window of my room looking out into the rainy night. I pressed my head against the cool glass and I thought, "You drank too much wine." Then I recalled a moment in Dickens's *Christmas Carol* where Scrooge, returning alone from dinner, encounters the face of his dead partner Jacob Marley on the knocker of his front door. "A bit of undigested beef," he says to explain the phenomenon. Marley's ghost proves all too real. My own "I drank too much wine" was a reflex of the same doubt. Unable to understand what I had been through, I sought to explain it away.

Now I stood with my head cooling on the window and I realized clearly that I had a choice. I could explain away this experience—reduce it to some mechanical cause—or I could accept it; I could keep faith with it and let it lead me. It was a Pascalian wager; it was an existential act. In that moment I decided I would call this event "real," and that I would make it the most real and important thing that had ever happened to me.

The Bible came alive for me that night; I tapped into its power; I set about on an uncharted course to learn how I might teach the Bible so that its vitality might strike others. As it had spoken to the imaginations of the poets, I wanted to find how it might speak to the imaginations of ordinary people. As it had touched me, my own most personal story, so I hoped to be able to discover how to bring the Bible into resonance with our personal stories. Whether I am a priest or not, only God knows, but I have learned to be some kind of teacher of the Bible. All that I learned in graduate school, and afterwards in my second career as a psychodramatist, I have poured into my vocation.

It is perhaps an ironic footnote to my story that the agent of my vocation was a Samuel. Samuel Klagsbrun was the man who first brought me years afterwards to a classroom where I had the chance to blend literature and psychodrama into what would in the end become Bibliodrama, as I have come to call my chosen métier. Sam, as he was called by me and all who knew him and worked for him at Four Winds Hospital, where he presided as founder, director, and visionary, was on the faculty at the Jewish Theological Seminary, and in those years he was teaching a course on leadership skills for rabbinical students about to enter their first pulpits. Urgent business was calling him away on a certain Tuesday, and he asked me to cover his class for him. With fear and trembling—aware that I was hardly qualified—I spent the hour of his class inviting students to imagine themselves in the role of Moses and to speak about the challenges each, as Moses, faced as a leader. I can see now, as I could not see then, that the seed of an old dream, planted fifteen years earlier when I was harrowed by many changes, was sending out its first green shoot.

I once saw the film version of Ray Bradbury's novel *Fahrenheit 451*. It faithfully rendered the story of the young man who, in that dis-topia of the future, was a fireman. Firemen in that time had the task of setting fires, not putting them out, and what they burned was books, for books were subversive in the eyes of the new regime. The hero gradually discovers that books are not the enemy, but rather sources of wonder and freedom. He finds he can no longer burn them; rather he wishes to find and to salvage them. His superiors learn of his defection and he is forced to flee. In his flight he finds an ally who brings him to a place in the wilderness where those who wish to preserve the old culture are gathered. It is winter and a snow is falling when his guide brings the young man to a grove in the middle of the forest; there we see men and women walking in pairs in a large circle under snow-covered trees. The sound track is silent, and only the ghosts of their breath make visible the words that are passing between these pairs. "Who are they and what are they doing?" the young man asks. His ally explains to him that one of each pair knows a book by heart and the other of the pair is committing it to memory by hearing it constantly repeated. It is on this scene that the film ends.

Twenty years ago I took my place in such a circle as a listener; I like to believe I have now been called to pass something on.

RABBI SANDY EISENBERG SASSO is an award-winning author of inspiring books for children of all faiths and backgrounds. The second woman to be ordained as a rabbi (1974) and the first rabbi to become a mother, she and her husband, Dennis, were the first rabbinical couple to jointly lead a congregation—Beth-El Zedeck in Indianapolis. Sasso holds a doctorate in ministry, is active in the interfaith community, and has written and lectured on the renewal of spirituality, women and religion, and the discovery of the religious imagination in children of all faiths.

I Am Not Supposed to Be Here

Rabbi Sandy Eisenberg Sasso

I responded to those who did not ask,
I was at hand to those who did not seek Me;
I said, "Here I am, here I am"
To a nation that did not invoke My Name.

(Isaiah 65: 1–2)

It wasn't supposed to happen this way. I was supposed to be heading home to Indianapolis after speaking at a rabbinical seminary's ordination ceremony and visiting my family in Philadelphia. I arrive at the airport ready for my return flight, anxious to get back to work, looking forward to a quiet dinner with my husband.

The flight is delayed. I am not overly concerned. This happens all the time. I decide to treat myself to a frozen yogurt. It won't spoil my appetite; dinner will be later than I thought. I call my husband to tell him that I'll be a little late, but to make reservations at our favorite Italian restaurant. We'll debrief over a glass of Chianti.

An hour passes and the flight attendant announces the boarding will commence. I board the plane confident that I'll be home in two hours. Three hours later, the plane is still on the runway. The book I have been trying to read isn't that good. The cabin is hot and I am thirsty. No one is serving drinks.

There is a teenager on the plane. It is her first flight. She's kept her composure, but her nerves are raw. You can tell she is afraid. I should offer a word of comfort, tell her all flights are not like this; everything will be fine. But everything isn't fine, and I don't say anything.

I am not supposed to be here. I have appointments the next morning and work waiting on my desk. I was supposed to have a quiet evening sipping a glass of wine with my husband before the start of a busy week. I've called him many times on the cell phone. He has canceled the dinner reservations. He's eaten the leftovers in the refrigerator. By my last call, he's tucked away in bed. I wish I were there. I am not supposed to be here.

Finally, the flight is canceled. It is past midnight. I wait another hour in line to rebook a flight for the next morning. There are many people in the same situation, but I am not especially friendly. I don't want to talk to anyone. The representative who rebooks my flight tells me that she is sorry but the airline cannot pay for my hotel room. I should understand. I don't.

I forget that she too is up at 1 A.M. and dealing with many disgruntled passengers. I think she could be a little more empathetic, more sympathetic to my plight. If she wants, I tell myself, she can get the airline to pay for the hotel. We both do not want to be where we are, and we make each other a little more miserable.

In the book of Genesis (28:10–16), Jacob finds a place to stop and sleep on his way from Beer Sheba to Haran. He dreams of a ladder set on the ground with its top to the sky, and angels of God going up and down on it. Jacob awakes from his dream and realizes that God was in that place, but he did not know it. If God is somewhere in this travel fiasco from Philadelphia to Indianapolis, I do not care to know it.

I finally find my way to a small hotel near the airport. It is past two in the morning. It is a short night. I do not dream of ladders with angels going up and down on them.

I wake up early, take a shower, and wash my hair. I plug in the hair dryer but it doesn't work. I push the reset button. It still doesn't work. I call the front desk. The hotel doesn't have another dryer. My hair is soaking wet and the weather has finally decided to cool off. I look terrible and I feel worse. I am not supposed to be here.

I return to the airport and eventually board the plane. I find myself seated next to a gentleman from Indianapolis. He, too, had been on the canceled flight the night before. We commiserate. Neither of us is supposed to be here.

We introduce ourselves to each other. I find out what he does and he finds out I am a rabbi. I am often hesitant to reveal my profession to strangers when I travel, in order to avoid engaging in long conversations about "religion." But I am too tired to fashion another identity.

"For years," my airplane companion begins, "I had questions I wanted to ask a rabbi. There are certain things about Judaism I don't understand. I am glad you are here." We talk, and somehow, despite only a few hours of sleep, the right words come. The two-hour flight passes quickly. By the time I arrive home, I am no longer irritable. I was supposed to be there.

I always thought that airline terminals and airplanes were merely necessary passageways to enable you to get to your destination. What is supposed to happen occurs either in the place where you are coming from or the place to which you are going. I had often wished that some Star Trek technology would allow me to be beamed to the location where I needed to be. Imagine how much more could be accomplished if we avoided the journey, that annoying interlude. If God is calling me to be present somewhere, why isn't it possible to do away with the long road to the appointed place?

A story is told of a young student who desperately wanted to meet Elijah. The boy's father assured him that if he would stay up all night and study with his whole heart, Elijah would come to greet him. The student did as his father instructed, yet nothing happened. Then one night while he was studying, there was a knock at the door. When he opened it, there was no one there but an old man who wanted something to eat. The student was too busy for such a distraction from his holy tasks, so he sent the man away.

When the boy told his father about the intrusion of the late-night visitor, the father sighed. "That intrusion," said the father, "was Elijah, and you have missed the opportunity of speaking with him. Now it is too late." From that day on, the boy always warmly greeted everyone he met, no matter how busy he was. He later became a rabbi.

I wasn't thinking at all about God during my airline delay. I was thinking about my missed appointments and assignments and all those intrusions that were keeping me from them. I was thinking about being somewhere other than where I was. But God was in the place I thought I wasn't supposed to be, and I did not know it.

The Jewish mystical tradition teaches that in everything there is a Divine spark, and we are in the places we find ourselves not by accident but to redeem the holy sparks present there. Everything invites us into relationship, but we often refuse. Everything calls to us— "Here I am"—but we aren't listening. Every situation wants to change us, but we are more focused on changing the situation. We hurry life along to get to "the point."

But the point isn't the beginning and the end, our place of origin or our destination. The journey is the point: the opportunity to hear the call and respond to the other. I learned that lesson on a flight from Philadelphia to Indianapolis. In responding to the man on the plane and to his questions about religion, I learned that you never know where, when, or through whom revelations may come.

RABBI ZALMAN SCHACHTER-SHALOMI is widely recognized as perhaps the most important contemporary Jewish spiritual teacher. A rabbi, he is also professor emeritus at Temple University and is on the faculty of Naropa University. His belief in the universality of spiritual truth has led him to study with Sufi masters, Buddhist teachers, Native American elders, Catholic monks, and humanistic and transpersonal psychologists. He is the founder of the Spiritual Eldering Institute in Boulder, Colorado, which sponsors nondenominational workshops to help people grow into elderhood. He is also the author of *From Age-ing to Sage-ing* and *Wrapped in a Holy Flame.*

The Challenge of Answering *Hineini*

Rabbi Zalman Schachter-Shalomi

When Adam heard God's voice calling him, *Ayekkah* (Where are you) (Genesis 3:9), he had hidden himself for shame, so he did not answer, *"Hineini."* Who knows what would have been had he stood up and taken responsibility for his actions before God, owning up to his disobedience? By seeking to shift blame, he invited blame on himself and punishment.

Each time I prepare to meet someone in a counseling session, a *Yehidut,* a moment of union, it calls for a safe and sacred space in which to meet. I prepare myself by recalling my own *hineini* moment, which nurtures my motivation to serve. I will describe such encounters in the hope that one or more will resonate in you.

A young rabbi came to see me about deeply troubling issues in his relationship with God, his congregation, and himself. I heard him out and felt with him his frustration, confusion, and the sense of his not being understood and of being abandoned. I asked him about what he did periodically to do maintenance on his soul. It seemed like a new question for him. Having been ordained and engaged by his community seemed like enough for him. Because he was a reasonably well-adjusted individual and otherwise not troubled, he had not confronted the issue of periodic *Heshbon ha-Nefesh,* spiritual review. Alas, in all the rabbinic seminaries the inner work is seldom addressed, as if professional development only related to how one counsels congregants, not how we sustain our own spiritual connection. All relationships need maintenance checks: marriage, parenting, employment, teaching, and the like. The greater one's responsibilities, the more people will be affected by one's inner balance, the more one needs to be recalibrated.

This young rabbi and I explored the motivation and the vocation of the rabbinic calling—yes, this is ultimately what we responded to when we pursued the learning and training for the rabbinate. The deeper we went, the more it became evident that we did not "choose, elect, opt, espouse" to become rabbis, but that somehow we were deployed in the mystery of *Nora' Alilot,* the Awesome Power at work in the world, who led us *b'ma'aglei tzedek,* by the circuitous routes of providence, to our work. As we went deeper yet, we got to the place where we knew that we heard the call: *"Et Mi Eshlah ummi yelekh lanu,"* "Whom shall I send and who will go for us" (Isaiah 6:8), and that we had said *"Hineini"* and that, while it was truly a free and deeply given consent, we had no real choice but to say *"Hineini."*

Each time we find ourselves *bein hametzarim,* in narrow places, it helps to visit the *hineini* place again. Here we draw strength that is not ours but that comes from the One who deploys us. Before parting that day the young rabbi and I looked deeply into each other's eyes past each other's egos to the God within, and from there we reaffirmed the calling and the assurance, *ki itkha ani,* I am surely with you.

Another colleague's board voted not to renew his contract. He was bitter, having stretched himself beyond his capacity to fulfill his *hineini.* He was burned out, and his health was suffering. His family felt his sadness and irritability, and he loathed himself.

Doubting his vocation, he wondered if he was destined to remain in the rabbinate. Most of his constituency were pleased with his ministry, but they were timid, while those who kept carping were those in power. We talked about his need for vindication in the face of the vindictiveness that faced him. How difficult it was to hold on to *ahavat Yisrael,* a love of the people of Israel, and to meet his people *b'sever panim yafot,* with a pleasant countenance.

We talked and I felt the tightness in his body, and a sense of despair and frustration oozing from his pores. We looked at Chapter 3 of the book of *Eichah,* Lamentations, and chanted it together in the special mode of the "blues" of that chapter:

> I, the one who is expected to be strong,
> have experienced
> the rod of His anger.
> Me, He has brought me into deepest darkness
> Shutting out all light.
> He has turned against me,
> day and night His hand is heavy on me....
> O Lord, all peace and prosperity
> have long since gone
> for You have taken them away,
> I have forgotten what enjoyment is...

We finished the chapter feeling the grief in that situation. He said, "I hurt too much." Deep, deep inside him there was hurt that even predated his current distress; all that fused together in a chorus that screamed, "You are worthless."

When we looked at the moment of his first awareness of the rabbinic vocation, he smiled a sad and somewhat bitter smile. "Yes. I thought it would be wonderful to serve as a rabbi. I felt that God would be in my corner, inspiring and sustaining me."

We reviewed some of the times when people had come to him and said, "What you did for me, what you said at that time changed my life for the better." We looked together at the people he had served

in bereavement and other life-cycle events and, yes, he felt a bit better; yes, he was inspired and sustained in his work.

After some time we got to the question: What needs to be done?

The burden of the resentment and the pain was too much to
bear. No champion would come to vindicate him and restore him to
his position. The cost of carrying the weight was beyond his energy.
He had to let go.

I suggested that he look again at the preamble to the *K'riat
sh'ma' sh'al hammittah,* the *Sh'ma* recited in bed [at night]: *"Hareini*
(like *hineini*) *mohel lelkhol mi sh'hikh'is v'hiqnit oti,"* "I forgive anyone who has angered and frustrated me—who has sinned against me,
causing hurt to my body, my finances, my reputation—any and all
things that pertain to me—whether under duress or willfully,
unawares or by intent, whether in this lifetime or any other incarna-
tion. Let no one be punished on my account."

One is not helped so quickly. There are times when reciting these
words will not feel true to his feelings, yet he does this knowing that
in the end it has to be.

Before he left, he sent blessings to those who opposed him and
vowed to smile at them when he saw them. He uses as his mantra the
passuq, the verse, *"hashivah li sesson yish'ekha v'ru'ah nedivah
tiysmekheni,"* Let me again rejoice in your help; let a vigorous spirit
sustain me (Psalms 51:14).

The story is not yet over. But the weight and the cost of *hineini*
are great. We cannot carry this weight alone without *Anokhi Anokhi
hu' m'enahemkhem,* I, I am the One who comforts you (Isaiah
51:12).

The Belzer Hassidic court with its rebbe, Reb Issakhar Ber
Rokeach, in Jerusalem is thriving today because of another great
example of *Mesirat Nefesh,* a self-sacrifice moment of *hinieni.* The
following incident occurred in the early years of the Holocaust. The
Gestapo, knowing how important the saintly leadership of the late
Belzer rebbe Reb Aharon Rokeach was to his followers, intended to
kill him and further demoralize the oppressed. When the Gestapo
burst into the house where the rebbe and some of his Hassidim were,
they asked, "Which one of you is the Rabbiner?" The rebbe's gabbai,

who attended him, was a physically more imposing figure than the rebbe himself. He stepped forward (I wish I had heard his name when I heard this story) and said his *hineini,* "I am the one." They shot him on the spot and left. This sacrifice made it possible that a renewed blossoming of a great heritage could continue. Subsequently, the Belzer rebbe and his brother Rabbi Mordechai, the Rav of Bilgorai, were disguised in Nazi uniforms and spirited to safe haven.

The numerical equivalent of *hineini* in Hebrew is 115, which is also the value of the letters in the words, *anachnu,* we, *aliyah,* ascent, and *ha'am,* the people. By being counted in *hineini,* we become part of the larger "we," *anachnu;* we experience an *ascent,* an *aliyah* of awareness that frees us from the narrow I-ness; and thus we become part of *ha'am,* the people.

Rabbi Harold M. Schulweis is the founding chairman of the Jewish Foundation for the Righteous, spiritual leader of Valley Beth Shalom in Encino, California, and author of *For Those Who Can't Believe*.

One *Hineini* Against Another

Rabbi Harold M. Schulweis

She entered the study clasping a large book in her hand, sat down on the chair across the desk, laid the Bible down, and pointed to the marked passage from Leviticus 18 that we had read at *Minchah* (Afternoon) Yom Kippur services the day before. "Rabbi, do you believe this?" She read the passage aloud, the one denouncing those who "lie with mankind as with womankind," an act of abomination deserving capital punishment.

"Rabbi, tell me. Is this right? Do you yourself believe this? Is my son an abomination?" She then told me how her son had been so taunted and tormented by his peers at a Jewish religious school of higher learning that he had left for San Francisco, where a psychologist was reputed to "make the crooked straight." Weeks later she received a cheerful call from her son indicating progress. He had such hopes that with therapy he would be like the others. Finally, he would be cured of the curse that tortured him. Then for a long spell, she didn't hear from him. She flew to San Francisco, and found a suicide note written by his hand. The therapy had not worked. He had taken his own life.

She looked me in the eyes, "You knew my son, Rabbi. Was he an abomination?"

What did she want from me—exoneration, consolation?

Neither. She wanted to know my rabbinic stance—where I stand as a rabbi and what I stand for on this issue. She wanted my *hineini* response to her cry. She wanted a rejection of the condemnatory mandate in Leviticus. She left the room sobbing and me in confusion.

I was caught between the voice of an anguished mother and the verse of a sacred book. Both voices had claims on me. Each called for an unequivocal response. I could not ignore the mother's deep hurt, nor could I dismiss the apodictic scriptural verse. To whose voice should I respond? Can you answer, "*Hineini*," to two contradictory imperatives?

I turned to that chapter in the Torah that the Rabbis chose to be read on Rosh ha-Shanah. This chapter, Genesis 22, contains *hineini* twice in response to two contradictory commands: The first *hineini* is Abraham's response to the command of *Elohim* to offer his son as a burnt offering. The voice is from *Elohim*, the Master Ruler, the sole name mentioned in the first ten verses of Genesis 22. Then another Divine voice is heard: "And the angel of the Lord called unto Abraham a second time out of heaven" (Genesis 22:15). The voice of *Adonai* counters the initial command of *Elohim:* "Do not raise your hand against the boy or do anything to him."

To which voice should Abraham listen—to the voice of the servant, the Angel of *Adonai,* or to the voice of the Master, *Elohim?* In a midrash on these verses, the sages ask rhetorically, "Whom does one obey, the voice of the Master or the voice of the Servant, God or the Angel?" Clearly, one follows the Master's voice.

Yet Abraham sides with the Divine echo, with the voice of the angelic servant of *Adonai,* and in so doing he de facto disobeys the initial command to sacrifice Isaac. For this disobedience (or higher obedience) Abraham is lauded (Genesis 22:16–18).

On what grounds does Abraham's second *hineini* prevail over the first? On the grounds of conscience, the same kind of conscience that inspires Abraham to confront God at Sodom: "Shall not the Judge of all the earth do justly?" (Genesis 18:25). That challenge of conscience is no capricious stance. It is informed by God, who is resolved not to hide from Abraham the Divine's designs and intention (Genesis 18:17). A moral covenant between the Divine and human justifies Abraham's expectation that God measure up to

God's covenantal duties and live up to God's revealed attributes of justice and fairness.

Abraham's conscience, symbolized by the term "angel of the Lord," does not violate God's sovereignty. Abraham's second *hineini*, which does not follow the mandate to sacrifice Isaac, is based on the deeper understanding of the nature of *Adonai*. God's initial imperative is questioned in the name of God. To question *Elohim* in the name of *Adonai* assumes a conscientious stance. For Abraham to reconsider his first *hineini* is a tribute to *Adonai* and to the maturity of Abraham's spiritual conscience.

God's one voice resonates with multiple echoes. Consider the profound insight in Pesikta de Rav Kahana, *Piska* 12: "David said, 'The voice of the Lord with strength.' It does not say, 'with God's strength' but with strength, which means according to the strength of each and every one. Therefore the Holy One says, 'Do not think that because you have heard many voices, there are many gods, for it is always "I." I am the Lord thy God.'" The voice of God is heard according to the strength of every man and woman. In the instance of the *Akeidah* story, the Torah celebrates the strength of the second *hineini*, the divinity of moral sensibility.

I am no Abraham, but I am his child. I have heard in my study the contradictory claims and voices that demand a *hineini* response. I am instructed by the biblical and rabbinic treatment of Abraham's posture and that of other Jewish prophets. I note that the tradition does not regard Abraham's challenge to God as *lèse majesté*. God's majesty is not injured but strengthened by the religious audacity of Abraham's dissent.

The angel of the Lord I translate as conscience. Conscience has too often been dismissed as capricious, relativistic, and arbitrary. But conscience, *con-scientia*, is a gift informed by wisdom and cultivated by patriarch, prophet, and the rabbinic tradition. Conscience is not an isolated single intuition, an idiosyncratic feeling pitted against single verses. Conscience grows and is developed in the collective instances of moral sensitivity reflected in Jewish law and lore throughout the ages.

The conscience that gnaws at me in the study, I regard as revelatory, and my struggle with it is not to be dismissed as merely subjective.

Moral conscience is indispensable to my faith. Consider, in this matter, the strong insight in the writings of Rabbi Abraham Isaac Kook in his *Oroth Ha-kodesh,* 3:11: "It is forbidden for religious behavior to compromise a person's natural moral sensibility. If it does, our fear of heaven is no longer pure. An indication of its purity is that our natural moral sense becomes more exalted as a consequence of religious inspiration. But if the opposite occurs, and the moral character of the individual or group is diminished by a religious observance, then we are certainly mistaken in our faith." The voice of the woman in my study is not a singular voice, and her concern is not religiously irrelevant. Both moral sensitivity and religious observance are complementary factors in my response.

I am heartened by Rabbi Kook's insight and instructed by the counsel of the sages (B. T. *Baba Batra* 43a): "To judge according to that which you see with your own eyes." What do I see? I see in the woman who came into my study and in the dozens more who have since come to me, the terror and pain of suffering pariahs, modern lepers of our society. I see people who have no more chosen their homosexual orientation than I have chosen my heterosexual orientation. For the most part this is their testimony, and I hear with my own ears and see with my own eyes those who "know their own bitterness" (Proverbs 14:10). I called the woman back to my study and thanked her for calling my attention to a reading that cannot be attributed to a tradition of compassion and understanding. Later, before the congregation, I affirmed my second *hineini:* "Let us not raise our hand or lift our voices against these innocent children of God in our midst. They are welcome in our congregation."

Hineini is not simply the obedient response to a single voice or verse. It is a response of sacred conscience, which more than once moved a rabbinic tradition to circumvent and even nullify the raw literal scriptural imperative. Who can be oblivious to the moral implications of the rabbinic tradition that struggled against the laws of the "rebellious son" (Deuteronomy 21:18), or the ordeal of the wife suspected of adultery (Numbers 5:12), or the heretical city tarnished with idolatry (Deuteronomy 13:13)? As Rabbi Kook would remind us, *hineini* must not run against the natural moral sensitivity rooted in the divinity that created us in the image of *Elohim-Adonai.*

Hineini must not be answered too quickly or too glibly. It is a response of the heart and the mind to a voice whose dictates must be carefully turned, questioned, and examined. For there are demonic voices in religious history, as Jewish history well knows. Satan is a ventriloquist and is skillful in projecting his voice into another. Abraham's second *hineini* spared his son from the death that flows from blind obedience. The second *hineini* has refined our tradition in the past and may in the future save it from distortions. The second *hineini* is tribute to the moral maturity of an endlessly evolving Jewish tradition.

PHYLLIS TRIBLE is university professor of biblical studies at Wake Forest University in North Carolina and Baldwin Professor of Sacred Literature, emerita, at Union Theological Seminary in New York. Her fields of scholarly interest include biblical theology, literary criticism, and feminism. Her most recent book is *Rhetorical Criticism: Context, Method, and the Book of Jonah*.

Beholding Esau

Phyllis Trible

Accepting the invitation to write a personal anecdote tied to one occurrence of *hineini* in the Bible brought difficulties I never anticipated. At first I heard strength and substance in the bold affirmation, "Behold, I," and looked forward to choosing a text and telling a story. Yet as I examined the fourteen occurrences, I sensed no particular rapport with any of them. After all, this marvelous rhetoric of relationship never appears in words of women or words to women. To undertake the assignment, then, I must do double work: Forge a connection with a text and transform its androcentric bias into a compatible idiom.

Gradually I found myself drawn to the *hineini* of the character Esau. He jolted my memory of things past. The memory took a circuitous route that comes with its own story. Many years ago in a conference of predominantly white women, held at Harvard Divinity School, an African American prefaced her remarks with the words: "Let me introduce myself. I am a daughter of Hagar outside the covenant." The introduction startled me. What did it mean to be "a daughter of Hagar outside the covenant?"

Reflecting now on that incident, I view it as a *hineini* occasion. The African-American woman was saying in effect, "Behold, I." She was relating to us through her own chosen self-identification, through a marginal character in our common biblical heritage, and through a part of that heritage that makes us uncomfortable, as it calls us to accountability. Her *hineini* turned academic exchange into personal encounter.

Beyond the encounter, she motivated me to see Hagar as an "I" in a narrative whose dominant story line would make her an "it" (Genesis 16:1–16 and 21:9–21). In time this outcast slave woman appeared before me as the first person in the Bible whom a Divine messenger visits; the only person who dares to name God; the only woman to receive a Divine promise of descendants; the first woman to hear an annunciation; and the first to weep for her dying child. Pondering these identities, I began to relate to Hagar in new ways. Sightings of her happened in my everyday world—in the faithful maid used, abused, and discarded by the ruling class; the pregnant young woman all alone; the surrogate mother; the expelled wife; the divorced mother with child; the homeless woman; and the shopping bag lady carrying bread and water in the wilderness of city streets. Hagar the Egyptian outside the covenant had moved to the center of my attention through her unspoken yet recoverable *hineini*. "Behold, I, Hagar."

Although I did not know it at the time, that move enabled me to hear Esau's spoken yet muted *hineini* (Genesis 27:1–3). The link came through an invitation to lecture on biblical lament. Struggling to develop the topic, I remembered Hagar weeping for her dying child. "She lifted up her voice and she wept" (Genesis 21:16). The Hebrew verb for weeping *(b-k-h)* first occurs here. Hagar the rejected unleashes the tears of Scripture. The next time the phrase to "lift up the voice and weep" occurs, it describes Esau the rejected (Genesis 27:38).

Esau, however, had never been high on my list of characters to study. Many times I wrestled with his brother Jacob, pitied his father Isaac, and entertained his mother Rebekah, but rarely did I even nod to Esau. Yet, his lachrymose affinity with Hagar turned my attention to him. Like her, he stands outside the covenant; like her, he becomes an "it" in the dominant story line of the biblical narrative.

The first reference to Esau lets us know that life will not go right for him. Though he will be the older of twins, Esau will serve his brother Jacob. So asserts God in a poem to the pregnant Rebekah (Genesis 25:23). As the twins mature, their parents respond differently to them. The split, ominous in itself, contains a more devastating difference. "Isaac loved Esau because he was fond of game; but Rebekah loved Jacob" (Genesis 25:28). Whether the pronoun "he" refers to the father or the son, Isaac's love for Esau is conditional but Rebekah's love for Jacob is unconditional. Divided brothers, divided parents, divided love supply all the ingredients for trouble. And as often happens in troubled families, one member, in particular, carries the demons. Esau is that one.

Moreover, as sometimes happens, observers of familial troubles account for them at the expense of the loser. Early on, when Jacob takes advantage of the famished Esau and so succeeds in purchasing his brother's birthright, the narrator faults Esau by charging that he "spurned his birthright" (Genesis 25:34). Later the narrator charges that Esau "made life bitter for Isaac and Rebekah" by marrying outside his kin (Genesis 26:34–35). Given the birth oracle, the ensuing incidents, and the narrator's interpretations, why would I want to embrace Esau?

The answer begins with the first meeting between father and son. Old, blind, and anticipating death, Isaac calls Esau into his presence (Genesis 27:1–3). He addresses him not by name but by the vocative of parental intimacy, "My son." The purpose of the meeting is to send Esau the skilled hunter into the field for game that he can turn into delicious food for his father. Eating the food, the aged Isaac will gain strength to bless his elder son. The scene resonates with the narrator's earlier report about Isaac's love for Esau, including its conditional element, "because he was fond of game."

To Isaac's call, Esau replies, *"Hineini"* (Behold, I). Concise, direct, and unequivocal, the reply signals continuity and commitment between generations. Esau is present to Isaac; he is there for his father. Whether the reply is wholly altruistic remains a moot question. Esau stands to reap blessing from fulfilling the request of his father; yet he hears about the blessing only after he has uttered *hineini,* here the language of filial responsibility. Unlike Isaac, however, Esau fails to relate through a vocative of personal intimacy. He does not say, *"Hineini,* my father," but simply, *"Hineini."* If Isaac's love for Esau is conditional, Esau's response is less than fulsome. But in their meeting these matters never surface.

From this scene of paternal call and filial reply, one might produce a reflection, if not a personal anecdote, on caring for elderly parents. Not unlike ancient figures, older people now live long lives well into infirmity and so need the help of a younger generation. The parent calls on the child. Whether the parent promises a specific reward, perhaps an inheritance, for the help requested, the child does not require it as a prerequisite for caring. Further, the parental need and the filial reply override whatever disquieting notes may lurk, often unacknowledged, in these relationships. Viewed this way, Esau's *hineini* becomes a model for a younger generation's response to the elderly.

For me, however, the *hineini* of Esau takes a different turn. In so answering the call of his blind father, Esau is calling on Isaac to see him—to behold him with understanding, to know him in an interior way, to perceive his inner self, to discern his precarious place in the family. I hear Esau's *hineini* in two contexts: the disturbing oracle to his mother that undermined him at birth by predicting the ascendancy of Jacob and the coming betrayal by his mother and brother (Genesis 27:5–40) that will undermine him in destiny by robbing him of the blessing that is rightfully his. Accordingly, Esau's *hineini* becomes for me an assertion of self-identity and a request for recognition. He is asking to be seen as Esau, apart from divine oracles and parental blinders. The explicit message, "Behold, I," is the same that I heard implicitly in the self-identification of the African-American woman at Harvard Divinity School and that I found implicitly in the biblical character Hagar.

Alas, Esau's *hineini* does not bring forth the response he desperately needs. The father upon whom the son relies is blind to the son upon whom the father relies. Isaac fails to behold Esau. As for Rebekah, she does not even try. Jacob is her son. Squeezed between a weak, impotent, and ineffectual father who loves him conditionally and a strong, domineering, and triumphal mother who never speaks to him (nor he to her), Esau becomes for both of his parents the rejected and discarded child supplanted by his sibling.

Contemporary sightings of Esau are legion, in countless neglected or rejected children. Their parents may be rich or poor. They may be hostile, well-meaning, or indifferent. Likewise, the siblings of these children may be manipulative, well-mannered, or insensitive. They may be older or younger. In many guises Esau walks our streets, attends our schools, works in our offices, and even resides in our homes. Further, through travel, television, and newsprint, he appears before us daily in children around the world.

Given the treatment that he received, is it any wonder that Esau "hated Jacob because of the blessing with which his father had blessed him" (Genesis 27:41) and so plotted to kill his brother? No, the wonder is that, many years later, Esau finds within himself forgiveness of his brother. One day, returning from exile, Jacob looks up and sees Esau coming toward him with four hundred men. But no threat is present. Instead, Esau "ran to meet him, and embraced him, and fell on his neck and kissed him, and they wept" (Genesis 33:4). Earlier Esau wept because Jacob had supplanted him. Now, as the brothers meet after so long a separation, their tears intermingle. Earlier Jacob cheated his brother; now Esau chooses not to retaliate.

Despite the fearful flattery that marks Jacob's verbal response, it can offer us delayed insight. Unharmed by Esau, Jacob avows, "...for truly to see your face is like seeing the face of God—since you have received me with such favor" (Genesis 33:10). If these beguiling words too easily lead away from Esau, back to Jacob the chosen one, that path we need not follow. As with the Hagar narrative, we can resist the dominant story line so as to behold the gracious face of Esau.

The story is not over; the *hineini* of Esau remains unfilled. This claim I anchor in a particular silence within the biblical narrative. The narrative reports the death of Isaac, with both sons present to bury him (Genesis 35:29); it reports the burial place in the cave near Mamre of both Isaac and Rebekah (Genesis 49:32); and it reports the death and subsequent burial of Jacob years later in the same place (Genesis 49:33; 50:7–14). Three members of this troubled family are at rest. But about Esau's death the narrative says nothing. Like Hagar, whose death is also unrecorded, Esau has no resting place. The stories of these two weepers outside the covenant remain unfinished. If for me the *hineini* of Esau elicits no personal anecdote, it nonetheless evokes a cri de coeur. "Behold, Esau."

Part III

A Guide to Creating Our Own Personal Midrash— Finding Your Own Voice in the Text

Since Midrash by definition is the process of finding contemporary meaning in the biblical text, we cannot merely read the midrashim produced by the Rabbis of old, nor even the powerful personal anecdotes of the teachers of our day. If we are serious about Torah study, then we must all bring ourselves to the text, with all of our questions, personal issues, and struggles. We need to find our own voices so we can give expression to who we are and to our aspirations. It is now our turn to create midrashim that represent our search for personal meaning.

Creating our own meaning cannot be done in a vacuum. It is not simply a matter of reading the biblical text and then immediately creating our own midrashim, even if we are able to read and interpret the text in Hebrew. If our modern midrashim are to have any lasting meaning, then we must move through three stages of engagement with the Bible.

First, we must commit ourselves to a close study of the Bible, searching out the meaning of the text in its own context. The initial phase of creating meaning for ourselves is understanding the *pshat* of a particular passage. Then, we modern readers must take advantage of the generations of rabbinic interpretations of the biblical text, realizing that the midrashim of the Rabbis reflect their own life situations. Whether Rabbi Akiba, Rabbi Ishmael, or Rabbi Meir of the second century; Rabbi Yohanan or Rabbi Yitzhak of the third century; or any of the other famous Rabbis of the first millenium, each found personal meaning as he interpreted any given passage. And, if the Rabbis of old could find relevancy in the Torah text for their day and for their lives, so can we.

Having established a firm base on which to create our own midrashic interpretations, by a close study of the Bible, enhanced by an immersion into the classical midrashim and from exposure to contemporary midrashic expressions, it is now our turn to wrestle with the words of Torah. The *hineini* passages we have studied demand that each of us engage them on the deepest level and, out of that engagement, create our own midrash.

Text Questions: Starting Points for the Creation of Contemporary Midrash

We need to develop our ability to raise questions about the biblical passages we study. These questions focus our attention on the problems, ambiguities, and missing details in the text, and serve as a hook on which we can append meaning. Questions about syntax, philology, literary structure and style, theology, historical context, and especially the humanistic questions that touch on the feelings, attitudes, and interactions of the biblical characters—all are bases on which we can shape our own midrashic responses.

To help get you started with your own questioning, allow me to note some of the questions that lie at the heart of my own midrashic interpretation of the fourteen biblical passages we have studied. In each case, I have included a range of questions to demonstrate the many ways one can enter the text, thereby discovering meaning that can inform our own creative process.

I would suggest that you first review the particular *hineini* passage in its biblical setting, as I have interpreted it in Part I, and then wrestle with the questions that I have specified. After that, you will surely come up with other questions that you feel are pivotal in understanding the message of the specific *hineini*.

1. GENESIS 22:1–2—RECOGNIZING THE OTHER

a. Why does Abraham respond, *"Hineini"*—indicating his willingness to act—when the task is not yet defined by God?

b. This is the last of God's ten trials of Abraham. What experiences does Abraham bring to this moment that enable him to respond to God's request?

c. Why is this the first time that *hineini* is used, even though God has spoken to and called to Abraham many times throughout his life?

d. In what way does Abraham experience God's call as a "trial"? Have you experienced a request by an other in your life as a trial or a test?

e. Why is Abraham willing to bring Isaac as a sacrifice, knowing that he—Isaac—is the guarantor of the future?

2. GENESIS 22:6–8—BEING ACCESSIBLE TO THE OTHER

a. What is the significance of Abraham using the very same word—*hineini*—to respond to Isaac that he used in responding to God? What does this say to you?

b. Isaac calls out, "my father," and Abraham reciprocates by saying, "my son." What does this communicate?

c. Why does Isaac ask, "Here *(hinei)* is the firebrand and the wood, but where is the lamb?" immediately after Abraham responds, *"Hineini"?* How does Abraham hear Isaac's question? Might he be wondering the very same thing?

d. In responding, "God will see to the lamb," what is Abraham communicating to his son?

e. Why is this the only interchange between father and son on the three-day journey to the mountain? What else might have transpired during the journey?

3. GENESIS 22:9–12—AWAKENING TO RELATIONSHIP

a. Why is it an angel who calls to Abraham here and not God?

b. Why is there a double calling of Abraham's name at this

moment? Can you think of circumstances when you have called to someone you love more than once?

c. How does Abraham feel when he hears the call at this climactic moment?

d. Put yourself in Isaac's place. What are Isaac's feelings? What does he say to his father?

e. Abraham descends from the mountain and returns to Beer Sheba with his servants. Why is Isaac not with them?

4. GENESIS 27:1–4—RESPONSE IN THE EVERYDAY

a. The text tells us that Isaac's eyes are too dim to see. What can't Isaac see?

b. Why doesn't Esau respond, "Here I am, my father," after Isaac says, "My son?"

c. What do you learn from the fact that the term *hineini,* which is used by Abraham to respond to God, is also used by Esau to respond to his father's request to hunt for him?

d. Why does Esau have to provide his father with food in order to receive the blessing?

e. What does this episode tell you about Esau's nature? How does he feel being the one who always provides his father with food?

5. GENESIS 27:15–19—UNQUALIFIED OPENNESS: THE CHALLENGE AND THE RISK

a. What is the nature of the question, "Who are you, my son?" Why does it follow Jacob's response, *"Hineini"?*

b. Does Isaac know who is standing before him?

c. What makes it difficult for Isaac to know which son it is?

d. If he knows it is Jacob, why does he bless him?

e. What is going through Jacob's mind when he responds, "I am Esau"?

6. GENESIS 31:1–13—FULFILLING PAST PROMISES

a. Why does the angel of God appear to Jacob in a dream?

b. Why does God call to Jacob at this point, when God didn't appear to him during all the years that he dwelt in Laban's house? What does this communicate to him?

c. Why is "seeing" associated with both Jacob and God in this narrative? What do they "see"?

d. Why does God identify the Divine Self as the God of Beth El?

e. Relationship with the other brings with it expectations. What does God expect of Jacob and why?

f. What is the vow that Jacob must fulfill (see Genesis 28:20–22) and how does it tie into the issue of Jacob's struggle with Laban over the flocks?

7. Genesis 37:11–14—The Significant Ramifications of Our Response to Others

a. Why does Jacob send Joseph out to his brothers, knowing how they feel about him?

b. Why does Joseph so readily respond to his father's request, knowing that his brothers hate him?

c. Is the challenge of *hineini* to be able to respond when the call is fraught with difficulty, even danger?

d. In journeying to Shechem to see his brothers, Joseph must think that he will be back in a very short time. How are we to know that our *hineini* responses may have consequences far beyond the initial request?

e. Jacob asks Joseph to bring him back word of his brothers. When is the next time that Joseph speaks to his father? How many of us realize that when we speak with someone we love, it may be the last opportunity we have to do so?

8. Genesis 46:1–4—Responding to the Other's Fears

a. Why does Jacob stop at Beer Sheba to sacrifice at the very outset of his journey down to Egypt?

b. What is the significance of God appearing to Jacob in a dream there? Where else does he have a dream in which God speaks to him?

c. Why did God call to him twice, "Jacob, Jacob"?

d. Why does God identify the Divine Self as the God of Jacob's father?

e. Why is Jacob so afraid of leaving the Land of Israel? And how is God's promise to be with him no different than when he set out for Haran in his youth?

f. Why does Jacob risk leaving the Land of Israel now?

9. Exodus 3:2–6—The Reticence to Respond

a. What does it take to see the other, to hear the call?

b. Why does God appear in the lowliest of plants, a scraggly bush?

c. Why is it emphasized that God *saw* him after Moses turned aside *to see* the bush?

d. Why does God have to call Moses twice here? What does it tell us about Moses at this point in his life? About God?

e. What is the point of stressing that Moses doesn't know that he is standing on holy ground?

f. Do we, like Moses, hide our faces from the other in our lives?

10. 1 Samuel 3:1–10—The Difficulty of Discerning the Call

a. Why does Samuel confuse the source of the call to him? Do we also not understand that God is calling when the call comes from human beings?

b. What enables Samuel to realize that God is calling him? What role does Eli play? Do we also need "mentors" to teach us about God's presence? Who are the mentors in your life?

c. Why does Eli refer to Samuel as "my son" the second time he hears the call?

d. Why does God call Samuel's name twice when the Divine appears to him?

e. What is the significance of Samuel leaving out God's name when he responds to the call the third time, even after Eli's directive?

11. 2 Samuel 1:1–16—Fabricating the Call

a. If the Amalekite's story is not true, why does he fabricate it? What does he think he will gain by lying? What do we think we will gain when we consciously do not tell the whole truth?

b. What is the import of the question Saul asks the young man, "Who are you?" and of David's question to him, "Where are you from?"

c. Why is the Amalekite constantly called a *na'ar,* a young lad?

d. When the king calls, the Amalekite responds, *"Hineini,"* seemingly showing his willingness to act on behalf of the king. However, he clearly has his own agenda. When we respond to the others in our lives, are we occasionally not so altruistic?

e. What does the lad's death tell you about the nature of how we respond to others?

12. Isaiah 65:1–2—The Ever-Present Other

a. What does it take to experience the other in our lives?

b. God is omnipresent, ever ready to be sought, to be found. Is that true of those whom we love?

c. Do we believe that God is always there, waiting for us to recognize the Divine Presence in the world?

d. What does God's double call of *hineini* mean? Can we understand what God is "feeling" here as we think about our own relationships?

e. What does the image of God spreading out the Divine hands communicate?

f. As you contemplate your own sense of what God means to you, what is the power of Isaiah putting the word *hineini* in God's mouth?

13. Isaiah 58:1–9—The Ultimate Call

a. Do we not sometimes delude ourselves into thinking that we are truly responding to the other, just as the Israelites of Isaiah's did?

b. When we think that we are merely responding to other human beings, do we understand that we are answering the call of the Divine?

c. Are you convinced that, when you cry out, God will be there, answering you?

d. How do you understand the notion that God responds to our call?

e. Do we believe that our actions can usher in the messianic age?

14. ISAIAH 52:1–6—THE ULTIMATE RESPONSE

a. The Israelites feel the pain of being cut off from God, suffering in exile. What does it feel like for you when you are cut off from the other in your life?

b. When you are suffering, do you think that you are alone?

c. What guarantees that we will one day experience wholeness and that all who feel oppressed will experience redemption?

d. What does it mean to know or learn God's name?

e. Why is God described here as the One who speaks, *medabber?*

f. What is the ultimate messianic vision?

THE TASK IS OURS

Now that we have absorbed the powerful meaning of the fourteen *hineini* passages in the Bible and the expression given to many of them through the creativity of our contemporary teachers, we may be like the impatient convert in the famous talmudic story of Hillel and Shammai, the well-known pair of first-century C.E. Palestinian rabbis (B. T. *Shabbat* 31a). The prospective convert wanted them to convert him while he stood on one foot. While Shammai drove him away, Hillel quoted to him the rabbinic understanding of the Golden Rule, Leviticus 19:18: "Love your neighbor as yourself," adding that this is the whole Torah; all the rest is commentary. He then directed the newly won convert: "*Zil g'mor* (go and learn it)."

Having tasted of the waters of Torah, you are now ready to "Go and learn it" for yourself. What is interesting is that the word *g'mor,* the imperative form of *gamar,* also means "finish, complete." Although we know that we can never complete the process of learning Torah, since it contains infinite meanings, our task at this time is to complete the process of creating meaning for ourselves out of our encounter with the *hineini* responses in the Bible. It is not enough that we have analyzed the fourteen biblical passages containing the word *hineini*, even with our immersion into the variety of associated rabbinic interpretations. It isn't even sufficient to have tasted the powerful messages of passionate and erudite modern teachers. No, the challenge is now ours—to find our own personal meaning in these texts, by creating our own modern midrashim.

As a first step, choose one of the *hineini* passages and answer the following questions about, and about it yourself:

1. What is the most intriguing question about this passage for you and why?
2. What problem in the text catches your attention?
3. What is the most powerful human dimension of the passage and how does it speak to your life situation?

As you begin to create your own midrash, remember the teaching of Hillel, cited above: The whole Torah is concerned with our response to other human beings; all else is commentary. As we create our own expressions of Torah by understanding how *hineini* works in our lives, may we have the wisdom to know that our encounter with the tradition must lead us to the others in our lives, those whom we love, the strangers whom we meet, and most important, the Other, the God of the universe who calls to us every moment of every day. May our midrashim enable us to better understand that it is only through the Other(s) that we ourselves can achieve wholeness in our lives. May we know the moment of calling, and may its power continue to sustain us, motivate us, and strengthen us.

Notes

PREFACE

1. R. Menahem Mendl of Kotzk, as quoted in Aharon Yaakov Greenberg, ed., *Itturey Torah* (Tel Aviv: Yavneh Publishing House, 1976) on Exodus.
2. Aviva Zornberg, *Genesis: The Beginning of Desire* (Philadelphia: Jewish Publication Society, 1995), p. 117.
3. *Bereshit Rabbah* 74:11.
4. Naomi Rosenblatt and Joshua Horwitz, *Wrestling with Angels* (New York: Dell Publishing, 1995), p. 203.

INTRODUCTION

1. Some of the initial material in the Introduction is based on an article I wrote for *Living Text: The Journal of Contemporary Midrash* 1 (July 1997), 12–16.
2. For more on the *PaRDeS* and the four categories of interpretation, see my *The Way Into Torah* (Woodstock, Vt.: Jewish Lights Publishing, 2000), pp. 78–86.
3. See *Midrash Ottiyyot d'Rabbi Akiba* and *Bamidbar Rabbah* 13:15 et. al.
4. B. T. *Shabbat* 88a.
5. J.P. Fokkelman, *Narrative Art in Genesis* (Amsterdam: Van Gorcum, 1975), pp. 3–4.
6. See, in this regard, Ezra 7:10, in which we read that "Ezra set his heart at searching out *(lidrosh)* the meaning of God's Torah."

7. *The Way Into Torah*, pp. 77ff.

8. Ibid., p. 74, and my citation of Wolfgang Iser's *The Art of Reading: A Theory of the Aesthetic Response* (Baltimore: Johns Hopkins University Press, 1979).

9. See also my *Self, Struggle and Change* (Woodstock, Vt.: Jewish Lights Publishing, 1995), p. 13.

10. Steven Kepnes, *The Text as Thou: Martin Buber's Dialogical Hermeneutics and Narrative Theology* (Bloomington and Indianapolis: Indiana University Press, 1992). On p. 76, Kepnes writes that "interpreting the text must involve assimilation of the text's meaning into the personal life of the interpreter. Application [of the text] should bring along with it a reorienting of the interpreter's life."

11. *The Way Into Torah*, pp. 74–75.

PART I: FOURTEEN BIBLICAL TEXTS, FOURTEEN OPPORTUNITIES FOR MEANING

CHAPTER 1: RECOGNIZING THE OTHER

1. All English translations are drawn from the *JPS Hebrew-English Tanakh* (Philadelphia: Jewish Publication Society, 1999).

2. Note, for example, Genesis 3:9–10, 4:6–9, and 6:13–22.

3. Genesis 22:2. Moriah is identified with Jerusalem based on 2 Chronicles 3:1.

4. The most complete rendition of Abraham's ten trials is found in a *Pirkei d'Rabbi Eliezer*, Chapters 26–31. This text is most probably an eighth-century C.E. Palestinian compilation. Shorter parallels are also found in other sources, including *Avot d'Rabbi Natan*, Version A, Chapter 33.

5. All of the tests mentioned here are part of the biblical account of Abraham's life, except for the story of the fiery furnace. The events surrounding Abraham's birth and youth in *Ur Chasdim* are not described in Genesis 11. They are found in the midrashic treatment of Abraham's life.

6. See *Pirkei d'Rabbi Eliezer*, Chapter 31 in this regard.

7. See, in this regard, Ramban's comment on Genesis 22:1.

8. In *Midrash Tanhuma Buber, Vayera* 44, the Rabbis differentiate among the various challenges which God presented to Abraham, to which he responded, *"Hineini."*

9. In describing the ten trials of Abraham, the author of *Avot d'Rabbi Natan*, in Version A, Chapter 33, emphasized that Abraham was tested

each time and in every one he was found to be *shalem,* complete or whole.

10. See Genesis 15:4–6 and Chapter 17.
11. Zornberg, *Genesis,* pp. 116–117. She draws on the Ishbitzer Rebbe from his *May ha-Shiloah.*
12. Many modern commentators note the power of the phrase *lech lecha* as pointing to Abraham's journey inward, including Samson Raphael Hirsch. See, in this regard, Zornberg's comments in *Genesis* pp. 74 and 87.
13. See, for example, *Bereshit Rabbah* 55:4.
14. Nahmanides's commentary to Genesis 22:1.
15. *Pirkei d'Rabbi Eliezer,* Chapter 30, extending the words of Genesis 21:11, "The matter distressed Abraham greatly."
16. Rosenblatt and Horwitz, *Wrestling with Angels,* p. 199.
17. See, among several parallel traditions, both Rashi and *Midrash Sekhel Tov* on Genesis 22:1.
18. See Zornberg, *Genesis,* pp. 12, 27, and 68 in this regard.
19. *Bereshit Rabbah* 55:6.
20. *'Or Ha-Hayyim* on Genesis 22:1.
21. See, in this regard, Elie Wiesel's comment in his *Messengers of God* (New York: Random House, 1976), p. 82.
22. See, for example *Midrash Tanhuma ha-Nidpas, Vayera* 22 and Rashi's comments on Genesis 22:1.
23. This interpretation is based on *Pesikta d'Rav Kahana* 23:9 and its parallel in *Pesikta Rabbati* 40:6.
24. See, in this regard, Isaac Arama's commentary, *Akeidat Yitzhak,* on our passage.
25. Rosenblatt and Horwitz, *Wrestling with Angels,* p. 201.
26. See the commentary *'Or Ha-Hayyim* on Genesis 22:1.
27. Zornberg, *Genesis,* p. 114.
28. Rosenblatt and Horwitz, *Wrestling with Angels,* pp. 202–203.
29. *Pesikta Rabbati* 40:6. The midrash plays on the mention of the word *ha-yom* (today or the day) in Genesis 22:14, implying that the day on which Isaac was brought to the mountain was *the* day of days, Rosh ha-Shanah, the very day on which the world was created. This is the basis on which the midrash juxtaposes the *Akeidah* and Rosh ha-Shanah.
30. Ibid.
31. In Isaiah 41:8, Abraham is called *Ohavi,* my friend or the one who loves me.

32. See, in this regard, B. T. *Sota* 31a and the Book of Jubilees 17:18.
33. *Yalkut Shimoni remez* 96.

CHAPTER 2: BEING ACCESSIBLE TO THE OTHER

1. Rosenblatt and Horwitz, *Wrestling with Angels,* p. 202.
2. Rabbi Joshua ben Levi was an early third-century C.E. Palestinian teacher.
3. B. T. *Sanhedrin* 98a.
4. See *Bereshit Rabbah* 56:7, *Yalkut Shimoni* Vol. 1, *remez* 101, and *Midrash Sekhel Tov* to Genesis 22:7 et al.
5. See, in this regard, the comment in *Pirkei d'Rabbi Eliezer,* Chapter 31, on Isaac calling out, "My father, here is the firestone and the wood, but where is the sheep for the burnt offering?" The Rabbis emphasize that when Isaac calls out to his father, he is giving voice to much more.
6. Aviva Zornberg, in her important work on Exodus, *The Particulars of Rapture: Reflections on Exodus* (New York: Doubleday, 2001), p. 84, cites Sefat Emet 40, which interprets Psalm 50:7: "Listen, my people, that I may speak," as "Your listening will enable me to speak."
7. Rosenblatt and Horowitz, *Wrestling with Angels,* p. 199.
8. See *Bereshit Rabbah* 56:7, *Midrash Tanhuma ha-Nidpas, Vayera* 22, *Pirkei d'Rabbi Eliezer,* Chapter 31, *Midrash Lekah Tov* to Genesis 22:8, *Midrash ha-Gadol* to Genesis 22:8, and *Sefer ha-Yashar* on Genesis 22.
9. See the commentary *K'li Yakar* to Genesis 22:7 in this regard.
10. *Sefer ha-Yashar* on Genesis 22.
11. See *Midrash Sekhel Tov* to Genesis 22:7 in this regard.
12. *Midrash ha-Gadol* to Genesis 22:8.
13. *K'li Yakar* to Genesis 22:7.
14. Both the *Targum Yerushalmi* and *Targum Yonatan* to Genesis 22:8 translate the word *yachdav* (together) with the Aramaic word *k'khada* (as one).
15. *Bereshit Rabbah* 56:7.
16. *Sefer ha-Yashar* on Genesis 22.
17. *Midrash ha-Gadol* to Genesis 22:8.

CHAPTER 3: AWAKENING TO RELATIONSHIP

1. Devora Steinmetz, *From Father to Son: Kinship, Conflict and Continuity in Genesis* (Louisville: John Knox Press, 1991), p. 52.

2. *ArtScroll Tanach Series, Sefer Bereshit* (New York: Mesorah Publications, Ltd., 1969), Vol. 2, p. 801, quotes Moses Alsheich's commentary, *Torat Moshe*, here.

3. This is a composite reworking of a midrash on Genesis 22:11–12 found in *Bereshit Rabbah* 56:7 and *Midrash Va-Yosha* et al.

4. See, in this regard, the comments of *K'li Yakar* and Ibn Ezra to Genesis 22:11. See also *Midrash Tanhuma Buber, Vayera* 46.

5. *ArtScroll, Sefer Bereshit*, p. 801.

6. Book of Jubilees 18:20.

7. For example, *Bereshit Rabbah* 56:8 and *Sefer ha-Yashar* on Genesis 22.

8. Steinmetz, *From Father to Son*, p. 64.

9. See, among others, *Bereshit Rabbah* 56:7 and Rashi to Genesis 22:11.

10. *K'li Yakar* to Genesis 22:11.

11. This interpretation is an adaptation of a comment in *Midrash Tanhuma Buber, Vayera* 46.

12. See the *Targum Yerushalmi* to Genesis 22:11 in this regard.

13. See, for example, *Bereshit Rabbah* 56:5 in this regard.

14. *Sefer ha-Yashar* on Genesis 22.

15. See *Vayikra Rabbah* 1:9 and its interpretation on Leviticus 1:1, which is applicable to Genesis 22:11–12.

16. Rashi's comment on Leviticus 1:1.

17. See *Bereshit Rabbah* 56:7 in this regard.

CHAPTER 4: RESPONSE IN THE EVERYDAY

1. Steinmetz, *From Father to Son*, p. 53.

2. See, for example, *Bereshit Rabbah* 63:6 and 65:1, in which Esau is equated with Rome.

3. Nehama Leibowitz, *Studies in the Weekly Sidra*, series 4/5718, on *Toldot*, World Zionist Organization Department of Torah Education and Culture in the Diaspora, pp. 2–3. She quotes *Midrash ve-ha-Ma'aseh* here.

4. *Midrash ha-Gadol* to Genesis 27:1.

5. See, for example, *Bereshit Rabbah* 65:10 in this regard.

6. Leibowitz, *Studies in the Weekly Sidra, Toldot*, p. 3, quotes *'Or Ha-Hayyim* on Genesis 27:1.

7. See my *Voices from Genesis: Guiding us through the Stages of Life* (Woodstock, Vt.: Jewish Lights Publishing, 1998), pp. 104–105.

8. An adaptation of Genesis 25:28, as well as our passage, Genesis 27:3–4.

9. Zornberg, *Genesis,* p. 170.

10. Steinmetz, *From Father to Son,* p. 40.

11. See, for example, *Genesis Rabbah 55:4.*

12. See my *Self, Struggle and Change,* pp. 103–104.

13. *Sidrei Devarim, pisqa* 336, *Bereshit Rabbah* 65:16 and 82:14, and especially *Devarim Rabbah* 1:14.

14. See *Sforno's* comment on Genesis 27:4 in this regard.

15. For example, Targum Yonatan to Genesis 27:1 and *Yalkut Shimoni,* Vol. 2, *remez* 11.

CHAPTER 5: UNQUALIFIED OPENNESS

1. Cohen, *Self, Struggle and Change,* pp. 107–108.

2. This is based on *Bereshit Rabbah* 65:16 and *Me'am Lo'az* to Genesis 27:17.

3. See Aviva Zornberg's perceptive analysis of this midrashic description of the crossing of the threshold in *Genesis,* pp. 174–175.

4. This is based on Genesis 25:27.

5. See, for example, *Tzena U'rena* on *Parashah Toldot* in this regard.

6. *Bereshit Rabbah* 65:15.

7. *Midrash Sekhel Tov* and *Midrash Aggadah* to Genesis 27:18.

8. *ArtScroll Series* to Genesis 27:18.

9. Zornberg, *Genesis,* pp. 170–171.

10. See Rashi on Genesis 27:19.

11. See *Sefat Emet* to Genesis 27:19 and Aviva Zornberg's comments on it, in *Genesis,* p. 172.

12. *Midrash ha-Hefetz* to Genesis 27:19.

13. See the Book of Jubilees 26:13 and *Me'am Lo'az* to Genesis 27:18 among many other sources.

14. Rashi on Genesis 27:19.

15. See this interpretation in *Bereshit Rabbah* 65:18.

16. *Bamidbar Rabbah* 10:6.

17. Zornberg, *Genesis,* p. 173.

CHAPTER 6: FULFILLING PAST PROMISES

1. Note Jacob's own words in this regard in Chapter 31, verses 7, 9.

2. *Midrash Sekhel Tov* to Genesis 31:13.

3. See Exodus 3:7, among other verses in this regard.

4. Note, for example, *Midrash Sekhel Tov* to Genesis 31:3.

5. *Midrash ha-Gadol* to Genesis 31:3.

6. *Midrash Tanhuma Buber, Va-yetze* 23.

7. *Midrash Tanhuma Buber, Va-yetze* 22, *Midrash Tanhuma ha-Nidpas, Va-yetze* 10 and *Me'am Lo'az* to Genesis 31:3.

8. Rashi to Genesis 31:3.

9. *Bereshit Rabbah* 74:1.

10. *Pirkei d'Rabbi Eliezer,* Chapter 36.

11. *Bereshit Rabbati* to Genesis 31:10. Compare Genesis 28:10ff to our passage in Chapter 31.

12. *Me'am Lo'az* and *Midrash Sekhel Tov* to Genesis 31:13.

13. *Targum Onkelos* to Genesis 31:13.

14. See, among many sources, Rashi and *Siftei Hachamim* on Genesis 31:13.

15. *Midrash ha-Gadol* to Genesis 31:13.

16. *Bereshit Rabbah* 74:3 and *Yalkut Shimoni, remez* 130.

17. *Midrash Sekhel Tov* to Genesis 31:11.

CHAPTER 7: THE SIGNIFICANT RAMIFICATIONS OF OUR RESPONSE TO OTHERS

1. Elie Wiesel, *Messengers of God,* p. 156f.

2. See, in this regard, Nahum Sarna, ed., *The JPS Torah Commentary Series: Genesis* (Philadelphia: Jewish Publication Society, 1989).

3. *Targum Yonatan* to Genesis 37:13.

4. *ArtScroll Series* to Genesis 37:13. See also Philo, *On Joseph* 10.

5. *Yafe To'ar* to Genesis 37:14. Note, too, how the Rabbis believed that an individual who is a *shaliach mitzvah,* who is an agent fulfilling a commandment—in this case, Joseph honoring his father—will surely not be harmed. See, for example, Moses Alsheikh's comments on Genesis 37:13–14.

6. This point is based on *Ba'al ha-Turim* to Genesis 37:14.

7. These words are placed in Jacob's mouth by Rabbi Hama bar Hanina in *Bereshit Rabbah* 84:13.

8. See, among many sources, *Sforno* to Genesis 37:14 and *'Or Ha-Hayyim* to Genesis 37:13.

9. *ArtScroll Series* to Genesis 37:13. See also *Midrash Sekhel Tov* to Genesis 37:14.

10. Moses Alsheikh's comment to Genesis 37:13.

11. See Devora Steinmetz's insightful textual analysis in her *From Father to Son*, pp. 57–58.

12. See *Midrash ha-Gadol* to Genesis 37:14 in this regard.

13. *ArtScroll Series* to Genesis 37:12.

14. Ramban's commentary to Genesis 37:14.

15. See Rashi and *Midrash Sekhel Tov* on Genesis 37:13 in this regard, among many similar comments throughout the Midrash and Commentary literatures.

16. Ibn Ezra to Genesis 37:13.

17. *Bereshit Rabbah* 84:13.

18. *Midrash Lekah Tov* and *Midrash Sekhel Tov* to Genesis 37:13.

19. This is based upon *Midrash Aggadah* to Genesis 37:13.

20. Pitzele, *Our Fathers' Wells*, p. 211.

21. *ArtScroll Series* to Genesis 37:13.

22. *Aggadat Bereshit*, Chapter 61.

23. See in this regard, the *ArtScroll Series* to Genesis 37:14, *Bereshit Rabbah* 84:13, *Targum Yonatan* to Genesis 37:14, B. T. *Sota* 11a, *Yalkut Shimoni remez* 141, and *Midrash ha-Gadol* to Genesis 37:14.

24. See my *Self, Struggle and Change*, pp. 156–158.

CHAPTER 8: RESPONDING TO THE OTHER'S FEARS

1. *Shemot Rabbah* 2:6.

2. Rosenblatt and Horowitz, *Wrestling with Angels*, pp. 369–370.

3. Leibowitz, *Studies in the Weekly Sidra, Vayiggash*. She points out that several commentators raise this very question.

4. *Sefer ha-Yashar, Parashat Vayigash*.

5. Sarna, *The JPS Torah Commentary Series: Genesis* to Genesis 46:1.

6. See Rashi and *Lekah Tov* to Genesis 46:3 in this regard, among many sources.

7. Rosenblatt and Horowitz, *Wrestling with Angels*, p. 370.

8. Leibowitz, *Studies in the Weekly Sidra, Vayiggash*.

9. *Midrash Sekhel Tov* to Genesis 46:3 and Ramban's comment on Genesis 46:1.

10. *Pirkei d'Rabbi Eliezer*, Chapter 39.

11. Leibowitz, *Studies in the Weekly Sidra, Vayiggash*.

12. Book of Jubilees 44:3.

13. Yet, *Hizkuni,* in his comments on Genesis 46:1, assumes that Jacob, following Isaac's example, built his own altar in Beer Sheba.

14. The Book of Jubilees 44:1.

15. See, among many similar traditions, *Bereshit Rabbati, Midrash Sekhel Tov, Me'am Lo'az,* and *Tzena U'rena* to Genesis 46:1.

16. *Bereshit Rabbah* 94:5 and *Yalkut Shimoni remez* 152.

17. Note Nehama Leibowitz's citations in this regard in her *Studies in the Weekly Sidra, Vayiggash,* especially from the *Meshekh Hokhma* of Rabbi Meir Simha of Dvinsk. The irony of course is that the redemption from Egypt begins in the middle of the night. See Exodus 12 in this regard.

18. See, for example, Rashi, *Torah Temimah, Midrash ha-Gadol* and *Midrash Sekhel Tov* to Genesis 46:2.

19. Steinmetz, *From Father to Son,* pp. 56–59.

20. Bereshit Rabbati to Genesis 46:3, which notes God's similar assurances to Abraham and to Isaac.

21. Zornberg, *Genesis,* p. 194.

22. *'Or Ha-Hayyim* to Genesis 46:4.

23. This is captured in the concept of *Shekhinta ba-Galuta,* the *Shekhinah* in Exile. See, for example, the *Mechilta d'Rabbi Ishmael, Massechta d'Shirta, parashah* 3 and *Shemot Rabbah* 15:16. The concept is based in part on Psalm 91:15: "I will be with him in distress."

24. See the breadth of commentary literature on Genesis 46:4, as well as *Bereshit Rabbati, Midrash Sekhel Tov,* and *Me'am Lo'az* to the same verse.

25. See the comments of Nehama Leibowitz in this regard, in her *Studies in the Weekly Sidra,* in which she cites *Haamek Davar.*

26. Zornberg, *Genesis,* p. 347.

27. *Bereshit Rabbah* 96:1.

28. *Bereshit Rabbah* 94:6 and *Midrash ha-Gadol* to Genesis 46:4.

CHAPTER 9: THE RETICENCE TO RESPOND

1. Most scholars believe that they are different mountains, one in Midian, the other in the Sinai Peninsula. They also make a distinction between them from a literary point of view: Horeb is assigned to the Elohist/Deuteronomist traditions, while Sinai belongs to Jehovist/Elohist.

2. The Rabbis make the connection between Horeb and Sinai, and see it as a narrative anticipation. See, for example, Shadal's comment on Exodus 3:1, as well as *Tzena U'rena* to Exodus 3:1.

3. Note, in this regard, *Midrash Lekah Tov* to Exodus 3:2; Sarna's comment on Exodus 3:2 in *The JPS Torah Commentary Series: Exodus;* and William Propp's note to Exodus 3:2 in *The Anchor Bible* on Exodus 1–18 (New York: Doubleday, 1964), p. 199.

4. For example, *Midrash Lekah Tov* to Exodus 3:2.

5. Rashi to Exodus 3:2.

6. Zornberg, *The Particulars of Rapture: Reflections on Exodus* (New York: Doubleday, 2000), p. 338.

7. Levi Meier, *Moses: The Prince, the Prophet* (Woodstock,Vt.: Jewish Lights Publishing, 1998), p. 31.

8. *Shemot Rabbah* 3:2.

9. See, in this regard, *Midrash ha-Gadol* and *K'li Yakar* to Exodus 3:2.

10. Psalm 91:15. This verse is repeated in numerous midrashic traditions to underscore God's presence when Israel suffers. For example, the *Mekhilta d'Rabbi Shimon ben Yohai* to Exodus 3:2, 8.

11. See, among many passages, *Pirkei d'Rabbi Eliezer,* Chapter 40, *Midrash Tanhuma Ha-Nidpas Shemot* 14, *Midrash Tanhuma Buber, Shemot* 13, *Yalkut Shimoni remazim* 167, 169, and *Midrash ha-Gadol* to Exodus 3:2.

12. *Shemot Rabbah* 2:5.

13. *Mekhilta d'Rabbi Shimon bar Yohai* to Exodus 3:8. This is represented in the concept of *Shechinta ba-Galuta,* the *Shekhinah* (God's presence), in exile with the people.

14. Meier, *Moses: The Prince, the Prophet,* p. 31.

15. *Shemot Rabbah* to Exodus 2:5. See also Philo, *On Moses* 1, 67.

16. *Shemot Rabbah* 2:1.

17. *Shemot Rabbah* 2:1 and Rashbam's comment on Exodus 3:1. Note, too, Exodus 2:12 and 3:17.

18. *Midrash Tanhuma Buber, Shemot* 13 and *Midrash Lekah Tov, Midrash Sekhel Tov,* and *Midrash Aggadah* to Exodus 3:3.

19. *Tzena U'rena* to Exodus 3:4.

20. *Yalkut Shimoni remez* 168 and *Midrash ha-Gadol* to Exodus 3:4.

21. The tradition underscores the urgency of the call based on the fact that there is no *meteg,* no vertical line, equivalent to a comma, between "Moses Moses," as there is in all other doubling of names when God calls, for example, Genesis 22:11, 46:2 and 1 Samuel 3:10. See *Shemot Rabbah* 2:6 in this regard.

22. *'Or Ha-Hayyim* and *Da'at Zekainim* to Exodus 3:4.

23. *Anchor Bible* to Exodus 3:3.

24. *Shemot Rabbah* 3:1. Some texts even say that God spoke to Moses in Amram's actual voice so as to comfort him. See, in this regard, *Shemot Rabbah* 2:6, *Yalkut Shimoni remez* 168 and *Midrash ha-Gadol* to Exodus 3:6.
25. *The JPS Torah Commentary Series: Exodus* 3:6.
26. Meier, *Moses: The Prince, the Prophet,* p. 32.

CHAPTER 10: THE DIFFICULTY OF DISCERNING THE CALL

1. Radak's comment on 1 Samuel 3:8.
2. *Sefer Shmuel,* a commentary by Yehudah Keel, on 1 Samuel 3:5. Samuel thought that his master needed his service.
3. Joseph Caro comment on 1 Samuel 3:1.
4. Yehudah Keel, *Sefer Shmuel,* 3:6.
5. Abravanel on I Samuel 3:1.
6. See the many comments to this effect on 1 Samuel 3:3, for example, Rashi, Radak, and Abravanel, as well as the *Targum Yonatan.* See also *Me'am Lo'az* to 1 Samuel 3:3.
7. *Targum Yonatan* to 1 Samuel 3:4.
8. See the comment in *Me'am Lo'az* to 1 Samuel 3:4, based on the verse from Job 37:4.
9. See, among many references, Rashi to 1 Samuel 3:4, *Midrash Shmuel* 9:5, *Yalkut Shimoni,* Vol. 2, *remez* 97, and *Me'am Lo'az* to 1 Samuel 3:3.
10. See, for example, Radak to 1 Samuel 3:3 and B. T. *Kiddushin* 72b in this regard.
11. *Bereshit Rabbah* 58:2, B. T. *Yoma* 38b, *Midrash Shmuel* 8:9, and *Me'am Lo'az* to 1 Samuel 3:3.
12. Ibid., 1 Samuel 3:3 and Abravanel's comment on 1 Samuel 3:7.
13. See the comment on the Proverbs text in B. T. *Shabbat* 113b.
14. See *Me'am Lo'az* to 1 Samuel 3:6 in thus regard, as well as Moshe Ginzberg and Shmuel Ahitov, eds., *Mikra Yisrael, 1 Samuel* (Tel Aviv: Am Oved, 1996), p. 81.
15. Note, among many parallels, the comments of Rashi, *Metzudat David,* and Abravanel to 1 Samuel 3:10.
16. *Me'am Lo'az* to 1 Samuel 3:10.
17. Abravanel to 1 Samuel 3:6, *Mikra Yisrael,* p. 81 and *Me'am Lo'az* to 1 Samuel 3:6.
18. Abravanel to 1 Samuel 3:4.
19. *Me'am Lo'az* to 1 Samuel 3:5.

20. *Midrash Shmuel* 9:8, *Yalkut Shimoni* Vol. 2, *remez* 97.

21. Yehudah Keel, *Sefer Shmuel* to 1 Samuel 3:4.

22. *Midrash Shmuel* 9:8 and Abravanel to 1 Samuel 3:3.

23. *Yalkut Shimoni*, Vol. 2, *remez* 97.

24. Note that *Targum Yonatan* translates Samuel's *"Hineini"* and God's *"Hinei Anochi"* in the same way: *"Ha Ana"* (Here I am).

CHAPTER 11: FABRICATING THE CALL

1. As noted in the beginning of our passage, 2 Samuel 1:1, referring to 1 Samuel Chapter 30.

2. John Mauchline, ed., *The New Century Bible, 1 and 2 Samuel,* (Greenwood, S.C.: Attic Press, 1971), p. 197.

3. Shimon bar Efrat, ed., *Mikra Yisrael, 2 Samuel,* pp. 4–5. See also A. S. Hartum, *Sifrei Mikra, Sefer Shmuel* (Tel Aviv: Yavneh, 1966), to 2 Samuel 1:10.

4. Robert Alter, *The David Story* (New York: W. W. Norton, 1999), p. 197.

5. 1 Chronicles 10:1–7. *Me'am Lo'az* to 1 Samuel 1:10.

6. Walter Brueggemann, *First and Second Samuel: Interpretation* (Louisville: John Knox Press, 1990), p. 211.

7. Eugene H. Peterson, ed., *Westminster Bible Companion, First and Second Samuel,* (Louisville: John Knox Press, 1999), p. 140.

8. Brueggemann, *First and Second Samuel,* p. 211.

9. Ibid., p. 212.

10. For example, Radak and Hartum to 2 Samuel 1:13.

11. *Me'am Lo'az* to 2 Samuel 1:13.

12. Alter, *The David Story,* p. 195, who cites J. P. Fokkelman.

13. See the commentary of Hartum and *Me'am Lo'az* to 2 Samuel 1:6 in this regard. *Me'am Lo'az.*

14. Genesis 27: 18.

15. Note, in this regard, the comments of Alter, *The David Story,* p. 195.

16. Alter, *The David Story,* p. 197.

17. Josephus, *The Books of Antiquities* VII, 1:1.

CHAPTER 12: THE EVER-PRESENT OTHER

1. Scholars have shown that the second half of the Book of Isaiah is the product of a different hand than the first half, labeling this section as Second Isaiah. Some even go so far as to indicate that part of it is the product of a Third Isaiah. In either case, Isaiah Chapters 40–66 clearly reflect a post-exilic context.

2. See, for example, Exodus 16 in this regard.

3. See the comparison of the murmurings of the desert generation and those described by the prophet Isaiah in *Shemot Rabbah* 25:4.

4. Paul Hanson, *Isaiah 40–66: Interpretation. A Bible Commentary for Teaching and Preaching* (Louisville: John Knox Press, 1995), p. 241.

5. Brevard Childs, *Isaiah, The Old Testament Library* (Louisville: John Knox Press, 2001), p. 535, as well the comments of classical biblical commentaries such as *Metzudat David* to Isaiah 65:1.

6. See, for example, Hartum to Isaiah 65:1.

7. See also Isaiah 51:1 and 58:2 in this regard.

8. See Radak, Ibn Ezra, and *Metzudat David* to Isaiah 65:1.

9. *Yalkut Shimoni* Vol. 2, *remezim* 509, 596.

10. R. N. Why Bray, ed., *The New Century Bible, Isaiah 40–66* (Greenwood, S.C.: The Attic Press, 1975), on Isaiah 65:1–2a. See also Childs, *Isaiah,* p. 535.

11. See, among many texts, *Targum Yonatan* and Rashi to Isaiah 65:1, and *The Book of Isaiah* (Hebrew), interpretation by Amos Hakham (Jerusalem: Mosad ha-Rav Kook, 1984), on Isaiah 65:1.

12. For example, Radak to Isaiah 65:2.

13. Rashi and Hartum to Isaiah 65:1.

14. *Shemot Rabbah* 25:4.

15. Rashi to Isaiah 65:1.

16. *Metzudat David* to Isaiah 65:1.

17. *Midrash Psalms* 10:2 and *Yalkut Shimoni,* Vol. 2, *remez* 508.

18. See, for example, Isaiah 1:15 and 4:31.

19. *The New Century Bible* on Isaiah 65:1–2a and Hakham, *The Book of Isaiah* on Isaiah 65:2.

20. Hakham, *The Book of Isaiah* on Isaiah 65:2, n. 3.

21. *Metzudat David* to Isaiah 65:2.

22. Hakham, *The Book of Isaiah* on Isaiah 65:2.

23. Rashi to Isaiah 65:2. Rashi's play on the description of the people as an *am sorer* who has turned *(sur)* from the right path, stands in contrast to

Moses in Exodus 3 who must turn from the beaten path to see the Burning Bush *(sar lirot)*. See, in this regard, Chapter 9, p. 72.

CHAPTER 13: THE ULTIMATE CALL

1. Claus Westermann, *Isaiah 40–66: A Commentary* (Philadelphia: The Westminster Press, 1969), p. 335 on Isaiah 58:2–3a.
2. *Metzudat David* to Isaiah 58:2.
3. *The New Century Bible* to Isaiah 58:2 and Hanson, *Isaiah 40–66*, p. 204.
4. *Targum Yonatan* to Isaiah 58:2.
5. Radak to Isaiah 58:2 and Westermann, *Isaiah 40–66*, p. 336.
6. *The New Century Bible* to Isaiah 58:5–7, as well as Radak's comment on Isaiah 58:5–7.
7. Hakham, *The Book of Isaiah* on Isaiah 58:3.
8. *The New Century Bible* to Isaiah 58:5–7.
9. Radak to Isaiah 58:6.
10. Hanson, *Isaiah 40–66*, p. 205.
11. See *Targum Yonatan* to Isaiah 58:7 in this regard.
12. Radak underscores this in his comment on Isaiah 58:7.
13. *Targum Yonatan* to Isaiah 58:8 and Radak to Isaiah 58:9.
14. Radak and *Metzudat David* to Isaiah 58:8.
15. *Targum Yonatan* to Isaiah 58:9.
16. See, for example, Hakham, *The Book of Isaiah,* on Isaiah 58:9.
17. See *Midrash Tanhuma ha-Nidpas, Shemot* 15, in this regard, and my remarks in Chapter 9, above.
18. Hakham, *The Book of Isaiah,* on Isaiah 58:8.

CHAPTER 14: THE ULTIMATE RESPONSE

1. Rashi to Isaiah 52:3.
2. See Klaus Baltzer in his work, *A Commentary on Isaiah 40–55,* Margaret Kohl, trans. (Minneapolis: Fortress Press, 2001), p. 374.
3. See also in this regard, Rashi to Isaiah 52:5.
4. See John Blenkinsopp's comment in *The Anchor Bible, Isaiah 40–55: A New Translation* (New York: Doubleday, 2000), p. 339.
5. For example, *Pesikta Rabbati* 22:7.

6. B. T. *Sukkah* 52b and *Yalkut Shimoni,* Vol. 2, *remez* 125, among several parallel traditions. The other three things God lamented were the creation of the Chaldeans, the Ishmaelites and the Evil Inclination.

7. Hakham, *The Book of Isaiah,* on Isaiah 52:5.

8. *Metzudat David* to Isaiah 52:1.

9. Radak to Isaiah 52:2.

10. Baltzer, *A Commentary on Isaiah 40–55,* p. 370.

11. Rashi and Hakham, *The Book of Isaiah,* on Isaiah 52:6.

12. Radak to Isaiah 52:6.

13. Baltzer, *A Commentary on Isaiah 40–55,* p. 377.

14. See in this regard, the *Targum Yonatan's* translation of the question, "What therefore do I gain here?" and Hartum's commentary to Isaiah 52:6.

15. *Midrash Psalms* 91:8 and *Yalkut ha-Machiri* to Isaiah 52:6.

16. Radak and *Metzudat David* to Isaiah 52:6.

17. Isaiah 52:9–10 and the comments of Hartum on these verses.

18. Radak to Isaiah 52:7.

Bar/Bat Mitzvah

The Bar/Bat Mitzvah Memory Book
An Album for Treasuring the Spiritual Celebration
By Rabbi Jeffrey K. Salkin and Nina Salkin
A unique album for preserving the spiritual memories of the day, and for recording plans for the Jewish future ahead. Contents include space for creating or recording family history; teachings received from rabbi, cantor, and others; mitzvot and *tzedakot* chosen and carried out, etc.
8 x 10, 48 pp, Deluxe Hardcover, 2-color text, ribbon marker, ISBN 1-58023-111-X **$19.95**

Bar/Bat Mitzvah Basics: A Practical Family Guide to Coming of Age Together
Edited by Helen Leneman. Foreword by Rabbi Jeffrey K. Salkin.
6 x 9, 240 pp, Quality PB, ISBN 1-58023-151-9 **$18.95**

For Kids—Putting God on Your Guest List: How to Claim the Spiritual Meaning of Your Bar or Bat Mitzvah *By Rabbi Jeffrey K. Salkin*
6 x 9, 144 pp, Quality PB, ISBN 1-58023-015-6 **$14.95** *For ages 11–12*

Putting God on the Guest List: How to Reclaim the Spiritual Meaning of Your Child's Bar or Bat Mitzvah *By Rabbi Jeffrey K. Salkin*
6 x 9, 224 pp, Quality PB, ISBN 1-879045-59-1 **$16.95**

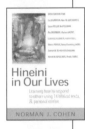

Tough Questions Jews Ask: A Young Adult's Guide to Building a Jewish Life
By Rabbi Edward Feinstein 6 x 9, 160 pp, Quality PB, ISBN 1-58023-139-X **$14.95** *For ages 13 & up*
Also Available: **Tough Questions Jews Ask Teacher's Guide**
8½ x 11, 72 pp, PB, ISBN 1-58023-187-X **$8.95**

Bible Study/Midrash

Hineini in Our Lives: Learning How to Respond to Others through 14 Biblical Texts, and Personal Stories *By Norman J. Cohen*
6 x 9, 240 pp, Hardcover, ISBN 1-58023-131-4 **$23.95**

Ancient Secrets: Using the Stories of the Bible to Improve Our Everyday Lives
By Rabbi Levi Meier, Ph.D. 5½ x 8½, 288 pp, Quality PB, ISBN 1-58023-064-4 **$16.95**

Moses—The Prince, the Prophet His Life, Legend & Message for Our Lives
By Rabbi Levi Meier, Ph.D.
6 x 9, 224 pp, Quality PB, ISBN 1-58023-069-5 **$16.95**; Hardcover, ISBN 1-58023-013-X **$23.95**

Self, Struggle & Change: Family Conflict Stories in Genesis and Their Healing Insights for Our Lives *By Norman J. Cohen* 6 x 9, 224 pp, Quality PB, ISBN 1-879045-66-4 **$16.95**

Voices from Genesis: Guiding Us through the Stages of Life *By Norman J. Cohen*
6 x 9, 192 pp, Quality PB, ISBN 1-58023-118-7 **$16.95**

Congregation Resources

Becoming a Congregation of Learners: Learning as a Key to Revitalizing Congregational Life *By Isa Aron, Ph.D. Foreword by Rabbi Lawrence A. Hoffman.*
6 x 9, 304 pp, Quality PB, ISBN 1-58023-089-X **$19.95**

Finding a Spiritual Home: How a New Generation of Jews Can Transform the American Synagogue *By Rabbi Sidney Schwarz*
6 x 9, 352 pp, Quality PB, ISBN 1-58023-185-3 **$19.95**

Jewish Pastoral Care: A Practical Handbook from Traditional & Contemporary Sources
Edited by Rabbi Dayle A. Friedman 6 x 9, 464 pp, Hardcover, ISBN 1-58023-078-4 **$35.00**

The Self-Renewing Congregation: Organizational Strategies for Revitalizing Congregational Life *By Isa Aron, Ph.D. Foreword by Dr. Ron Wolfson.*
6 x 9, 304 pp, Quality PB, ISBN 1-58023-166-7 **$19.95**

Or phone, fax, mail or e-mail to: **JEWISH LIGHTS Publishing**
Sunset Farm Offices, Route 4 • P.O. Box 237 • Woodstock, Vermont 05091
Tel: (802) 457-4000 • Fax: (802) 457-4004 • www.jewishlights.com
Credit card orders: **(800) 962-4544** (8:30AM–5:30PM ET Monday–Friday)
Generous discounts on quantity orders. SATISFACTION GUARANTEED. Prices subject to change.

Children's Books

Because Nothing Looks Like God
By Lawrence and Karen Kushner
What is God like? The first collaborative work by husband-and-wife team Lawrence and Karen Kushner introduces children to the possibilities of spiritual life. Real-life examples of happiness and sadness invite us to explore, together with our children, the questions we all have about God, no matter what our age.
11 x 8½, 32 pp, Full-color illus., Hardcover, ISBN 1-58023-092-X **$16.95** *For ages 4 & up*

Also Available: **Because Nothing Looks Like God Teacher's Guide**
8½ x 11, 22 pp, PB, ISBN 1-58023-140-3 **$6.95** *For ages 5–8*

Board Book Companions to *Because Nothing Looks Like God*
5 x 5, 24 pp, Full-color illus., SkyLight Paths Board Books, **$7.95** each *For ages 0–4*
What Does God Look Like? ISBN 1-893361-23-3
How Does God Make Things Happen? ISBN 1-893361-24-1
Where Is God? ISBN 1-893361-17-9

The 11th Commandment: Wisdom from Our Children
by The Children of America
"If there were an Eleventh Commandment, what would it be?" Children of many religious denominations across America answer this question—in their own drawings and words.
8 x 10, 48 pp, Full-color illus., Hardcover, ISBN 1-879045-46-X **$16.95** *For all ages*

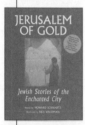

Jerusalem of Gold: Jewish Stories of the Enchanted City
Retold by Howard Schwartz. Full-color illus. by Neil Waldman.
A beautiful and engaging collection of historical and legendary stories for children. Each celebrates the magical city that has served as a beacon for the Jewish imagination for three thousand years. Draws on Talmud, midrash, Jewish folklore, and mystical and Hasidic sources.
8 x 10, 64 pp, Full-color illus., Hardcover, ISBN 1-58023-149-7 **$18.95** *For ages 7 & up*

The Book of Miracles: A Young Person's Guide to Jewish Spiritual Awareness
By Lawrence Kushner. All-new illustrations by the author.
6 x 9, 96 pp, 2-color illus., Hardcover, ISBN 1-879045-78-8 **$16.95** *For ages 9–13*

In Our Image: God's First Creatures
By Nancy Sohn Swartz
9 x 12, 32 pp, Full-color illus., Hardcover, ISBN 1-879045-99-0 **$16.95** *For ages 4 & up*

From SKYLIGHT PATHS PUBLISHING

Becoming Me: A Story of Creation
By Martin Boroson. Full-color illus. by Christopher Gilvan-Cartwright.
Told in the personal "voice" of the Creator, a story about creation and relationship that is about each one of us. In simple words and with radiant illustrations, the Creator tells an intimate story about love, about friendship and playing, about our world—and about ourselves.
8 x 10, 32 pp, Full-color illus., Hardcover, ISBN 1-893361-11-X **$16.95** *For ages 4 & up*

Ten Amazing People: And How They Changed the World
By Maura D. Shaw. Foreword by Dr. Robert Coles. Full-color illus. by Stephen Marchesi.
Black Elk • Dorothy Day • Malcolm X • Mahatma Gandhi • Martin Luther King, Jr. • Mother Teresa • Janusz Korczak • Desmond Tutu • Thich Nhat Hanh • Albert Schweitzer • This vivid, inspirational, and authoritative book will open new possibilities for children by telling the stories of how ten of the past century's greatest leaders changed the world in important ways.
8½ x 11, 48 pp, Full-color illus., Hardcover, ISBN 1-893361-47-0 **$17.95** *For ages 6–10*

Where Does God Live? *By August Gold and Matthew J. Perlman*
Using simple, everyday examples that children can relate to, this colorful book helps young readers develop a personal understanding of God.
10 x 8½, 32 pp, Full-color photo illus., Quality PB, ISBN 1-893361-39-X **$8.95** *For ages 3–6*

Children's Books
by Sandy Eisenberg Sasso

Adam & Eve's First Sunset: God's New Day
Engaging new story explores fear and hope, faith and gratitude in ways that will delight kids and adults—inspiring us to bless each of God's days and nights.
9 x 12, 32 pp, Full-color illus., Hardcover, ISBN 1-58023-177-2 **$17.95** *For ages 4 & up*

But God Remembered: Stories of Women from Creation to the Promised Land
Four different stories of women—Lillith, Serach, Bityah, and the Daughters of Z—teach us important values through their faith and actions.
9 x 12, 32 pp, Full-color illus., Hardcover, ISBN 1-879045-43-5 **$16.95** *For ages 8 & up*

Cain & Abel: Finding the Fruits of Peace
Full-color illus. by Joani Keller Rothenberg
Shows children that we have the power to deal with anger in positive ways. Provides questions for kids and adults to explore together.
9 x 12, 32 pp, Full-color illus., Hardcover, ISBN 1-58023-123-3 **$16.95** *For ages 5 & up*

God in Between
Full-color illus. by Sally Sweetland
If you wanted to find God, where would you look? This magical, mythical tale teaches that God can be found where we are: within all of us and the relationships between us.
9 x 12, 32 pp, Full-color illus., Hardcover, ISBN 1-879045-86-9 **$16.95** *For ages 4 & up*

God's Paintbrush
Wonderfully interactive, invites children of all faiths and backgrounds to encounter God through moments in their own lives. Provides questions adult and child can explore together.
11 x 8½, 32 pp, Full-color illus., Hardcover, ISBN 1-879045-22-2 **$16.95** *For ages 4 & up*

Also Available: **God's Paintbrush Teacher's Guide**
8½ x 11, 32 pp, PB, ISBN 1-879045-57-5 **$8.95**

God's Paintbrush Celebration Kit
A Spiritual Activity Kit for Teachers and Students of All Faiths, All Backgrounds
Additional activity sheets available:
8-Student Activity Sheet Pack (40 sheets/5 sessions), ISBN 1-58023-058-X **$19.95**
Single-Student Activity Sheet Pack (5 sessions), ISBN 1-58023-059-8 **$3.95**

In God's Name
Full-color illus. by Phoebe Stone
Like an ancient myth in its poetic text and vibrant illustrations, this award-winning modern fable about the search for God's name celebrates the diversity and, at the same time, the unity of all people.
9 x 12, 32 pp, Full-color illus., Hardcover, ISBN 1-879045-26-5 **$16.95** *For ages 4 & up*

Also Available as a Board Book: **What Is God's Name?**
5 x 5, 24 pp, Board, Full-color illus., ISBN 1-893361-10-1 **$7.95** *for ages 0–4 (A SkyLight Paths book)*

Also Available: **In God's Name video and study guide**
Computer animation, original music, and children's voices. 18 min. **$29.99**

Also Available in Spanish: **El nombre de Dios**
9 x 12, 32 pp, Full-color illus., Hardcover, ISBN 1-893361-63-2 **$16.95** *(A SkyLight Paths book)*

Noah's Wife: The Story of Naamah
When God tells Noah to bring the animals of the world onto the ark, God also calls on Naamah, Noah's wife, to save each plant on Earth. Based on an ancient text.
9 x 12, 32 pp, Full-color illus., Hardcover, ISBN 1-58023-134-9 **$16.95** *For ages 4 & up*

Also Available as a Board Book: **Naamah, Noah's Wife**
5 x 5, 24 pp, Full-color illus., Board, ISBN 1-893361-56-X **$7.95** *For ages 0–4 (A SkyLight Paths book)*

For Heaven's Sake: Finding God in Unexpected Places
9 x 12, 32 pp, Full-color illus., Hardcover, ISBN 1-58023-054-7 **$16.95** *For ages 4 & up*

God Said Amen: Finding the Answers to Our Prayers
9 x 12, 32 pp, Full-color illus., Hardcover, ISBN 1-58023-080-6 **$16.95** *For ages 4 & up*

Current Events/History

The Story of the Jews: A 4,000-Year Adventure—A Graphic History Book
Written & illustrated by Stan Mack
Through witty, illustrated narrative, we visit all the major happenings from biblical times to the twenty-first century. Celebrates the major characters and events that have shaped the Jewish people and culture.
6 x 9, 288 pp., illus., Quality PB, ISBN 1-58023-155-1 **$16.95**

The Jewish Prophet: Visionary Words from Moses and Miriam to Henrietta Szold and A. J. Heschel   *By Rabbi Michael J. Shire*
6½ x 8½, 128 pp, 123 full-color illus., Hardcover, ISBN 1-58023-168-3 **$25.00**

Shared Dreams: Martin Luther King, Jr. & the Jewish Community
By Rabbi Marc Schneier. Preface by Martin Luther King III.
6 x 9, 240 pp, Hardcover, ISBN 1-58023-062-8 **$24.95**

"Who Is a Jew?": Conversations, Not Conclusions *By Meryl Hyman*
6 x 9, 272 pp, Quality PB, ISBN 1-58023-052-0 **$16.95**

Ecology

Ecology & the Jewish Spirit: Where Nature & the Sacred Meet
Edited by Ellen Bernstein 6 x 9, 288 pp, Quality PB, ISBN 1-58023-082-2 **$16.95**

Torah of the Earth: Exploring 4,000 Years of Ecology in Jewish Thought
Vol. 1: Biblical Israel: One Land, One People; Rabbinic Judaism: One People, Many Lands
Vol. 2: Zionism: One Land, Two Peoples; Eco-Judaism: One Earth, Many Peoples
Edited by Rabbi Arthur Waskow
Vol. 1: 6 x 9, 272 pp, Quality PB, ISBN 1-58023-086-5 **$19.95**
Vol. 2: 6 x 9, 336 pp, Quality PB, ISBN 1-58023-087-3 **$19.95**

Grief/Healing

Against the Dying of the Light: A Parent's Story of Love, Loss and Hope
By Leonard Fein
In this unusual exploration of heartbreak and healing, Leonard Fein chronicles the sudden death of his 30-year-old daughter and shares the hard-earned wisdom that emerges in the face of loss and grief.
5½ x 8½, 176 pp, Hardcover, ISBN 1-58023-110-1 **$19.95**

Grief in Our Seasons: A Mourner's Kaddish Companion *By Rabbi Kerry M. Olitzky*
4½ x 6½, 448 pp, Quality PB, ISBN 1-879045-55-9 **$15.95**

Healing of Soul, Healing of Body: Spiritual Leaders Unfold the Strength & Solace in Psalms *Edited by Rabbi Simkha Y. Weintraub, C.S.W.*
6 x 9, 128 pp, 2-color illus. text, Quality PB, ISBN 1-879045-31-1 **$14.95**

Jewish Paths toward Healing and Wholeness: A Personal Guide to Dealing with Suffering *By Rabbi Kerry M. Olitzky. Foreword by Debbie Friedman.*
6 x 9, 192 pp, Quality PB, ISBN 1-58023-068-7 **$15.95**

Mourning & Mitzvah, 2nd Edition: A Guided Journal for Walking the Mourner's Path through Grief to Healing *By Anne Brener, L.C.S.W.*
7½ x 9, 304 pp, Quality PB, ISBN 1-58023-113-6 **$19.95**

The Perfect Stranger's Guide to Funerals and Grieving Practices
A Guide to Etiquette in Other People's Religious Ceremonies *Edited by Stuart M. Matlins*
6 x 9, 240 pp, Quality PB, ISBN 1-893361-20-9 **$16.95** *(A SkyLight Paths book)*

Tears of Sorrow, Seeds of Hope: A Jewish Spiritual Companion for Infertility and Pregnancy Loss *By Rabbi Nina Beth Cardin*
6 x 9, 192 pp, Hardcover, ISBN 1-58023-017-2 **$19.95**

A Time to Mourn, A Time to Comfort: A Guide to Jewish Bereavement and Comfort *By Dr. Ron Wolfson* 7 x 9, 336 pp, Quality PB, ISBN 1-879045-96-6 **$18.95**

When a Grandparent Dies: A Kid's Own Remembering Workbook for Dealing with Shiva and the Year Beyond *By Nechama Liss-Levinson, Ph.D.*
8 x 10, 48 pp, 2-color text, Hardcover, ISBN 1-879045-44-3 **$15.95** *For ages 7–13*

Life Cycle

Parenting

The New Jewish Baby Album: Creating and Celebrating the Beginning of a Spiritual Life—A Jewish Lights Companion
By the Editors at Jewish Lights. Foreword by Anita Diamant. Preface by Sandy Eisenberg Sasso.
A spiritual keepsake that will be treasured for generations. More than just a memory book, *shows you how—and why it's important*—to create a Jewish home and a Jewish life. Includes sections to describe naming ceremony, space to write encouragements, and pages for writing original blessings, prayers, and meaningful quotes throughout.
8 x 10, 64 pp, Deluxe Padded Hardcover, Full-color illus., ISBN 1-58023-138-1 **$19.95**

The Jewish Pregnancy Book: A Resource for the Soul, Body & Mind during Pregnancy, Birth & the First Three Months
By Dr. Sandy Falk, M.D., and Rabbi Daniel Judson, with Steven A. Rapp
Includes medical information on fetal development, pre-natal testing and more, from a liberal Jewish perspective; prenatal *aleph-bet* yoga; and ancient and modern prayers and rituals for each stage of pregnancy.
7 x 10, 144 pp, Quality PB, Layflat binding, b/w illus., ISBN 1-58023-178-0 **$16.95**

Celebrating Your New Jewish Daughter: Creating Jewish Ways to Welcome Baby Girls into the Covenant—New and Traditional Ceremonies
By Debra Nussbaum Cohen 6 x 9, 272 pp, Quality PB, ISBN 1-58023-090-3 **$18.95**

The New Jewish Baby Book: Names, Ceremonies & Customs—A Guide for Today's Families *By Anita Diamant* 6 x 9, 336 pp, Quality PB, ISBN 1-879045-28-1 **$18.95**

Parenting As a Spiritual Journey: Deepening Ordinary and Extraordinary Events into Sacred Occasions *By Rabbi Nancy Fuchs-Kreimer*
6 x 9, 224 pp, Quality PB, ISBN 1-58023-016-4 **$16.95**

Embracing the Covenant: Converts to Judaism Talk About Why & How
Edited and with introductions by Rabbi Allan Berkowitz and Patti Moskovitz
6 x 9, 192 pp, Quality PB, ISBN 1-879045-50-8 **$16.95**

The Guide to Jewish Interfaith Family Life: An InterfaithFamily.com Handbook
Edited by Ronnie Friedland and Edmund Case 6 x 9, 384 pp, Quality PB, ISBN 1-58023-153-5 **$18.95**

Making a Successful Jewish Interfaith Marriage: The Jewish Outreach Institute Guide to Opportunities, Challenges and Resources
By Rabbi Kerry Olitzky with Joan Peterson Littman 6 x 9, 176 pp, Quality PB, ISBN 1-58023-170-5 **$16.95**

The Perfect Stranger's Guide to Wedding Ceremonies
A Guide to Etiquette in Other People's Religious Ceremonies *Edited by Stuart M. Matlins*
6 x 9, 208 pp, Quality PB, ISBN 1-893361-19-5 **$16.95** *(A SkyLight Paths book)*

How to Be a Perfect Stranger, 3rd Edition
The Essential Religious Etiquette Handbook
Edited by Stuart M. Matlins and Arthur J. Magida
The indispensable guidebook to help the well-meaning guest when visiting other people's religious ceremonies.
   A straightforward guide to the rituals and celebrations of the major religions and denominations in the United States and Canada from the perspective of an interested guest of any other faith, based on information obtained from authorities of each religion. Belongs in every living room, library, and office.
6 x 9, 432 pp, Quality PB, ISBN 1-893361-67-5 **$19.95** *(A SkyLight Paths book)*

Divorce Is a Mitzvah: A Practical Guide to Finding Wholeness and Holiness When Your Marriage Dies *By Rabbi Perry Netter. Afterword by Rabbi Laura Geller.*
6 x 9, 224 pp, Quality PB, ISBN 1-58023-172-1 **$16.95**

A Heart of Wisdom: Making the Jewish Journey from Midlife through the Elder Years
Edited by Susan Berrin. Foreword by Harold Kushner. 6 x 9, 384 pp, Quality PB, ISBN 1-58023-051-2 **$18.95**

So That Your Values Live On: Ethical Wills and How to Prepare Them
Edited by Jack Riemer and Nathaniel Stampfer 6 x 9, 272 pp, Quality PB, ISBN 1-879045-34-6 **$18.95**

Spirituality/Women's Interest

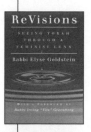

Lifecycles, Vol. 1: Jewish Women on Life Passages & Personal Milestones
Edited and with introductions by Rabbi Debra Orenstein
6 x 9, 480 pp, Quality PB, ISBN 1-58023-018-0 **$19.95**

Lifecycles, Vol. 2: Jewish Women on Biblical Themes in Contemporary Life
Edited and with introductions by Rabbi Debra Orenstein and Rabbi Jane Rachel Litman
6 x 9, 464 pp, Quality PB, ISBN 1-58023-019-9 **$19.95**

Moonbeams: A Hadassah Rosh Hodesh Guide *Edited by Carol Diament, Ph.D.*
8½ x 11, 240 pp, Quality PB, ISBN 1-58023-099-7 **$20.00**

ReVisions: Seeing Torah through a Feminist Lens *By Rabbi Elyse Goldstein*
5½ x 8½, 224 pp, Quality PB, ISBN 1-58023-117-9 **$16.95**

White Fire: A Portrait of Women Spiritual Leaders in America
By Rabbi Malka Drucker. Photographs by Gay Block.
7 x 10, 320 pp, Hardcover, 30+ b/w photos, ISBN 1-893361-64-0 **$24.95** *(A SkyLight Paths book)*

Women of the Wall: Claiming Sacred Ground at Judaism's Holy Site
Edited by Phyllis Chesler and Rivka Haut
6 x 9, 496 pp, Hardcover, b/w photos, ISBN 1-58023-161-6 **$34.95**

The Women's Torah Commentary: New Insights from Women Rabbis on the 54
Weekly Torah Portions *Edited by Rabbi Elyse Goldstein*
6 x 9, 496 pp, Hardcover, ISBN 1-58023-076-8 **$34.95**

The Year Mom Got Religion: One Woman's Midlife Journey into Judaism
By Lee Meyerhoff Hendler
6 x 9, 208 pp, Quality PB, ISBN 1-58023-070-9 **$15.95**; Hardcover, ISBN 1-58023-000-8 **$19.95**

See Holidays for *The Women's Passover Companion: Women's Reflections on the Festival of Freedom* and *The Women's Seder Sourcebook: Rituals & Readings for Use at the Passover Seder.*

Theology/Philosophy

Aspects of Rabbinic Theology
By Solomon Schechter. New Introduction by Dr. Neil Gillman.
6 x 9, 448 pp, Quality PB, ISBN 1-879045-24-9 **$19.95**

Broken Tablets: Restoring the Ten Commandments and Ourselves
Edited by Rachel S. Mikva. Introduction by Lawrence Kushner. Afterword by Arnold Jacob Wolf.
6 x 9, 192 pp, Quality PB, ISBN 1-58023-158-6 **$16.95**; Hardcover, ISBN 1-58023-066-0 **$21.95**

Creating an Ethical Jewish Life
A Practical Introduction to Classic Teachings on How to Be a Jew
By Dr. Byron L. Sherwin and Seymour J. Cohen
6 x 9, 336 pp, Quality PB, ISBN 1-58023-114-4 **$19.95**

The Death of Death: Resurrection and Immortality in Jewish Thought
By Dr. Neil Gillman 6 x 9, 336 pp, Quality PB, ISBN 1-58023-081-4 **$18.95**

Evolving Halakhah: A Progressive Approach to Traditional Jewish Law
By Rabbi Dr. Moshe Zemer
6 x 9, 480 pp, Quality PB, ISBN 1-58023-127-6 **$29.95**; Hardcover, ISBN 1-58023-002-4 **$40.00**

Hasidic Tales: Annotated & Explained
By Rabbi Rami Shapiro. Foreword by Andrew Harvey, SkyLight Illuminations series editor.
5½ x 8½, 192 pp, Quality PB, ISBN 1-893361-86-1 **$16.95** *(A SkyLight Paths Book)*

A Heart of Many Rooms: Celebrating the Many Voices within Judaism
By Dr. David Hartman
6 x 9, 352 pp, Quality PB, ISBN 1-58023-156-X **$19.95**; Hardcover, ISBN 1-58023-048-2 **$24.95**

Judaism and Modern Man: An Interpretation of Jewish Religion
By Will Herberg. New Introduction by Dr. Neil Gillman.
5½ x 8½, 336 pp, Quality PB, ISBN 1-879045-87-7 **$18.95**

Keeping Faith with the Psalms: Deepen Your Relationship with God Using the
Book of Psalms *By Daniel F. Polish*
6 x 9, 272 pp, Hardcover, ISBN 1-58023-179-9 **$24.95**

(continued next page)

Theology/Philosophy *(continued)*

The Last Trial
On the Legends and Lore of the Command to Abraham to Offer Isaac as a Sacrifice
By Shalom Spiegel. New Introduction by Judah Goldin.
6 x 9, 208 pp, Quality PB, ISBN 1-879045-29-X **$18.95**

A Living Covenant: The Innovative Spirit in Traditional Judaism
By Dr. David Hartman 6 x 9, 368 pp, Quality PB, ISBN 1-58023-011-3 **$18.95**

Love and Terror in the God Encounter
The Theological Legacy of Rabbi Joseph B. Soloveitchik
By Dr. David Hartman
6 x 9, 240 pp, Quality PB, ISBN 1-58023-176-4 **$19.95**; Hardcover, ISBN 1-58023-112-8 **$25.00**

Seeking the Path to Life
Theological Meditations on God and the Nature of People, Love, Life and Death
By Rabbi Ira F. Stone 6 x 9, 160 pp, Quality PB, ISBN 1-879045-47-8 **$14.95**

The Spirit of Renewal: Finding Faith after the Holocaust
By Rabbi Edward Feld 6 x 9, 224 pp, Quality PB, ISBN 1-879045-40-0 **$16.95**

Tormented Master: *The Life and Spiritual Quest of Rabbi Nahman of Bratslav*
By Dr. Arthur Green 6 x 9, 416 pp, Quality PB, ISBN 1-879045-11-7 **$18.95**

Your Word Is Fire: The Hasidic Masters on Contemplative Prayer
Edited and translated by Dr. Arthur Green and Barry W. Holtz
6 x 9, 160 pp, Quality PB, ISBN 1-879045-25-7 **$15.95**

Travel

Israel—A Spiritual Travel Guide: A Companion for the Modern Jewish Pilgrim
By Rabbi Lawrence A. Hoffman
4¾ x 10, 256 pp, Quality PB, illus., ISBN 1-879045-56-7 **$18.95**

Also Available: **The Israel Mission Leader's Guide**
Prepared with the assistance of Rabbi Elliott Kleinman
5½ x 8½, 16 pp, PB, ISBN 1-58023-085-7 **$4.95**

12 Steps

100 Blessings Every Day
Daily Twelve Step Recovery Affirmations, Exercises for Personal Growth &
Renewal Reflecting Seasons of the Jewish Year
By Rabbi Kerry M. Olitzky. Foreword by Rabbi Neil Gillman.
Using a one-day-at-a-time monthly format, this guide reflects on the rhythm of
the Jewish calendar to help bring insight to recovery from addictions and com-
pulsive behaviors of all kinds. Its exercises help us move from *thinking* to *doing*.
4½ x 6½, 432 pp, Quality PB, ISBN 1-879045-30-3 **$14.95**

Recovery from Codependence: A Jewish Twelve Steps Guide to Healing Your Soul
By Rabbi Kerry M. Olitzky 6 x 9, 160 pp, Quality PB, ISBN 1-879045-32-X **$13.95**

Renewed Each Day: Daily Twelve Step Recovery Meditations Based on the Bible
By Rabbi Kerry M. Olitzky and Aaron Z.
Vol. I—Genesis & Exodus:
6 x 9, 224 pp, Quality PB, ISBN 1-879045-12-5 **$14.95**
Vol. 2—Leviticus, Numbers & Deuteronomy:
6 x 9, 280 pp, Quality PB, ISBN 1-879045-13-3 **$14.95**

Twelve Jewish Steps to Recovery
A Personal Guide to Turning from Alcoholism & Other Addictions—Drugs, Food,
Gambling, Sex...
By Rabbi Kerry M. Olitzky and Stuart A. Copans, M.D. Preface by Abraham J. Twerski, M.D.
6 x 9, 144 pp, Quality PB, ISBN 1-879045-09-5 **$14.95**

Abraham Joshua Heschel

The Earth Is the Lord's: The Inner World of the Jew in Eastern Europe
5½ x 8, 128 pp, Quality PB, ISBN 1-879045-42-7 **$14.95**

Israel: An Echo of Eternity *New Introduction by Susannah Heschel.*
5½ x 8, 272 pp, Quality PB, ISBN 1-879045-70-2 **$19.95**

A Passion for Truth: Despair and Hope in Hasidism
5½ x 8, 352 pp, Quality PB, ISBN 1-879045-41-9 **$18.95**

Holidays/Holy Days

7th Heaven: Celebrating Shabbat with Rebbe Nachman of Breslov
By Moshe Mykoff with the Breslov Research Institute
Based on the teachings of Rebbe Nachman of Breslov. Explores the art of consciously observing Shabbat and understanding in-depth many of the day's traditional spiritual practices.
5¼ x 8¼, 224 pp, Deluxe PB w/flaps, ISBN 1-58023-175-6 **$18.95**

The Women's Passover Companion
Women's Reflections on the Festival of Freedom
Edited by Rabbi Sharon Cohen Anisfeld, Tara Mohr, and Catherine Spector
A groundbreaking collection that captures the voices of Jewish women who engage in a provocative conversation about women's relationships to Passover as well as the roots and meanings of women's seders.
6 x 9, 352 pp, Hardcover, ISBN 1-58023-128-4 **$24.95**

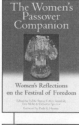

The Women's Seder Sourcebook
Rituals & Readings for Use at the Passover Seder
Edited by Rabbi Sharon Cohen Anisfeld, Tara Mohr, and Catherine Spector
This practical guide gathers the voices of more than one hundred women in readings, personal and creative reflections, commentaries, blessings, and ritual suggestions that can be incorporated into your Passover celebration as supplements to or substitutes for traditional passages of the haggadah.
6 x 9, 384 pp, Hardcover, ISBN 1-58023-136-5 **$24.95**

Hanukkah, 2nd Edition: The Family Guide to Spiritual Celebration
By Dr. Ron Wolfson with Joel Lurie Grishaver
7 x 9, 240 pp, illus., Quality PB, ISBN 1-58023-122-5 **$18.95**

The Jewish Gardening Cookbook: Growing Plants & Cooking for Holidays & Festivals *By Michael Brown*
6 x 9, 224 pp, 30+ illus., Quality PB, ISBN 1-58023-116-0 **$16.95**;
Hardcover, ISBN 1-58023-004-0 **$21.95**

Passover, 2nd Edition: The Family Guide to Spiritual Celebration
By Dr. Ron Wolfson with Joel Lurie Grishaver
7 x 9, 352 pp, Quality PB, ISBN 1-58023-174-8 **$19.95**

Shabbat, 2nd Edition: The Family Guide to Preparing for and Celebrating the Sabbath
By Dr. Ron Wolfson 7 x 9, 320 pp, illus., Quality PB, ISBN 1-58023-164-0 **$19.95**

Sharing Blessings: Children's Stories for Exploring the Spirit of the Jewish Holidays
By Rahel Musleah and Michael Klayman
8½ x 11, 64 pp, Full-color illus., Hardcover, ISBN 1-879045-71-0 **$18.95** *For ages 6 & up*

The Jewish Family Fun Book: Holiday Projects, Everyday Activities, and Travel Ideas with Jewish Themes
By Danielle Dardashti and Roni Sarig. Illus. by Avi Katz.
With almost 100 easy-to-do activities to re-invigorate age-old Jewish customs and make them fun for the whole family, this complete sourcebook details activities for fun at home and away from home, including meaningful everyday and holiday crafts, recipes, travel guides, enriching entertainment and much, much more. Illustrated.
6 x 9, 288 pp, 70+ b/w illus. & diagrams, Quality PB, ISBN 1-58023-171-3 **$18.95**

Inspiration

God in All Moments
Mystical & Practical Spiritual Wisdom from Hasidic Masters
Edited and translated by Or N. Rose with Ebn D. Leader
Hasidic teachings on how to be mindful in religious practice and how to cultivate everyday ethical behavior—*hanhagot.*
5½ x 8½, 120 pp, Quality PB, ISBN 1-58023-186-1 **$14.95**

The Dance of the Dolphin: Finding Prayer, Perspective and Meaning in the Stories of Our Lives By Karyn D. Kedar 6 x 9, 176 pp, Hardcover, ISBN 1-58023-154-3 **$19.95**

The Empty Chair: Finding Hope and Joy—Timeless Wisdom from a Hasidic Master, Rebbe Nachman of Breslov *Adapted by Moshe Mykoff and the Breslov Research Institute*
4 x 6, 128 pp, 2-color text, Deluxe PB w/flaps, ISBN 1-879045-67-2 **$9.95**

The Gentle Weapon: Prayers for Everyday and Not-So-Everyday Moments—Timeless Wisdom from the Teachings of the Hasidic Master, Rebbe Nachman of Breslov
Adapted by Moshe Mykoff and S. C. Mizrahi, together with the Breslov Research Institute
4 x 6, 144 pp, 2-color text, Deluxe PB w/flaps, ISBN 1-58023-022-9 **$9.95**

God Whispers: Stories of the Soul, Lessons of the Heart By Karyn D. Kedar
6 x 9, 176 pp, Quality PB, ISBN 1-58023-088-1 **$15.95**

An Orphan in History: One Man's Triumphant Search for His Jewish Roots
By Paul Cowan. Afterword by Rachel Cowan. 6 x 9, 288 pp, Quality PB, ISBN 1-58023-135-7 **$16.95**

Restful Reflections: Nighttime Inspiration to Calm the Soul, Based on Jewish Wisdom
By Rabbi Kerry M. Olitzky & Rabbi Lori Forman
4½ x 6½, 448 pp, Quality PB, ISBN 1-58023-091-1 **$15.95**

Sacred Intentions: Daily Inspiration to Strengthen the Spirit, Based on Jewish Wisdom
By Rabbi Kerry M. Olitzky and Rabbi Lori Forman
4½ x 6½, 448 pp, Quality PB, ISBN 1-58023-061-X **$15.95**

Kabbalah/Mysticism/Enneagram

Seek My Face: A Jewish Mystical Theology
By Dr. Arthur Green
This classic work of contemporary Jewish theology, revised and updated, is a profound, deeply personal statement of the lasting truths of Jewish mysticism and the basic faith claims of Judaism. A tool for anyone seeking the elusive presence of God in the world. 6 x 9, 304 pp, Quality PB, ISBN 1-58023-130-6 **$19.95**

Zohar: Annotated & Explained
Translation and annotation by Dr. Daniel C. Matt. Foreword by Andrew Harvey, SkyLight Illuminations series editor.
Offers insightful yet unobtrusive commentary to the masterpiece of Jewish mysticism that explains references and mystical symbols, shares wisdom of spiritual masters, and clarifies the *Zohar's* bold claim: We have always been taught that we need God, but in order to manifest in the world, God needs us.
5½ x 8½, 160 pp, Quality PB, ISBN 1-893361-51-9 **$15.95** *(A SkyLight Paths book)*

Cast in God's Image: Discover Your Personality Type Using the Enneagram and Kabbalah
By Rabbi Howard A. Addison
7 x 9, 176 pp, Quality PB, Layflat binding, 20+ journaling exercises, ISBN 1-58023-124-1 **$16.95**

Ehyeh: A Kabbalah for Tomorrow By Dr. Arthur Green
6 x 9, 224 pp, Hardcover, ISBN 1-58023-125-X **$21.95**

The Enneagram and Kabbalah: Reading Your Soul By Rabbi Howard A. Addison
6 x 9, 176 pp, Quality PB, ISBN 1-58023-001-6 **$15.95**

Finding Joy: A Practical Spiritual Guide to Happiness By Dannel I. Schwartz with Mark Hass
6 x 9, 192 pp, Quality PB, ISBN 1-58023-009-1 **$14.95**; Hardcover, ISBN 1-879045-53-2 **$19.95**

The Gift of Kabbalah: Discovering the Secrets of Heaven, Renewing Your Life on Earth
By Tamar Frankiel, Ph.D.
6 x 9, 256 pp, Quality PB, ISBN 1-58023-141-1 **$16.95**; Hardcover, ISBN 1-58023-108-X **$21.95**

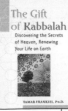

The Way Into Jewish Mystical Tradition By Lawrence Kushner
6 x 9, 224 pp, Hardcover, ISBN 1-58023-029-6 **$21.95**

Meditation

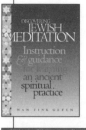

The Handbook of Jewish Meditation Practices

A Guide for Enriching the Sabbath and Other Days of Your Life
By Rabbi David A. Cooper
Easy-to-learn meditation techniques for use on the Sabbath and every day, to help us return to the roots of traditional Jewish spirituality where Shabbat is a state of mind and soul. 6 x 9, 208 pp, Quality PB, ISBN 1-58023-102-0 **$16.95**

Discovering Jewish Meditation: Instruction & Guidance for Learning an Ancient Spiritual Practice *By Nan Fink Gefen, Ph.D.* 6 x 9, 208 pp, Quality PB, ISBN 1-58023-067-9 **$16.95**

A Heart of Stillness: A Complete Guide to Learning the Art of Meditation
By Rabbi David A. Cooper

5½ x 8½, 272 pp, Quality PB, ISBN 1-893361-03-9 **$16.95** *(A SkyLight Paths book)*

Meditation from the Heart of Judaism: Today's Teachers Share Their Practices, Techniques, and Faith *Edited by Avram Davis*
6 x 9, 256 pp, Quality PB, ISBN 1-58023-049-0 **$16.95**

Silence, Simplicity & Solitude: A Complete Guide to Spiritual Retreat at Home
By Rabbi David A. Cooper
5½ x 8½, 336 pp, Quality PB, ISBN 1-893361-04-7 **$16.95** *(A SkyLight Paths book)*

Three Gates to Meditation Practice: A Personal Journey into Sufism, Buddhism, and Judaism *By Rabbi David A. Cooper*
5½ x 8½, 240 pp, Quality PB, ISBN 1-893361-22-5 **$16.95** *(A SkyLight Paths book)*

The Way of Flame: A Guide to the Forgotten Mystical Tradition of Jewish Meditation
By Avram Davis 4½ x 8, 176 pp, Quality PB, ISBN 1-58023-060-1 **$15.95**

Ritual/Sacred Practice

The Jewish Dream Book

The Key to Opening the Inner Meaning of Your Dreams
By Vanessa L. Ochs with Elizabeth Ochs; Full-color Illus. by Kristina Swarner
Vibrant illustrations, instructions for how modern people can perform ancient Jewish dream practices, and dream interpretations drawn from the Jewish wisdom tradition help make this guide the ideal bedside companion for anyone who wants to further their understanding of their dreams—and themselves.
8 x 8, 120 pp, Full-color illus., Deluxe PB w/flaps, ISBN 1-58023-132-2 **$16.95**

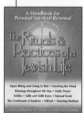

The Rituals & Practices of a Jewish Life: A Handbook for Personal Spiritual Renewal *Edited by Rabbi Kerry M. Olitzky and Rabbi Daniel Judson*
6 x 9, 272 pp, illus., Quality PB, ISBN 1-58023-169-1 **$18.95**

The Book of Jewish Sacred Practices: CLAL's Guide to Everyday & Holiday Rituals & Blessings *Edited by Rabbi Irwin Kula and Vanessa L. Ochs, Ph.D.*
6 x 9, 368 pp, Quality PB, ISBN 1-58023-152-7 **$18.95**

Science Fiction/ Mystery & Detective Fiction

Mystery Midrash: An Anthology of Jewish Mystery & Detective Fiction
Edited by Lawrence W. Raphael. Preface by Joel Siegel.
6 x 9, 304 pp, Quality PB, ISBN 1-58023-055-5 **$16.95**

Criminal Kabbalah: An Intriguing Anthology of Jewish Mystery & Detective Fiction
Edited by Lawrence W. Raphael. Foreword by Laurie R. King.
6 x 9, 256 pp, Quality PB, ISBN 1-58023-109-8 **$16.95**

More Wandering Stars: An Anthology of Outstanding Stories of Jewish Fantasy and Science Fiction *Edited by Jack Dann. Introduction by Isaac Asimov.*
6 x 9, 192 pp, Quality PB, ISBN 1-58023-063-6 **$16.95**

Wandering Stars: An Anthology of Jewish Fantasy & Science Fiction
Edited by Jack Dann. Introduction by Isaac Asimov.
6 x 9, 272 pp, Quality PB, ISBN 1-58023-005-9 **$16.95**

Spirituality

The Alphabet of Paradise: An A–Z of Spirituality for Everyday Life
By Rabbi Howard Cooper
In twenty-six engaging chapters, Cooper spiritually illuminates the subjects of our daily lives—A to Z—examining these sources by using an ancient Jewish mystical method of interpretation that reveals both the literal and more allusive meanings of each. 5 x 7¼, 224 pp, Quality PB, ISBN 1-893361-80-2 **$16.95** *(A SkyLight Paths book)*

Does the Soul Survive?: A Jewish Journey to Belief in Afterlife, Past Lives & Living with Purpose *By Rabbi Elie Kaplan Spitz. Foreword by Brian L Weiss, M.D.*
Spitz relates his own experiences and those shared with him by people he has worked with as a rabbi, and shows us that belief in afterlife and past lives, so often approached with reluctance, is in fact true to Jewish tradition.
6 x 9, 288 pp, Quality PB, ISBN 1-58023-165-9 **$16.95**; Hardcover, ISBN 1-58023-094-6 **$21.95**

First Steps to a New Jewish Spirit: Reb Zalman's Guide to Recapturing the Intimacy & Ecstasy in Your Relationship with God
By Rabbi Zalman M. Schachter-Shalomi with Donald Gropman
An extraordinary spiritual handbook that restores psychic and physical vigor by introducing us to new models and alternative ways of practicing Judaism. Offers meditation and contemplation exercises for enriching the most important aspects of everyday life. 6 x 9, 144 pp, Quality PB, ISBN 1-58023-182-9 **$16.95**

God In Our Relationships: Spirituality between People from the Teachings of Martin Buber *By Rabbi Dennis S. Ross*
On the eightieth anniversary of Buber's classic work, we can discover new answers to critical issues in our lives. Inspiring examples from Ross's own life—as congregational rabbi, father, hospital chaplain, social worker, and husband—illustrate Buber's difficult-to-understand ideas about how we encounter God and each other. 5½ x 8½, 160 pp, Quality PB, ISBN 1-58023-147-0 **$16.95**

The Jewish Lights Spirituality Handbook: A Guide to Understanding, Exploring & Living a Spiritual Life *Edited by Stuart M. Matlins*
What exactly is "Jewish" about spirituality? How do I make it a part of my life? Fifty of today's foremost spiritual leaders share their ideas and experience with us.
6 x 9, 456 pp, Quality PB, ISBN 1-58023-093-8 **$18.95**; Hardcover, ISBN 1-58023-100-4 **$24.95**

Bringing the Psalms to Life: How to Understand and Use the Book of Psalms
By Dr. Daniel F. Polish
6 x 9, 208 pp, Quality PB, ISBN 1-58023-157-8 **$16.95**; Hardcover, ISBN 1-58023-077-6 **$21.95**

God & the Big Bang: Discovering Harmony between Science & Spirituality
By Dr. Daniel C. Matt 6 x 9, 216 pp, Quality PB, ISBN 1-879045-89-3 **$16.95**

Godwrestling—Round 2: Ancient Wisdom, Future Paths
By Rabbi Arthur Waskow 6 x 9, 352 pp, Quality PB, ISBN 1-879045-72-9 **$18.95**

One God Clapping: The Spiritual Path of a Zen Rabbi *By Rabbi Alan Lew with Sherril Jaffe*
5½ x 8½, 336 pp, Quality PB, ISBN 1-58023-115-2 **$16.95**

The Path of Blessing: Experiencing the Energy and Abundance of the Divine
By Rabbi Marcia Prager 5½ x 8½, 240 pp., Quality PB, ISBN 1-58023-148-9 **$16.95**

Six Jewish Spiritual Paths: A Rationalist Looks at Spirituality *By Rabbi Rifat Sonsino*
6 x 9, 208 pp, Quality PB, ISBN 1-58023-167-5 **$16.95**; Hardcover, ISBN 1-58023-095-4 **$21.95**

Soul Judaism: Dancing with God into a New Era
By Rabbi Wayne Dosick 5½ x 8½, 304 pp, Quality PB, ISBN 1-58023-053-9 **$16.95**

Stepping Stones to Jewish Spiritual Living: Walking the Path Morning, Noon, and Night *By Rabbi James L Mirel and Karen Bonnell Werth*
6 x 9, 240 pp, Quality PB, ISBN 1-58023-074-1 **$16.95**; Hardcover, ISBN 1-58023-003-2 **$21.95**

There Is No Messiah... and You're It: The Stunning Transformation of Judaism's Most Provocative Idea *By Rabbi Robert N. Levine, D.D.*
6 x 9, 192 pp, Hardcover, ISBN 1-58023-173-X **$21.95**

These Are the Words: A Vocabulary of Jewish Spiritual Life *By Dr. Arthur Green*
6 x 9, 304 pp, Quality PB, ISBN 1-58023-107-1 **$18.95**

Spirituality/Lawrence Kushner

The Book of Letters: A Mystical Hebrew Alphabet
Popular Hardcover Edition, 6 x 9, 80 pp, 2-color text, ISBN 1-879045-00-1 **$24.95**
Deluxe Gift Edition with slipcase, 9 x 12, 80 pp, 4-color text, Hardcover, ISBN 1-879045-01-X **$79.95**
Collector's Limited Edition, 9 x 12, 80 pp, gold foil embossed pages, w/limited edition silkscreened print, ISBN 1-879045-04-4 **$349.00**

The Book of Miracles: A Young Person's Guide to Jewish Spiritual Awareness
All-new illustrations by the author
6 x 9, 96 pp, 2-color illus., Hardcover, ISBN 1-879045-78-8 **$16.95** *For ages 9–13*

The Book of Words: Talking Spiritual Life, Living Spiritual Talk
6 x 9, 160 pp, Quality PB, ISBN 1-58023-020-2 **$16.95**

Eyes Remade for Wonder: A Lawrence Kushner Reader
Introduction by Thomas Moore
6 x 9, 240 pp, Quality PB, ISBN 1-58023-042-3 **$18.95**; Hardcover, ISBN 1-58023-014-8 **$23.95**

God Was in This Place & I, i Did Not Know
Finding Self, Spirituality and Ultimate Meaning
6 x 9, 192 pp, Quality PB, ISBN 1-879045-33-8 **$16.95**

Honey from the Rock: An Introduction to Jewish Mysticism
6 x 9, 176 pp, Quality PB, ISBN 1-58023-073-3 **$16.95**

Invisible Lines of Connection: Sacred Stories of the Ordinary
5½ x 8½, 160 pp, Quality PB, ISBN 1-879045-98-2 **$15.95**

Jewish Spirituality—A Brief Introduction for Christians
5½ x 8½, 112 pp, Quality PB Original, ISBN 1-58023-150-0 **$12.95**

The River of Light: Jewish Mystical Awareness
6 x 9, 192 pp, Quality PB, ISBN 1-58023-096-2 **$16.95**

The Way Into Jewish Mystical Tradition
6 x 9, 224 pp, Hardcover, ISBN 1-58023-029-6 **$21.95**

Spirituality/Prayer

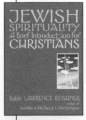

Pray Tell: A Hadassah Guide to Jewish Prayer
By Rabbi Jules Harlow, with contributions from Tamara Cohen, Rochelle Furstenberg, Rabbi Daniel Gordis, Leora Tanenbaum, and many others
A guide to traditional Jewish prayer enriched with insight and wisdom from a broad variety of viewpoints—from Orthodox, Conservative, Reform, and Reconstructionist Judaism to New Age and feminist. Offers fresh and modern slants on what it means to pray as a Jew, and how women and men might actually pray. 8½ x 11, 400 pp, Quality PB, ISBN 1-58023-163-2 **$29.95**

My People's Prayer Book Series
Traditional Prayers, Modern Commentaries
Edited by Rabbi Lawrence A. Hoffman
Provides diverse and exciting commentary to the traditional liturgy, helping modern men and women find new wisdom in Jewish prayer, and bring liturgy into their lives.

Each book includes Hebrew text, modern translation, and commentaries from all perspectives of the Jewish world.

Vol. 1—The *Sh'ma* and Its Blessings
7 x 10, 168 pp, Hardcover, ISBN 1-879045-79-6 **$23.95**

Vol. 2—The *Amidah*
7 x 10, 240 pp, Hardcover, ISBN 1-879045-80-X **$24.95**

Vol. 3—*P'sukei D'zimrah* (Morning Psalms)
7 x 10, 240 pp, Hardcover, ISBN 1-879045-81-8 **$24.95**

Vol. 4—*Seder K'riat Hatorah* (The Torah Service)
7 x 10, 264 pp, Hardcover, ISBN 1-879045-82-6 **$23.95**

Vol. 5—*Birkhot Hashachar* (Morning Blessings)
7 x 10, 240 pp, Hardcover, ISBN 1-879045-83-4 **$24.95**

Vol. 6—*Tachanun* and Concluding Prayers
7 x 10, 240 pp, Hardcover, ISBN 1-879045-84-2 **$24.95**

Vol. 7—Shabbat at Home
7 x 10, 240 pp (est), Hardcover, ISBN 1-879045-85-0 **$24.95**

Spirituality/The Way Into... Series

The Way Into... Series offers an accessible and highly usable "guided tour" of the Jewish faith, people, history and beliefs—in total, an introduction to Judaism that will enable you to understand and interact with the sacred texts of the Jewish tradition. Each volume is written by a leading contemporary scholar and teacher, and explores one key aspect of Judaism. *The Way Into...* enables all readers to achieve a real sense of Jewish cultural literacy through guided study.

The Way Into Encountering God in Judaism   *By Neil Gillman*
6 x 9, 240 pp, Hardcover, ISBN 1-58023-025-3 **$21.95**

Also Available: **The Jewish Approach to God: A Brief Introduction for Christians**
By Neil Gillman 5½ x 8½, 192 pp, Quality PB, ISBN 1-58023-190-X **$16.95**

The Way Into Jewish Mystical Tradition   *By Lawrence Kushner*
6 x 9, 224 pp, Hardcover, ISBN 1-58023-029-6 **$21.95**

The Way Into Jewish Prayer   *By Lawrence A. Hoffman*
6 x 9, 224 pp, Hardcover, ISBN 1-58023-027-X **$21.95**

The Way Into Torah   *By Norman J. Cohen*
6 x 9, 176 pp, Hardcover, ISBN 1-58023-028-8 **$21.95**

Spirituality in the Workplace

Being God's Partner
How to Find the Hidden Link Between Spirituality and Your Work
By Rabbi Jeffrey K. Salkin. Introduction by Norman Lear.
6 x 9, 192 pp, Quality PB, ISBN 1-879045-65-6 **$17.95**

The Business Bible: 10 New Commandments for Bringing Spirituality & Ethical Values into the Workplace   *By Rabbi Wayne Dosick*
5½ x 8½, 208 pp, Quality PB, ISBN 1-58023-101-2 **$14.95**

Spirituality and Wellness

Aleph-Bet Yoga
Embodying the Hebrew Letters for Physical and Spiritual Well-Being
By Steven A. Rapp. Foreword by Tamar Frankiel, Ph.D., and Judy Greenfeld. Preface by Hart Lazer
7 x 10, 128 pp, Quality PB, Layflat binding, b/w photos, ISBN 1-58023-162-4 **$16.95**

Entering the Temple of Dreams
Jewish Prayers, Movements, and Meditations for the End of the Day
By Tamar Frankiel, Ph.D., and Judy Greenfeld
7 x 10, 192 pp, illus., Quality PB, ISBN 1-58023-079-2 **$16.95**

Minding the Temple of the Soul
Balancing Body, Mind, and Spirit through Traditional Jewish Prayer, Movement, and Meditation   *By Tamar Frankiel, Ph.D., and Judy Greenfeld*
7 x 10, 184 pp, illus., Quality PB, ISBN 1-879045-64-8 **$16.95**
Audiotape of the Blessings and Meditations: 60 min. **$9.95**
Videotape of the Movements and Meditations: 46 min. **$20.00**

About Jewish Lights

People of all faiths and backgrounds yearn for books that attract, engage, educate, and spiritually inspire.

Our principal goal is to stimulate thought and help all people learn about who the Jewish People are, where they come from, and what the future can be made to hold. While people of our diverse Jewish heritage are the primary audience, our books speak to people in the Christian world as well and will broaden their understanding of Judaism and the roots of their own faith.

We bring to you authors who are at the forefront of spiritual thought and experience. While each has something different to say, they all say it in a voice that you can hear.

Our books are designed to welcome you and then to engage, stimulate, and inspire. We judge our success not only by whether or not our books are beautiful and commercially successful, but by whether or not they make a difference in your life.

For your information and convenience, at the back of this book we have provided a list of other Jewish Lights books you might find interesting and useful. They cover all the categories of your life:

Bar/Bat Mitzvah	Life Cycle
Bible Study / Midrash	Meditation
Children's Books	Parenting
Congregation Resources	Prayer
Current Events / History	Ritual / Sacred Practice
Ecology	Spirituality
Fiction: Mystery, Science Fiction	Theology / Philosophy
Grief / Healing	Travel
Holidays / Holy Days	Twelve Steps
Inspiration	Women's Interest
Kabbalah / Mysticism / Enneagram	

Stuart M. Matlins, Publisher

Or phone, fax, mail or e-mail to: **JEWISH LIGHTS Publishing**
Sunset Farm Offices, Route 4 • P.O. Box 237 • Woodstock, Vermont 05091
Tel: (802) 457-4000 • Fax: (802) 457-4004 • www.jewishlights.com
Credit card orders: **(800) 962-4544** (8:30AM–5:30PM ET Monday–Friday)
Generous discounts on quantity orders. SATISFACTION GUARANTEED. Prices subject to change.